UNIVERSITY OF NORTH CAROLINA AT CHAPEL HILL
DEPARTMENT OF ROMANCE LANGUAGES

NORTH CAROLINA STUDIES
IN THE ROMANCE LANGUAGES AND LITERATURES

ESSAYS; TEXTS, TEXTUAL STUDIES AND TRANSLATIONS; SYMPOSIA

Founder: URBAN TIGNER HOLMES

Distributed by:

UNIVERSITY OF NORTH CAROLINA PRESS
CHAPEL HILL
North Carolina 27514
U.S.A.

NORTH CAROLINA STUDIES IN THE
ROMANCE LANGUAGES AND LITERATURES

Number 178

THE DRAMA OF SELF IN
GUILLAUME APOLLINAIRE'S *ALCOOLS*

THE DRAMA OF SELF IN GUILLAUME APOLLINAIRE'S *ALCOOLS*

BY

RICHARD HOWARD STAMELMAN

CHAPEL HILL

NORTH CAROLINA STUDIES IN THE ROMANCE
LANGUAGES AND LITERATURES

U.N.C. DEPARTMENT OF ROMANCE LANGUAGES

1976

Library of Congress Cataloging in Publication Data

Stamelman, Richard Howard.
  The drama of self in Guillaume Apollinaire's Alcools.

  (North Carolina studies in the Romance languages and literatures; 178)
  Bibliography: p.
  Includes index.
  1. Apollinaire, Guillaume, 1880-1918. Alcools.
I. Title. II. Series.

PQ2601.P6A727   841'.9'12   76-22801
ISBN 0-8078-9178-9

I. S. B. N. 0-8078-9178-9

DEPÓSITO LEGAL: V. 2.449 - 1976   I.S.B.N. 84-399-5235-X
ARTES GRÁFICAS SOLER, S. A. - JÁVEA, 28 - VALENCIA (8) - 1976

To Becky

Voici de quoi est fait le chant symphonique de l'amour

—"Le Chant d'amour," *Calligrammes*

ACKNOWLEDGMENTS

I would like to express my great indebtedness and appreciation to Wallace Fowlie of Duke University who never tired of encouraging and advising me, especially at those times when encouragement was most needed, and who listened so patiently to my interpretations of Apollinaire's poems. I am grateful also to Joseph H. McMahon of Wesleyan University for his careful reading of the manuscript and for his helpful suggestions and comments. In addition, I wish to thank Duke University and Wesleyan University for their generous financial assistance without which this study would not have been possible. Finally, my deepest gratitude goes to my wife for her advice, her support, and her love during the writing of this book. The patience and the understanding she showed will never be forgotten.

Parts of this study have been published in a somewhat different form in professional journals. "The Dramatic Structure of Apollinaire's 'Merlin et la vieille femme'" appeared in the *French Review*, XLVI (Special Issue, No. 5, *Studies in French Poetry*, Spring, 1973), and "Apollinaire's 'Cortège': The Poetics of Introspection" was published in *Papers on Language and Literature*, 9 (Fall, 1973).

R. H. S.

Middletown, Connecticut

July 1973

CONTENTS

	Page
ACKNOWLEDGMENTS	9
INTRODUCTION: THE SEARCH FOR SELF	13

PART 1. THE DRAMAS OF SELF

I. THE DRAMA OF FRAGMENTATION	25
"Palais"	25
"Cortège"	39
II. THE DRAMA OF DISPERSION	56
"Nuit rhénane"	56
III. THE DRAMA OF REINTEGRATION	62
"Mai"	62
"Merlin et la vieille femme"	78

PART 2. THE METAPHORS OF SELF

IV. HARLEQUIN: THE PROTEAN SELF	103
V. PARIS: THE POETIC MONTAGE OF SELF	119
VI. SONG: THE CATHARSIS OF SELF	165
VII. CONCLUSION	210
BIBLIOGRAPHY OF WORKS CITED	219
GENERAL INDEX	224

Introduction

THE SEARCH FOR SELF

> And out of what one sees and hears and out
> Of what one feels, who could have thought to make
> So many selves, so many sensuous worlds,
> As if the air, the mid-day air, was swarming
> With the metaphysical changes that occur
> Merely in living as and where we live.[1]

The search for self and identity is the major concern of Guillaume Apollinaire's poetry in *Alcools* (1913) and in *Calligrammes* (1918). Throughout these collections Apollinaire strives first to find, then to identify and, finally, to know his elusive, multiple, and protean self. In poem after poem he attempts to define his *moi* through a poetic style of extreme self-consciousness, as the following lines from "Cortège" show:

> Un jour
> Un jour je m'attendais moi-même
> Je me disais Guillaume il est temps que tu viennes [2]

or those from the poem "Zone," where his life is compared to

> ... un tableau pendu dans un sombre musée
> Et quelquefois tu vas le regarder de près
> (*O. P.*, p. 41)

---

[1] Wallace Stevens, "Esthétique du Mal," *Collected Poems* (New York: Alfred A. Knopf, 1964), p. 326.
[2] Guillaume Apollinaire, *Œuvres poétiques* ("Bibliothèque de la Pléiade"; Paris: Gallimard, 1959), p. 74; hereafter cited in the text as *O. P.*

In "Le Brasier" Apollinaire describes the self undergoing fragmentation and purification by fire:

> Je flambe dans le brasier à l'ardeur adorable
> Et les mains des croyants m'y rejettent multiple innombrablement
>
> (O. P., p. 109)

and in "L'Emigrant de Landor Road" the self is portrayed as

> Une tapisserie sans fin
> Qui figurait son histoire
>
> (O. P., p. 106)

In "Palais" the poet watches his fragmented selves as they head towards a supernatural *soirée*: "On voit venir au fond du jardin mes pensées" (O. P., p. 61). In "Les Fiançailles" the poet casts a harsh eye on his past life:

> J'ai eu le courage de regarder en arrière
> Les cadavres de mes jours
> Marquent ma route et je les pleure
>
> (O. P., p. 131)

and in "La Chanson du Mal-Aimé" the body's shadow becomes the image, the mourning double, of the poet's self: "O mon ombre en deuil de moi-même" (O. P., p. 54). Similarly, in the poem "Les Collines" Apollinaire sees a multiple vision of himself:

> Je m'arrête pour regarder
> Sur la pelouse incandescente
> Un serpent erre c'est moi-même
> Qui suis la flûte dont je joue
> Et le fouet qui châtie les autres
>
> (O. P., p. 174)

An orphic communion between the poet's self and the universe takes place in the poem "Vendémiaire":

> J'ai soif villes de France et d'Europe et du monde
> Venez toutes couler dans ma gorge profonde
> ... ...

> Ecoutez-moi je suis le gosier de Paris
> Et je boirai encore s'il me plaît l'univers
>
> (*O. P.*, pp. 149 and 154)

and in "Le Musicien de Saint-Merry" Apollinaire describes his desire to create a poetry that will be a song of himself:

> Je ne chante pas ce monde ni les autres astres
> Je chante toutes les possibilités de moi-même hors de
>   ce monde et des astres
> Je chante la joie d'errer et le plaisir d'en mourir
>
> (*O. P.*, p. 188)

As these passages illustrate, Apollinaire is hypnotized by the mystery and complexity of his own being. In many of the poems of *Alcools* he calls the self by different names (it answers to *je, tu, nous,* and *vous*) in an attempt to realize Socrates' celebrated command to "Know thyself." But his search for self-knowledge is rendered difficult by the protean nature of the self. It continually changes form, even as it is being defined. It is "not a state but a process of becoming."[3] It includes not only those selves that have already been born, but also all the selves yet to be born, for as Jung has said, "'just as man is always that which he once was, so he is always that which he is yet to become.'"[4] It is these qualities of elusiveness and multiplicity that make the poet's search for self so formidable an undertaking.

How, then, is the poet to define his "I," when it is not one but many? How is he to locate the self, when it is composed of myriad selves that are clothed in different costumes, painted in different colors, and hidden behind different masks? Within the self, a world of kaleidoscopic fragments divides, shifts, and re-forms into new patterns and configurations. Confronted by this fragmented world, how is the poet to grasp the unity of the self? How can he define the quality of "I-ness" that distinguishes him from all men, if the "I" multiplies so rapidly that it is never the same at any one moment?

---

[3] Bruno Bettelheim, *The Empty Fortress. Infantile Autism and the Birth of the Self* (New York: The Free Press, 1967), p. 37.

[4] *Psychological Reflections. An Anthology of the Writtings of C. G. Jung,* selected and ed. by Jolande Jacobi ("Bollingen Series" XXXI; New York: Pantheon, 1953), pp. 272-273, cited by Herbert Read, *Icon and Idea: The Function of Art in the Development of Human Consciousness* (Cambridge: Harvard University Press, 1955), p. 114.

These are obstacles to self-knowledge, but not insurmountable ones; they can be overcome by the creation of a work of art.

The self is fluid, mercurial, difficult to hold, like water slipping through closed fingers. But water can be contained in a glass and held; and in similar fashion the poet can place the self in a tight container which will allow him to grasp and hold the self without losing it. That container is, of course, the work of art, the poem. By placing the "I" in his poems Apollinaire succeeds in capturing his elusive self and studying its nature. It becomes that "tableau pendu dans un sombre musée" or that "tapisserie sans fin" to which he sometimes returns to take a closer look.

But the argument can be raised that the self is never the same at any moment of existence, and therefore, the self or selves fixed in one poem are not those captured in another. This is quite true. But, since diversity is the nature of the self, a work of art should aim at recording this diversity and at painting the different selves that belong to it. Montaigne, whose *Essais* remain to this day one of the most complete records of the different states of self, recognized the need for painting the flux:

> Le monde n'est qu'une branloire perenne. Toutes choses y branlent sans cesse.... La constance mesme n'est autre chose qu'un branle plus languissant. Je ne puis asseurer mon objet. Il va trouble et chancelant, d'une yvresse naturelle. Je le prens en ce point, comme il est, en l'instant que je m'amuse a luy. Je ne peints pas l'estre. Je peints le passage: non un passage d'aage en autre, ou, comme dict le peuple, de sept en sept ans, mais de jour en jour, de minute en minute. Il faut accommoder mon histoire a l'heure. Tant y a que je me contredis bien a l'aventure, mais la verite, comme disoit Demades, je ne la contredy point. Si mon ame pouvait prendre pied, je ne m'essaierois pas, je me resoudrois; elle est tousjours en apprentissage et en espreuve.[5]

And Apollinaire appears to suggest as much when, in *Les Peintres cubistes,* he writes that

> On ne découvrira jamais la réalité une fois pour toutes. La vérité sera toujours nouvelle.[6]

---

[5] Michel de Montaigne, *Essais* (2 vols.; Paris: Garnier, 1962), II, 222.

[6] Ed. by L. C. Breunig, and J.-Cl. Chevalier (Coll. "Miroirs de l'Art"; Paris: Hermann, 1965), p. 48.

For him every poem constitutes a new reality, a new truth, and a new identity.

Like Montaigne's *Essais*, *Alcools* contains the diverse and often contradictory selves that compose Apollinaire's self. They are all different selves of the same "I" — different species, so to speak, of the same genus. But they are in conflict and often at war with each other. A state of tension, confusion and disorder exists within the self. The poet, compelled by his "rage for order" to tidy up this chaotic situation, to untangle this Gordian knot and thus to come to know himself, is engaged in a noble struggle, a struggle that may be called the drama of self.

The drama of self is the poet's dramatic search for self-knowledge; it exists within him and performs in voices that he alone can understand. The drama of self is a private affair. But when that drama is made actual and performed in the form of a poem, three things occur: first, the private drama existing within the poet's self becomes the "text" or the "script" to be followed during the "performance" of the poem; second, the poet's selves which constitute the self are objectified, externalized and then called on to act out this drama; third, the poet becomes the *metteur-en-scène* overseeing the entire production — its staging, décor, lighting, costumes, masks. In this manner, the *drama* of self within the poet is transformed into a *dramatization* of self in the poem. [7]

---

[7] Interestingly, Jean-Claude Chevalier in his brilliant formalist analysis of *Alcools* ("*Alcools*" *d'Apollinaire: essai d'analyse des formes poétiques* ["Bibliothèque des lettres modernes," vol. XVII; Paris: Minard, 1970]) makes the same point in a discussion of Apollinaire's "Le Larron," "L'Ermite," and "Merlin et la vieille femme." Speaking of "Le Larron" in particular, he writes:

> Le poète "se met en scène" sous la transposition de personnages de drame; ceux-ci "jouent" la comédie de l'existence sur laquelle pèse le regard du créateur, qui s'est institué spectateur par le seul fait d'écrire. Aussi les éléments du dialogue sont-ils soulignés.... Le dialogue du Je et du Tu entre les personnages symboliques d'une allégorie introduit donc l'idée d'un drame par lequel l'écrivain confie à ses personnages la tâche d'élucider le douloureux problème qui le tourmente; il enferme dans une scène, à des fins heuristiques, les éléments de son propre drame. C'est une des possibilités de la poésie que d'ordonner en plans ce qui, dans la réalité quotidienne, n'aurait pas de profondeur; le poète peut organiser une représentation (au double sens du terme) et, par là, se trouver une signification. (pp. 46-47)

M. Chevalier calls this dramatic representation "la transposition hamlétique," and he describes it as follows:

The text — the drama as it exists within the self — remains the blueprint, the ideal; but the actors' interpretation and the director's "staging" may fail to realize this ideal. The performance may not actualize the text. But there is no printed libretto for us, the "audience," to follow during the performance, no printed copies of the "text" by which to form our own opinions. All we see is the performance, and we must judge the drama of self solely on its dramatized form. Although the poet knows both the drama and its dramatization, we know only the latter. For us, therefore, the dramatization *is* the drama.

The difference between the text and its performance is the difference between the drama and its dramatization, between the ideal and the reality. We can only work with the reality and isolate from it the different selves of the poet that are involved. But the poet is able to compare and judge between the internal drama of self and its external dramatized form. Moreover, it is through the act of writing the dramatization, as he watches the performance as a spectator, that Apollinaire arrives at the greatest degree of self-awareness. As M. Chevalier states, Apollinaire "s'est institué spectateur par le seul fait d'écrire." [8] In a sense, Apollinaire gives to his poems the responsibility of defining his identity; more particularly, he yields to the language of his poems — to their images, metaphors, rhymes, and rhythms — and at the very moment that he is writing them, the task

> La poésie figure le drame du poète et de l'homme, lui donne non seulement sens, mais, plus, existence, exactement comme Hamlet fait représenter par les comédiens le drame qui le hante et lui donne une existence qui était dissoute dans les phantasmes de sa folie. (p. 103)

However, M. Chevalier does not believe, as I do, that the dramatic structure of Apollinaire's early poems informs all of the poetry in *Alcools*. In fact, he identifies a different poetic structure — "une fonction lyrique" rather than "une fonction dramatique" (p. 33) — as being at the heart of the later poems of *Alcools*, especially those poems that date from 1908-1910 ("1909," "Les Fiançailles," "Le Brasier," "Cortège," and others). According to his interpretation, a dramatic poetry of representation and imitation, characterized by the use of pastiche, dialogue, allegory, and *récit*, and by the repetition of consonants, is replaced by a lyric poetry of creation, where qualities of multiplicity, proliferation, and expansiveness predominate. This new poetry exhibits formal characteristics quite distinct from the earlier poetry, and significantly, the *Je*, *Tu*, and *Il* personages that constitute it are presented in a new configuration of relations (see pp. 95, 105-6, 111-12, 204-5, 223-25, 267).

[8] *Ibid.*, p. 46.

of discovering and revealing an image of himself. By means of poetic language Apollinaire quite literally organizes a self. The poem is for him what the work of art is for Jean Rousset:

> Avant d'être production ou expression, l'œuvre est pour le sujet créateur un moyen de se révéler à lui-même.... L'œuvre est donc pour l'artiste un instrument privilégié de découverte. [9]

Poetry for Apollinaire is presence, the possession of himself in the immediacy and the immanence of the poetic act, in the *hic et nunc* of the poem. And the words of that poem enact, play out, and live Apollinaire's search for self. As the poet Yves Bonnefoy, for whom poetry is also a quest [10] (though towards ends different from Apollinaire's), has written:

> ... les mots peuvent être avant tout notre acte. Leur pouvoir-être, leur avenir infini d'associations prétendues verbales, dites gratuites, nous retrouverons qu'il n'est que la métaphore de notre rapport infini avec la moindre chose réelle, de la nature subjective de toute chose profonde.... [11]

The dramatization of self in Apollinaire's poetry can be described in more detail as involving a process that the French word "chosification" ("thingification") best describes. The poet's inner selves, which are in a continual process of becoming, are objectified and embodied in outward forms; they are made into things, objects. In the act of dramatization the protean self of a given moment is exteriorized and fixed in an unchanging form: the poem. Thus, trans-

---

[9] *Forme et signification. Essais sur les structures littéraires de Corneille à Claudel* (Paris: Corti, 1962), pp. vi and ix. In another passage, M. Rousset, quoting Camus, remarks:

> L'artiste ne connaît pas d'autre instrument de l'exploration et de l'organisation de soi-même que la composition de son œuvre; "une œuvre d'homme n'est rien d'autre que ce long cheminement pour retrouver par les détours de l'art les deux ou trois images simples et grandes sur lesquelles le cœur, une première fois, s'est ouvert."
> (p. vi)

[10] "Poésie et voyage sont d'une même substance, d'un même sang,..." "Les Tombeaux de Ravenne" (1953), in his *Du Mouvement et de l'immobilité de Douve* (Coll. "Poésie"; Paris: Gallimard, 1970), p. 31.

[11] "L'Acte et le lieu de la poésie" (1958), in *Ibid.*, p. 207.

formed the selves lose their egocentricity, their "I-ness," and develop a new identity, a feeling of "other-ness." The dramatization of the self through art results in a divorce between the poet and his selves; while he belongs to the world of self, they have been transposed to the world of things. Yet, this alienation is a necessary prerequisite to self-contemplation. The externalization of the internal prepares the way for self-awareness. Poetry, therefore, becomes a means of achieving self-knowledge, and in Apollinaire the search for self and the creation of poetry are inseparable enterprises.

Almost a decade before Apollinaire's birth another French poet had stressed the importance of self-objectification in poetry. In his famous letter to Paul Demeny on May 15, 1871 Arthur Rimbaud called for a new vision of poetry and a new definition of self:

> Car JE est un autre. Si le cuivre s'éveille clairon, il n'y a rien de sa faute. Cela m'est évident: j'assiste à l'éclosion de ma pensée: je la regarde, je l'écoute: je lance un coup d'archet: la symphonie fait son remuement dans les profondeurs ou vient d'un bond sur la scène.[12]

The image of the symphony unfolding and developing "dans les profondeurs" until in a crescendo of sound it bursts forth and onto a stage is a striking expression of how the self is externalized and given dramatic form. Although the poet's *I* is a spectator, watching the birth of its thought and listening to its first movements, it does draw the first bow-stroke, thus initiating a stirring of selves within the self. This restless movement of selves grows more intense and more agitated until, like the symphony, it reaches a climax and projects the selves out of the poet and onto a stage, that stage being for Apollinaire the poem. The *I* becomes embodied in visible and dramatic form; it becomes something or somebody else, an object, a form, a *persona*, the other: "Car JE est un autre."

The following chapters will attempt to examine the drama of self in Apollinaire's *Alcools* by a close analysis of the different experiences expressed in certain poems of the collection; my aim is to identify and to define the self or selves that are inextricably linked with those experiences and that are, therefore, dramatized in those poems. In

---

[12] Arthur Rimbaud, *Œuvres complètes* ("Bibliothèque de la Pléiade"; Paris: Gallimard, 1954), p. 270.

Alcools Apollinaire dramatizes his search for self-knowledge through three distinct "dramatic" experiences, what may be called the drama of fragmentation, the drama of dispersion, and the drama of reintegration. The drama of fragmentation is characterized by a *dédoublement* of the poet's self; the self is divided into many fragments, and the fragmented selves are closely analyzed by the poet. The drama of dispersion involves the scattering of fragmented selves like seeds on a wind, so that the poet becomes ubiquitous in the universe; Apollinaire's self takes on a plasticity and a fluidity that enable it to unite with all objects. The drama of reintegration reverses the movements towards fragmentation and dispersion by reunifying the fragmented and dispersed selves into a complete and undivided self; in this way the poet can see the clearest possible portrait of himself. In addition, Apollinaire uses three key metaphors to represent his search for self-identity: namely, Harlequin, who symbolizes the protean, mercurial nature of the self; the city of Paris, which becomes the landscape through which the self searches for its identity; and song, through which Apollinaire's self expresses its inner conflicts and sorrows, and thus succeeds, through a lyric and, above all, cathartic experience, to know itself. Whether through dramatization or through the use of images, it is always a question in Apollinaire's poetry of the search for self-knowledge. [13]

---

[13] While my study is based on the thesis that three fundamental dramatic experiences structure Apollinaire's search for self, as it takes place in and through his poetry (namely, fragmentation, dispersion, and reintegration), it might be noted that Philippe Renaud in his valuable study of Apollinaire's poetry (*Lecture d'Apollinaire* [Lausanne: L'Age d'Homme, 1969]) identifies a "dialectics of self" at work at different points in Apollinaire's poetry: "lue 'de l'intérieur,' elle [l'œuvre d'Apollinaire] nous paraît fondée sur une dialectique de la dispersion et du remembrement du Moi passant par une sorte de mort" (p. 17). *Alcools* in particular, states M. Renaud,

> retrace la geste d'un héros qui se donne pour mage et Suprême savant, un *fondé en poésie* hanté par le désir de métamorphoser en *carmen*, de ressusciter en paroles ce qui est soumis au destin; qui va jusqu'à une sorte de suicide de son Moi épars dans le monde pour le réunir et le récupérer par un regard lié à la naissance du Souffle, qui est le centre mystérieux de l'opération poétique. (p. 21)

My analysis of Apollinaire's search for self-knowledge in *Alcools* was developed independently of the ideas that M. Renaud presents in his book, which had not yet appeared at the time my study was being written (1966-1967). Although we agree on a number of points — for example, we are in agreement, first, that it is in and through his poetry and by means of the act of poetic creation that Apollinaire seeks simultaneously to find himself and to immortalize what he has discovered, and second, that *Alcools* creates, in the words of M. Renaud "un lien vivant, sensible, presque matériel entre le lecteur et le Moi qui habite le livre" (p. 457) — and although some of our ideas concerning such poems as "Merlin et la vieille femme" and "Cortège" converge, nevertheless, we disagree on many points, and our methods of approaching Apollinaire's poetry differ considerably.

As the following pages will demonstrate, I do not agree that the Apollinarian self must sacrifice itself through suicide, "dans le dessein de renaître en poésie" (Renaud, p. 138). Nor can I agree with M. Renaud's statement that "le Moi d'Apollinaire, dans *Alcools*, n'offre aucune richesse 'psychologique'" (p. 153), nor that in Apollinaire "'cet instinct ou connaissance de soi-même' n'implique aucune idée d'introspection" (p. 98). Moreover, unlike M. Renaud, who suggests that the appearance of the "other" is a characteristic of Apollinaire's second work of poetry, *Ondes* ("dans *Ondes*, le dédoublement de soi, fondamental dans *Alcools*... cède le pas à l'intervention d'un Autre," p. 339), I would maintain that the "other" is present much earlier, in certain poems of *Alcools*. Finally, I do not agree with M. Renaud's contention that the splitting up of Apollinaire's personality into "un Moi narrateur et un Moi *poète*" (p. 420) is what constitutes the newness of the Apollinarian self as presented in the later *poèmes de guerre*. It seems to me that this particular kind of *dédoublement* is in evidence much earlier, in such poems of *Alcools* as "Merlin et la vieille femme" and "Crépuscule."

PART 1

THE DRAMAS OF SELF

> See, now they vanish,
> The faces and places, with the self which,
>   as it could, loved them,
> To become renewed, transfigured, in
>   another pattern.
>
> (T. S. Eliot, "Little Gidding,"
> *Four Quartets*)

Chapter I

THE DRAMA OF FRAGMENTATION

"PALAIS"

Images of decapitation and cerebral dissection create a drama of self-fragmentation in Apollinaire's poem, "Palais" (O. P., pp. 61-62). In a macabre and burlesque fashion Apollinaire describes a giant banquet, where the guests are served the insides of his own mind, prepared and impeccably garnished according to the fine art of French cuisine. Like Picasso, of whom he wrote in *Les Peintres cubistes*, "Un Picasso étudie un objet comme un chirurgien dissèque un cadavre," [1] Apollinaire performs surgery on his own self, meticulously probing and dissecting its different regions and innumerable layers. Like the cubists, who fragmented objects so that they could observe them from different perspectives, Apollinaire studies the self from every possible angle. As is common in Apollinaire's poems, the autopsy of self is accompanied by a strong feeling of self-deprecation and ridicule.

"Palais" was first published in the *Revue Littéraire de Paris et de Champagne* (no. 32) in November 1905 with the title "Dans le Palais de Rosemonde." It is improbable that the manuscript, written on a page torn from a bank ledger, was composed before 1902 when Apollinaire first began work as a bank clerk. [2] The poem, however, is dedicated to Max Jacob whom Apollinaire met in the summer of 1904,

---

[1] p. 51.
[2] LeRoy C. Breunig, "The Chronology of Apollinaire's *Alcools*," PMLA, LXVII (December, 1952), 916.

and, in all probability, it was written between that summer and its publication the following year.[3]

In "Palais" Apollinaire describes a fantasy journey undertaken by his own personnified thoughts to the enchanted palace of Rosamond buried deep in a dream world. Historically, the story of Rosamond Clifford, who because of her exquisite beauty was known as "Fair Rosamond," is surrounded by a paucity of fact and a wealth of fiction.[4] According to many legends, Rosamond was the mistress of King Henry the Second of England and bore him two sons: Geoffrey, later Archbishop of York, and William Longword, later Earl of Salisbury. To protect Rosamond from the jealous rage of his queen, Eleanor of Aquitaine, Henry built a palace near Woodstock which he surrounded with a labyrinth through which he alone knew the way. After one of his visits to Rosamond Henry inadvertently drew a silken thread out of the labyrinth with him. Queen Eleanor, spying the thread, made her way through the maze and confronted the usurper of her bed whom she then poisoned. Rosamond's body was laid to rest in Godstow Nunnery near Oxford. Also related to the legend is the episode that recounts how Huth, the Bishop of Lincoln, while visiting the Nunnery in 1192, discovered Rosamond's elaborate tomb bright with candles and was so scandalized that he ordered her bones removed to some less sacrosanct spot.

The Rosamond of Apollinaire's "Palais" is undoubtedly the "Fair Rosamond" of English history. But there is also an allusion to another historical figure named Rosamond, who, as queen of the Lombards, predates Henry's mistress by at least six centuries. This Rosamond

---

[3] Marie-Jeanne Durry, *Guillaume Apollinaire: Alcools* (3 vols.; Paris: Société d'Edition d'Enseignement Supérieur, 1964), II, 29. Another fact that points to the probability of 1905 as the date of composition is the similarity between "Palais" and the play, "Le Roi Bombance," by the Italian futurist, Marinetti, which was published between February and June 1905. In the play three apprentice cooks ("Marmitons") revolt against the King who is faced at the same time with an uprising of the "Affamés." The latter ask for food and later capture the King whom they then devour. A discussion of the similarities between the two works is found in Francis J. Carmody, *The Evolution of Apollinaire's Poetics, 1901-1914* ("University of California Publications in Modern Philology," vol. LXX; Berkeley: University of California Press, 1963), pp. 33-36.

[4] The following is taken from Virgil B. Heltzel, *Fair Rosamond. A Study of the Development of a Literary Theme* ("Northwestern University Studies in the Humanities," no. 16; Evanston: "Northwestern University Studies, 1947), pp. 1-13.

was forced to marry Alboin, king of the Lombards, around 566. In a moment of drunken hysteria he forced her to drink out of a chalice made from her father's skull. In revenge she stabbed Alboin in his sleep.[5] Apollinaire alludes to this earlier figure in the line: "Madame Rosemonde roule avec mystère/ Ses petits yeux tout ronds pareils aux yeux des Huns."[6]

The title of "Palais" has a historical, a physiological, and an erotic meaning. In addition to referring to the palace at Woodstock built by King Henry, "Palais" also alludes to the roof of the mouth, the palate. The Rabelaisian images of carnivorous appetite and the nauseating menu served at the end of the poem indicate the importance of the palate and of the sense of taste in the poem. However, M. André Rouveyre, in his *Amour et poésie d'Apollinaire*,[7] offers a third meaning that emphasizes the erotic quality of the poem. The palate, the boned, vaulted roof of the mouth, where the pleasure of the lips and the craving of appetite are satisfied, is a palace, so to speak, of love. Here, the first words and kisses of love are born; but, as M. Rouveyre points out, it suggests another vaulted region of the female body also devoted to love, pleasure, and satisfaction:

---

[5] "Rosamond," *Grand Larousse encyclopédique* (1964), vol. IX.

[6] Rosamond and her marvelous palace are popular figures in Apollinaire's poetry. In a poem written in June 1901 and sent on the back of a post card to one of his early loves Apollinaire makes his first allusion to Henry's courtesan (*O. P.*, p. 327). A year later in "Le Dôme de Cologne," composed during a stay in Germany, he referred to Rosamond's palace as one of the architectural marvels of the world. Rosamond also gives her name to a poem in *Alcools*, but this Rosamond is an unknown woman whom Apollinaire follows through the streets of Amsterdam during a visit in August 1905. Through a clever play on words the name "Rosemonde" is transformed into the mystical "Rose du Monde." In *Le Bestiaire* (1908) Apollinaire emphasizes once again that the palace of Rosamond is one of the great wonders of the world (*O. P.*, p. 15). In a note to the poem he presents detailed information concerning the palace:

> Voici, touchant ce palais, témoignage de l'amour que le roi d'Angleterre éprouvait pour sa maîtresse, ce couplet d'une complainte dont je ne connais point l'Auteur:
> > Pour mettre Rosemonde à l'abri de la haine
> > Que lui portait la reine
> > Le roi fit construire un palais
> > Tel qu'on n'en vit jamais.

(*O. P.*, p. 34)

[7] (Paris: Editions du Seuil, 1955), pp. 184-186.

> Par faveur les femmes ont deux palais. L'un et l'autre composés et mouvementés pareillement. Apollinaire, en mettant le titre de son poème, considérait en imagination celui de leurs deux palais qui est le plus intime, le plus ardent et le plus tourmenté. [8]

In "Palais" a mock-serious, symbolist tone mixes with passages of Verlainesque charm and grace. The comic and the serious, and the sacred and the profane, are blended together. The scatological is married to the holy. Every line is a new experience and a surprising, unexpected encounter. The poetic effects of surprise, which Apollinaire called the distinguishing feature of "l'esprit nouveau," [9] are found everywhere in "Palais." Moreover, by effectively using burlesque and black humor Apollinaire preserves and even exaggerates the horrible and the macabre in his poem. This, too, is in accord with the "esprit nouveau," as he later defined it:

> L'esprit nouveau ne cherche pas à transformer le ridicule, il lui conserve un rôle qui n'est pas sans saveur. De même, il ne veut pas donner à l'horrible le sens du noble. Il le laisse horrible et n'abaisse pas le noble. [10]

Rimbaud, in his celebrated letter to Paul Demeny, spoke of witnessing the birth of his own thought ("j'assiste à l'éclosion de ma pensée: je la regarde, je l'écoute"). Similarly, in "Palais" Apollinaire watches a procession of his own thoughts, as they wend their way toward a dream world:

> 1 Vers le palais de Rosemonde au fond du Rêve
> Mes rêveuses pensées pieds nus vont en soirée
> Le palais don du roi comme un roi nu s'élève
> Des chairs fouettées des roses de la roseraie
>
> 5 On voit venir au fond du jardin mes pensées
> Qui sourient du concert joué par les grenouilles
> Elles ont envie des cyprès grandes quenouilles
> Et le soleil miroir des roses s'est brisé

---

[8] *Ibid.*, pp. 185-186.
[9] "L'Esprit nouveau et les poètes," *Mercure de France*, CXXX (1er décembre, 1918), 391.
[10] *Ibid.*, pp. 390-391.

Le stigmate sanglant des mains contre les vitres
10   Quel archer mal blessé du couchant le troua
La résine qui rend amer le vin de Chypre
Ma bouche aux agapes d'agneau blanc l'éprouva

Sur les genoux pointus du monarque adultère
Sur le mai de son âge et sur son trente et un
15   Madame Rosemonde roule avec mystère
Ses petits yeux tout ronds pareils aux yeux des Huns

Dame de mes pensées au cul de perle fine
Dont ni perle ni cul n'égale l'orient
Qui donc attendez-vous
20   De rêveuses pensées en marche à l'Orient
Mes plus belles voisines

Toc toc Entrez dans l'antichambre le jour baisse
La veilleuse dans l'ombre est un bijou d'or cuit
Pendez vos têtes aux patères par les tresses
25   Le ciel presque nocturne a des lueurs d'aiguilles

On entra dans la salle à manger les narines
Reniflaient une odeur de graisse et de graillon
On eut vingt potages dont trois couleurs d'urine
Et le roi prit deux œufs pochés dans du bouillon

30   Puis les marmitons apportèrent les viandes
Des rôtis de pensées mortes dans mon cerveau
Mes beaux rêves mort-nés en tranches bien saignantes
Et mes souvenirs faisandés en godiveaux

Or ces pensées mortes depuis des millénaires
35   Avaient le fade goût des grands mammouths gelés
Les os ou songe-creux venaient des ossuaires
En danse macabre aux plis de mon cervelet

Et tous ces mets criaient des choses nonpareilles
       Mais nom de Dieu!
40   Ventre affamé n'a pas d'oreilles
Et les convives mastiquaient à qui mieux mieux

Ah! nom de Dieu! qu'ont donc crié ces entrecôtes
Ces grands pâtés ces os à moelle et mirotons
Langues de feu où sont-elles mes pentecôtes
45   Pour mes pensées de tous pays de tous les temps

(*O. P.*, pp. 61-62)

Between the first and second stanzas of "Palais" there is a change of perspective. While in the first strophe the palace is seen in the distance, and the "pensées rêveuses" are *going* toward it, in the second the thoughts are seen at the far end of the garden *coming* toward the palace. In the first instance, the poet sees the palace from his thoughts' point of view; in the second, he observes his thoughts from the palace's point of view.

The change of perspective indicates the poet's vacillating position in the poem. He is both engaged in and disengaged from his "rêveuses pensées." On the one hand, he identifies with the self, and on the other, he dissociates himself from it. At one moment he is subjective, looking at things through the eyes of his thoughts; during these moments he uses the first person possessive adjective ("*mes* rêveuses pensées," "*ma* bouche," "*mes* beaux rêves," "*mes* souvenirs"). But, at other moments, he is objective, looking at his "rêveuses pensées" through the eyes of an outsider, a spectator. To indicate his separation from the self and his identification with the outsider the poet uses the impersonal pronoun, on ("*on* voit venir," "*on* entra dans la salle," "*on* eut vingt potages"). It is only in the role of spectator that the poet can analyze the self. To perceive the self through the senses of taste, sight, and smell the poet must objectify and externalize it. He must, to paraphrase Rimbaud, make his "Je" into "un autre." This he does in "Palais" where his "rêveuses pensées" are diced, chopped, and ground, and the fragments used as the basic ingredients in different dishes, which are then tasted by him. In this way he experiences and knows his own self.

The poet's "rêveuses pensées" walk naively through the twilight garden that surrounds the palace (ll. 1-2). Insouciant and graceful, they are on their way to spend an evening at Rosamond's palace. They are barefooted, as if they were going to a *fête champêtre* rather than to a palace ball. Their careless state of undress contrasts sharply with the portrait of the *mondaine* Rosamond, who appears in the fourth strophe bedecked in great elegance (l. 14). These "rêveuses pensées" have the simple grace of Verlaine's charming *bergamasques,* and the palace garden resembles his magical parks and lawns.

But the delicate charm of the poem's opening lines is quickly destroyed. The garden's peace is deceptive; the frogs' concert and the dark silhouettes of the cypresses are mere appearances (ll. 6-7), for the palace is a den of erotic pleasure and sexual violence: "Le palais don du roi comme un roi nu s'élève / Des chairs fouettées des roses de la roseraie." The palace majestically rises from and looms above the decimated petals of the rose garden. In many ways it resembles the king who built it, Henry the Second, whose amorous pleasures and sexual appetite were notorious. It is a monument to this great lover-king, who stands regally, in naked splendor, above the flesh that he has both loved and beaten.

The palace of Rosemond is a castle of erotic and sadistic pleasure. Here, eroticism leads eventually to destruction. All things — flesh, roses, the sun, and above all, the poet's "rêveuses pensées" — will be ripped to pieces, shattered or dissected. Yet, the "rêveuses pensées," like butterflies innocently falling into a spider's web, stray closer and closer to the palace, naively unaware of the danger they approach. They desire the twilight serenity beneath the cypress trees ("Elles ont envie des cyprès grandes quenouilles"), but are unaware that the cypress portends death and that the distaff, which the cypress resembles, symbolizes the thread of life that can be cut at any moment. Heedless of the physical appearance of things, which to an experienced eye would signal danger, and unconscious of the destroyed roses, the shattered sun (l. 8), and the bloody handprints on the palace windows (l. 9), the "rêveuses pensées" continue to stroll toward the palace.

Both the first and second stanzas end with sexual images of destruction: the trampled rose garden and the shattered sun ("Le soleil miroir des roses s'est brisé"). Literally, this fragmented sun describes the red glow of sunset, as night falls. Symbolically, however, it has a sexual connotation. According to a Freudian explanation, blossoms and flowers in general represent female sex organs, and the rose, in particular, represents the vulva.[11] The association of the sun with the rose is an image of sexual union:

> The symbol of a rose or rose-shaped flower vitalized by an omnipotent sun, which was later to culminate in Dante's Catholic *Comedy*, was central among the earliest organized attempts of man to comprehend the universe around him. This ancient integration of sun and flower was intended to symbolize simultaneously the sexual union of male and female

---

[11] Barbara Seward, *The Symbolic Rose* (New York: Columbia University Press, 1960), p. 7.

creative forces, the physical fertility of all natural things, and the spiritual attainment of ultimate harmony.[12]

The image of "le soleil miroir des roses s'est brisé" thickens the cloud of sexuality and amplifies the air of eroticism that hang heavily over Rosamond's palace. The roses, symbols of sexual love, are reflected in the giant celestial mirror, the sun; but when the sun is fragmented into myriad pieces, its reflection of the roses is also multiplied. Instead of one giant reflection there are millions of tiny ones: each fragment, a reflection; each facet, a mirror image.

Moreover, the shattered sun, whose surface has become pockmarked with a network of tiny facets and fragments, resembles the poet's fragmented self, as it is found at the conclusion of "Palais"; there, the poet's *I* is cracked and splintered, the pieces are chopped and diced, and then served in different courses of a meal.

With the third strophe there is a further amplifying of reflection. The sun, which mirrors the roses in each of its fragments, is, in its turn, reflected by the glass windows of the palace: "Le stigmate sanglant des mains contre les vitres." The roses, therefore, are reflected twice and fragmented twice: once by the sun and again by the windows. This *dédoublement* of fragments and reflections creates a hectic *jeu de lumière*. Reality is confused, illusion multiplied. Even before the "pensées" enter the labyrinthine palace and its mazy dream world, things have already become disturbingly confused, and hopelessly fragmented.

The palace is bathed in the red rays of the shattered and dying sun which leave a bloody mark on the palace windows (l. 9). The bloodied hands against these windows belong to the poet's thoughts which have now reached the palace proper. As they peer through the windows, their hands touch the glass and are covered with the blood-red light reflected there. However, there is another, more magical explanation for these bloodied hands. Mme Durry believes, and rightly so, that the "pensées" are wounded by the archer who is the palace guard (l. 10).[13] But, while she holds that the poet's thoughts are met at the castle as enemies, it would seem, however, that they are neither

---

[12] *Ibid.*, p. 10.
[13] II, 39.

enemies nor, for that matter, simple trespassers. Rather, they are going to spend an evening at the palace at the invitation of Rosamond, who now awaits them ("Qui donc attendez-vous/De rêveuses pensées en marche à l'Orient/Mes plus belles voisines").

If one considers, moreover, the identity of the archer who defends Rosamond's palace of love, it is clear that anyone who strayed near enough would have to be pierced by his arrows. This archer is Eros, the son of Aphrodite, and his presence is suggested in the allusion to Cyprian wine (l. 11), for the island of Cyprus was the birthplace and home of his mother. He wounds the poet's thoughts with his arrows of love and thus prepares them for their entrance into the palace. In his turn, Eros is wounded by the setting sun, pierced by those darting rays that strike the palace windows and ricochet off ("archer mal blessé du couchant").

The association of the spiritual with the temporal and the sacred with the profane is obvious throughout the poem, but nowhere as striking as in the third stanza. Pierced by Eros's arrows the "rêveuses pensées" lose their purity and innocence, just as the sun, symbol of spirituality, was corrupted when it reflected the rose, symbol of earthly love. The wine from Cyprus, a pagan allusion to Aphrodite's birthplace, refers also to the transsubstantiation of wine into the blood of Christ. Furthermore, the bloody mark left on the windows of the palace is a reference to Christ's wounds on the Cross. Finally, the agapes or love feasts (l. 12) of primitive Christianity contrast sharply with the gluttonous feast that occurs at the end of the poem.

Apollinaire's allusion to the agapes practiced during the early years of Christianity is ironical. The agape, a common religious meal which originated from Christ's Last Supper, was characterized until the end of the second century by the celebration of the Eucharist and in some churches by the sacrifice of the paschal lamb. Both events are symbolically recreated by the poet who tastes Cyprian wine and white lamb (ll. 11-12). But more importantly, agapes were meals of brotherhood, manifestations of that Christian love of neighbor, itself called *Agape*, and as such they represent a love very different from the destructive *eros* that dominates all of "Palais."

The New Testament allusion to the love feast is found in Jude 12: "These men are stains on your *love feasts*, where they banquet together irreverently and set their hearts on feeding themselves alone."[14] Since the purpose of the love feast was to express the solidarity and joy of the communicants, nothing could have been more contrary to its goal than for certain diners to go off and eat apart in little groups.[15] This is exactly what happens during the banquet at the end of "Palais." There is no fraternal communion during the meal, and each diner cares for nothing but his own stomach: "Ventre affamé n'a pas d'oreilles/Et les convives mastiquaient à qui mieux mieux."

While the poet mixes the sacred with the profane in the third strophe, in the two following stanzas he integrates the courtly with the scatological. The king addresses Rosamond, who, dressed to the teeth, sits on his pointed knees and rolls her eyes like some carnivorous animal (ll. 13-16). The scene is ridiculous; the language the king speaks is burlesque. He uses the rhetoric of chivalry and the courtly language of love to address his fair lady and to praise the erotic beauty of her body: "Dame de mes pensées au cul de perle fine." Like an accomplished troubadour he invents a poetic conceit, a precious *jeu de mots*: "Dont ni perle ni cul n'égale l'orient." Not only are the courtly and the scatological mixed here, but also the ideal, unattainable woman of courtly romance ("Dame de mes pensées") is associated with the courtesan ("cul de perle fine"). Moreover, the king's pun on the word "l'orient," which means either the eastern point on the horizon where the sun rises or the orient or shine produced by the reflections of a pearl, is taken up by Rosamond and complicated further when she tells him that she is awaiting "De rêveuses pensées en marche à l'Orient."[16]

---

[14] Ceslaus Spicq, *Agape in the New Testament*, trans. by Sister Marie Aquinas McNamara and Sister Mary Honoria Richter (3 vols.; St. Louis: B. Herder Book Co., 1965), II, 368.

[15] *Ibid.*, p. 371.

[16] The comparison by Apollinaire between Rosamond and the orient of a pearl bears a curious similarity to an old English poem, "The Ballad of Fair Rosamond." The third stanza of the "Ballad" describes Henry's mistress:

> "Her crisped lockes like threads of golde
> Appeard to each mans sight;
> Her sparkling eyes, like *Orient pearles*,
> Did cast a heavenleye light" [italics mine]

(Thomas Percy, *Reliques of Ancient English Poetry* [3 vols.; London, 1857], II, 156-157, cited by Amy Kelly, *Eleanor of Aquitaine and the Four Kings* [Cambridge: Harvard University Press, 1950], p. 150.)

Throughout "Palais" there is a lowering of lights; scenes become progressively dimmer, as the "pensées" approach the palace. When they finally enter the castle antechamber in the sixth strophe, night has almost fallen. The light in the palace, however, is completely artificial and luxurious. All illumination and reflection come from precious stones and gems. Rosamond's buttocks shine with the nacre of pearl, and the night light in the antechamber is a golden jewel: "La veilleuse dans l'ombre est un bijou d'or cuit" (l. 23).

The walls of Rosamond's palace enclose an elaborate mass of rooms and corridors which contain an intricate dream world of fantasy, illusion, and horror. Not until the poet's thoughts enter the palace (l. 22) do they become part of the "Rêve," and even then, they are only on the threshold. In order to leave the antechamber and pass into the labyrinth of the dream palace they must first remove their heads and surrender their intellectual power: "Pendez vos têtes aux patères par les tresses." Self-decapitation is the price of their admission to the irrational, dream world of the palace proper. By hanging their heads on pegs, as a polite visitor walking into a vestibule would hang up his coat before proceeding farther, the "pensées" leave rationality and reason behind them. While they are in the palace, however, their heads are taken down and sent to the kitchen to be prepared for dinner. The poet's thoughts have literally and figuratively lost their heads.

The poet's decapitated thoughts have surrendered their power to think. The skulls that housed their cerebral power are now in the kitchen being carefully skinned, plucked, boned, and carved, prior to being boiled in bouillon, roasted, rolled into slightly decomposed, but still tasty, meat ball pies ("mes souvenirs faisandés en godiveaux"), cut in raw slices, ground into "pâtés," chopped up, and placed in stews ("mirotons").

The poet enters the palace dining room and the unpleasant odor of burnt grease and bad cooking greets him (ll. 26-27). The first course of this nauseating feast is "vingt potages dont trois couleurs d'urine." As the meal continues, and the poet tastes more and more of himself, he realizes how dead, sterile, and tasteless are the different regions of his mind and the diverse parts of the self. His once beautiful dreams are stillborn, his memories, decomposed by time (ll. 31-34). Unrealized thoughts that atrophied and died in his brain have been preserved there like some frozen, grotesque, prehistoric animal. Now that he tastes them they are insipid and dull: "Or ces pensées mortes depuis des millénaires/Avaient le fade goût des grands mammouths gelés." He realizes that his is a charnel-house mind, devoted to necrophilia and overly attracted by the chimera and horror of the grave (ll. 36-37). Although this is both a nauseating meal and a disgusting revelation about his own self, the poet is able to stomach both meal and revelation alike. Despite his cynical self-deprecation the poet faces the truth about himself; he achieves self-knowledge. [17]

---

[17] Images of Rabelaisian gourmandise are frequent in Apollinaire's poetry, prose, and other writings. In fact, gourmandise was often associated with his personality, as the following menu written by Max Jacob on the occasion of a banquet organized by Pierre Reverdy and other young poets of the *Nord-Sud* circle in honor of Apollinaire, reveals; in many ways, this menu echoes the menu which the poet eats in "Palais," although it is without the vulgarity and the pessimism of the latter:

MENU
Déjeuner Guillaume Apollinaire
31 Décembre 1916

Hors-d'œuvre cubistes, orphistes, futuristes, etc.
Poisson de l'ami Méritarte
Zone de contrefilet à la Croniamantal
Arétin de chapon à l'Hérésiarque
Méditations esthétiques en salade
Fromages en Cortège d'Orphée
Fruits du Festin d'Esope
Biscuits du Brigadier Masqué

Vin blanc de l'Enchanteur
Vin rouge de la Case d'Armons
Champagne des Artilleurs
Café des Soirées de Paris
Alcools   (Collection Adéma)

(Guillaume Apollinaire, *Œuvres complètes*, ed. by Marcel Adéma and Michel Décaudin [4 vols. and facsimiles; Paris: Balland et Lecat, 1966], IV, 971-72 and facsimiles)

The allusions to characters in his prose works ("l'ami Méritarte" of a story of the same name in *Le Poète assassiné*, "Croniamantal" of *Le Poète assassiné*, "l'Hérésiarque" of *L'Hérésiarque et Cie*, "le Brigadier masqué" of the story "Cas du Brigadier masqué c'est-à-dire le poète ressuscité" found in *Le Poète assassiné*, "l'Enchanteur" of *L'Enchanteur pourrissant*), the references to his poetic works ("Zone," "Cortège d'Orphée," subtitle of *Le Bestiaire*, "Case d'Armons," title of one of the sections of *Calligrammes*, "Alcools"), the mention of the reviews on which he collaborated (*Le Festin d'Esope* and *Les Soirées de Paris*), and other references to his literary productions (*Méditations esthétiques, L'Œuvre du Divin Arétin*, an edition of Aretino's erotic writings which Apollinaire published in *Les Maîtres de l'amour* collection), and to his war experiences ("Artilleurs") — all these constitute a biography and a

The poet, however, is not the only diner at the banquet of self, although it appears that he is the only one who finds the dinner disagreeable. The other guests gluttonously devour the food served them (ll. 40-41). Their hunger is so great that they are deaf to the surprising and unique revelations ("des choses nonpareilles") that the dishes cry out. The celebrated proverb, which Apollinaire wisely and humorously incorporates into this stanza with a minor change, is undoubtedly true: "Ventre affamé n'a point d'oreilles." The poet, moreover, criticizes the insensitivity of his audience of starving gluttons. He alone is responsible for the dinner that is given them. It is his mind that has been dissected, his *moi* that has been carved up and served as a disgusting meal, and the only reaction he gets, the only understanding he receives, is the licking of lips and the chewing of teeth: "Les convives mastiquaient à qui mieux mieux." He expresses his frustration by swearing, "Mais nom de Dieu!"

"Palais" ends with an irreverent pun. In the last stanza Apollinaire rhymes "entrecôtes" with "pentecôtes" and associates the "langues de feu," last dish served at the dinner (ll. 42-44), with the Pentecostal tongues of fire that descended on Christ's apostles fifty days after Easter:

> And suddenly a sound came from heaven like the rush of a mighty wind, and it filled all the house where they were sitting. And there appeared to them tongues as of fire, distributed and resting on each one of them. And they were all filled with the Holy Spirit and began to speak in other tongues, as the spirit gave them utterance.
> (Acts 2:2-4, *Revised Standard Bible,* 1952)

Apollinaire's allusion to "langues de feu" and to "mes pentecôtes" refers not only to the Christian holiday of Pentecost but also to the Jewish holiday of pentecost or Shavuot, which commemorates the giving of the Ten Commandments. Both holidays celebrate a descent and an incarnation of the divine. The Holy Spirit descends, invades the Apostles, and brings them the gift of tongues, the gift of universal communication. God speaks to Moses and writes the Ten Command-

---

bibliography of Guillaume Apollinaire expressed through the art of *haute cuisine*: a portrait of the Apollinarian self as food and nourishment for future generations of poets.

ments with His finger on two stone tablets. In each case, divine words are communicated and incarnated; and in each case, the spiritual assumes human forms.

The containment and incarnation of the spiritual is what the poet in "Palais" desires. To resuscitate his mind and self he desperately needs a gift of tongues, a gift, that is, of poetry. Where, he asks, is the descent of spirit and the indwelling of poetic inspiration that will preserve my thoughts by making them ubiquitous and eternal: "où sont-elles mes pentecôtes/Pour mes pensées de tous pays de tous les temps"? Where is the gift of poetry that can negate the limits of space and time ("tous pays," "tous les temps") and disseminate my thoughts? Where are the poems tongued with fire that will contain my timeless and limitless thoughts and transform the insipid "pensées mortes" I have just tasted?[18]

In the concluding strophe of the poem Apollinaire raises a serious question about the role of self-knowledge in the creation of poetry. What, he asks, is the next step for a poet after self-knowledge, after the poet has come face to face with his dead thoughts, stillborn dreams and decomposed memories? How can the poet discover the poetic fire needed to transform this bitter self-knowledge into poetry, a poetry that will preserve for all times and for all peoples (l. 45) the different forms of his protean self? But Apollinaire gives no answers; instead, he illustrates how elusive and ephemeral self-knowledge can be. The poet in "Palais" slowly loses the self-knowledge he has gained during the feast. Now that the dinner has ended he is no longer certain what those dishes told him: "Ah! nom de Dieu! qu'ont donc crié ces entrecôtes/Ces grands pâtés ces os à moelle et mirotons." Unfortunately, he does not possess the poetic inspiration — the necessary pentecostal fire — to prevent the knowledge he has just acquired from disappearing. Thus, in "Palais" Apollinaire expresses, through a dark and bitter example, the truth about his search for self; it is

---

[18] A similar interpretation of these last two lines is developed by Lionel Follet in his detailed study of "Palais," entitled "Du 'Palais' de Rosemonde à l'univers poétique," in Lionel Follet and Marc Poupon, Lecture de "Palais" d'Apollinaire ("Archives des lettres modernes," no. 138; Paris: Minard, 1972), pp. 15-102; see especially, pp. 45-7. M. Follet presents an interesting comparison between "Palais" and "Merlin et la vieille femme," demonstrating quite conclusively the close thematic and stylistic resemblance of the two poems (pp. 49-56, 68-70).

a quest that can only be accomplished through poetry, whose pentecostal fire offers the best chance of capturing the fleeting and multiple essence of the self. Without the power to create poetry there can be no hope of defining what the self is.

Castle of a sexually powerful king, den of iniquity, pleasure dome of erotic and sadistic love, nightmarish château of a dream world, the palace of Rosamond has many identities, and, it seems, many rooms of torture: an abbatoir where the poet's self is slaughtered, an operating room where his mind is dissected and his brain lobotomized, a kitchen where dreams and memories are the ingredients for macabre dishes, and a dining room where the self is chewed by a group of carnivorous gluttons. Throughout this meal the poet, stripped of his illusions and his dignity, bravely faces public scrutiny and, above all, the brute, disgusting reality of his own being. Unfortunately, he is unable to make poetic use of what he has learned. In "Palais" the drama of fragmentation leads to an ephemeral understanding of the self. In the poem "Cortège," however, it leads much further.

"CORTÈGE"

"Cortège" [19] is composed of what appears to be three different poems: a section of mystical, hermetic, and metaphysical poetry (ll. 1-18), a very long passage of personal, carefree, prosaic enumerations (ll. 19-65), and finally two concluding stanzas of alexandrines (ll. 66-73), which contrast sharply with the preceding *vers libres* and give the poem a classical ending quite suitable to the subtle allusion to Boileau in the last line.

This lack of stylistic continuity is even more evident if one looks at the three manuscript versions of "Cortège," which were composed at different times between 1906 and 1912, when the poem appeared in the revue *Poème et Drame*. The first manuscript, a loose sheet of paper that is impossible to date, contains a very early version of the poem's second part. The second, a manuscript of lines 24 through 48, is written on the back of a subscription announcement for the third year (1906) of the revue, *Vers et Prose*; and the third contains an unfinished version of the poem's first part, as it appeared under

---

[19] See below, pp. 54-55 for the text of the poem.

the title "Brumaire" in *L'Année républicaine,* a *recueil* that was proposed by Apollinaire in 1909 but never completed.[20]

Yet, despite the farrago of prosaic and noble styles, of free and conventional rhythms, and of seemingly unrelated passages, "Cortège" has a surprising unity. A desire for self-knowledge informs and unites the entire poem. From the lofty and mystical bird in the opening three stanzas to the poet's myriad sensual experiences in the second section to the shining past that grows within him at the end, there is a movement towards introspection and towards an inner vision.

As the title suggests, "Cortège" describes a procession; but this is not an ordinary parade. What marches in review before the poet are images of himself, pieces that have been fragmented from the self and then objectified. As in "Palais," where waiters bearing dishes that have been prepared from fragments of the poet's self ("Des rôtis de pensées mortes dans mon cerveau / Mes beaux rêves mort-nés en tranches bien saignantes") serve the poet, so in "Cortège" the participants in the procession carry before the poet the real and imaginary elements, or selves, that constitute his identity; when all these fragments are accumulated they give a full portrait of the poet's *moi*. The drama of fragmentation in "Cortège" leads ultimately, by the accumulation of fragments, to self-knowledge.

"Cortège" begins with a description of a mythic bird that lays its eggs in the sky (ll. 1-5). As Michel Décaudin in his *Le Dossier d'"Alcools"* has pointed out,[21] this non-terrestrial bird is not a creation of Apollinaire's fertile imagination, for in *Le Monde enchanté, cosmographie et histoire naturelle fantastiques du Moyen Age* (Paris, 1845) by Ferdinand Denis, with which Apollinaire was acquainted, is found the following passage from the *Voyages* (1608-9) of Jean Mocquet:

> "L'un de ces mariniers me montra un petit oyseau qui n'estoit pas plus gros qu'une linotte, et me dict qu'il ne bougeait de la mer et n'alloit jamais à terre, et que lorsque la femelle veut pondre ses œufs, elle monte fort haut jusqu'à ce qu'on ne la peut voir, et pond ainsi ses œufs, et un à chaque fois qu'elle monte (...)"

---

[20] Michel Décaudin, *Le Dossier d' "Alcools"* ("Publications romanes et françaises," vol. LXVII; Geneva: Droz, 1965), pp. 126-127.
[21] p. 127.

Denis's work also points out that the European explorers who discovered the New World also discovered that the Bird of Paradise lived eternally in the sky.[22]

But if Apollinaire did not invent this perpetually flying bird, neither did Francis Picabia, who also speaks of it in the second chapter of his *Jésus-Christ Rastaquouère*, written in 1920:[23]

> "Il est une espèce d'oiseau d'une grande rareté et bien difficile à connaître, car ces oiseaux ne se posent jamais; le [sic] femelle pond ses œufs dans les airs à une grande hauteur et l'éclosion des petits a lieu avant qu'ils n'aient eu le temps d'arriver jusqu'à terre; volant sans cesse, ignorant le repos, les battements de leurs ailes sont semblables aux battements de notre cœur, arrêt signifie mort. Ces oiseaux existent partout, ils ont, semble-t-il, toujours existé, mais d'où proviennent-ils, de quelle planète? La connaissance de leur origine préoccupe beaucoup de cerveaux..."[24]

In the opening stanza of "Cortège" this legendary bird, which represents the poet, makes its nest deep in the outer regions of the atmosphere (ll. 1-3). But the startling feature about the bird's flight is that it flies *upwards* toward an earth that shines with the blinding intensity of the sun, an earth situated in the position normally occupied by the sun. The bird's flight therefore is a "vol inverse," for its habits are the contrary of those of other birds: rather than laying its eggs on the ground it lays them in the sky; instead of

---

[22] "Jouet éternel des vagues de l'air, l'oiseau de paradis ne trouva d'autre asile que le souffle des vents, d'autre nourriture qu'une céleste rosée. La nature, qui l'avait paré des reflets de l'émeraude et des rayons dorés de la topaze, ne lui avait donné que des ailes, comme pour l'inviter à de célestes amours que la terre ne devait jamais souiller." Ferdinand Denis, *Le Monde enchanté. Cosmographie et histoire naturelle fantastiques du moyen âge* (1845; rpt. New York: Burt Franklin, n.d.), p. 150.

[23] Marguerite Bonnet, "A Propos de 'Cortège': Apollinaire et Picabia," *La Revue des lettres modernes*, nos. 85-89 (automne, 1963), p. 63. In fact, Picabia learned about this bird from Apollinaire. (Hereafter, *La Revue des lettres modernes* will be referred to as *R. L. M.*)

[24] *Ibid.*, citing *Jésus-Christ Rastaquouère*, Collection Dada, n.d., n.p., p. 33. As Mme Bonnet points out, Apollinaire's use of the mythic bird and Picabia's are diametrically opposed. While in "Cortège" the legend illustrates the importance of the past, in Picabia's work it illustrates the importance of the future, and, above all, of movement. The unceasing flight of the bird represents for him the twentieth century poet, who never stops to rest but is continually moving forward (pp. 70-72).

flying downward, its flight is perpetually directed upward. Along with the bird's inverted flight there is a corresponding inversion in the universe: the earth and the sun have traded positions to create a new solar system.

Thus, the opening stanza of "Cortège" announces that the universe has been turned upside down, that perspectives have been considerably altered. The result is a new universe and with it a new manner of perceiving the world. The bird is blinded by this new reality (ll. 4-5) because its eyesight is accustomed to looking at the universe as it was in the past. Since perspectives have been changed, and the earth now occupies the shining center of a new Ptolemaic cosmos, normal vision is neither effective nor reliable. A transformed universe requires a new optic, a new way of looking at the world, and this is symbolized by the bird, which, in lowering its "deuxième paupière," renounces its outmoded point-of-view. In so doing it shuts out the view of the exterior world and turns its glance inward to contemplate itself. Its new vision is one that looks into the self rather than out to the world; it is one of *in-sight*. An optic of introspection replaces one of extrospection, and the bird becomes the symbol of the poet's new vision of reality, a "Nouvel oiseau d'une nouvelle réalité,"[25] as Apollinaire called it in the "Brumaire" manuscript of the poem.

While in the first stanza of "Cortège" the movement inward towards introspection is set in motion, it is not until the third stanza that this movement is accomplished. In between, however, there is a transitional strophe that makes the change from the exterior to the interior world (ll. 6-11). With this stanza the poet's "I" makes its first direct appearance in the poem. But it has a double identity; two opposing selves answer to the name, "I." Like the solar earth of the first stanza, which is a combination of the sun's light ("brille") and the earth's mass ("sol"), the poet is a mixture of two different selves: an earthy, corporeal self and a solar, spiritual one. The material self is somber and opaque (l. 6). It is the poet's body which, like a fog, a hand, and a vault, is capable of shutting out light (ll. 7-9). Strongly attached to the exterior world, by what Apollinaire calls in one of the poem's manuscripts "de grouillantes chaînes,"[26] this grounded

---

[25] Décaudin, *Le Dossier*, p. 127.
[26] *Ibid.*

self opposes the more spiritual, air-borne self, which, since it is capable of self-illumination, lights up the shadows of the material self (ll. 10-11). Because of its power of illumination and because it recedes into a night sky that appears to represent the poet's past (for the allusion to "des astres bien-aimés" suggests ambiguously an intimacy existing between the poet and this sky) the solar self is that part of the poet responsible for self-knowledge and for insight. Like the bird which closes its eye to the exterior world, the solar self shuts out the sight of the earthy self by moving away from it ("Je m'éloignerai"); it therefore begins a voyage of introspection into the hidden reaches of the poet's *moi*, which is represented in concrete terms as a region "d'ombres/Et d'alignements d'yeux des astres bien-aimés."

The third stanza (ll. 12-18) begins with the magical bird of the first strophe flying the same inverted flight; in fact, it repeats almost word for word the opening four lines of the poem, but with an important difference.[27] From the second stanza on an interiorization of the landscape has taken place. The region described is that of the poet's self. The bird no longer flies in the atmosphere but instead makes its nest in the poet's memory (ll. 13-14). Here, as before, it is forced to close its eye, but this time not because of a shining earth but because of the blinding light of a meteor ("ce feu oblong"). In keeping with the inverted movements of objects in the poem the oblong

---

[27] As M. Chevalier has observed, Apollinaire makes extensive and extraordinary use of repetition in his poetry:

> Nul n'a mieux marqué qu'Apollinaire, de façon plus ouverte, cette faculté de reprise et de transformation qui est l'essence même de la poésie. (p. 92)

A possible explanation of Apollinaire's fascination with repetition is offered by M. Chevalier:

> Apollinaire, jusqu'à l'obsession, s'est réutilisé lui-même, il reprend ses manuscrits, les refond, il récupère des textes anciens, les réutilise à d'autres fins. (p. 28)

Apollinaire's use of repetition — and one thinks of the line from "Nuit rhénane" ("Le Rhin le Rhin est ivre...," *O. P.*, p. 111), or the one that opens "Mai" ("Le mai le joli mai...," *O. P.*, p. 112), or the final line of "Zone" ("Soleil cou coupé," *O. P.*, p. 44), or the line from "La Chanson du Mal-Aimé" ("...un cul de dame damascène," *O. P.*, p. 55), and the list could go on forever — constitutes a fundamental structure of his poetry, one which M. Chevalier has identified with the quality of formal, semantic, phonetic, temporal, and spatial circularity which many of the poems of *Alcools* seem to possess (see Chevalier, pp. 29-33, 78-85, 158-61, 243-51, *et passim*).

fire refers to a meteor or a falling star which, instead of falling towards earth or disintegrating as it speeds through the universe, rises and becomes more intense. Eventually, its light will become so bright that it will become "l'unique lumière" (ll. 17-18). It is a symbol of the poet's memory, which becomes brighter, paradoxically, the farther it recedes into the past. In the natural world governed by time, the more distant the past gets from the present the more vague, somber, and dead it becomes. But within the timelessness of the poet's self the reverse occurs. The more distant the past is from the present the brighter it becomes. At the end of "Cortège" the past will be called a "passé luisant" (l. 71).[28] Memory is intensified to the point that it becomes the solar center of the self. What begins as a meteor will in the future be transformed into a sun. At the center of this universe will shine a light that may be called the "empyrean" of the poet's self; it resembles the lofty region described by Apollinaire in his poem "Le Brasier":

> Descendant des hauteurs où pense la lumière
> Jardins rouant plus haut que tous les ciels mobiles
> L'avenir masqué flambe en traversant les cieux
> (O. P., p. 110)

But if the oblong fire refers to the poet's memory it also refers to the work of art, which in Apollinaire's poetry is closely related to memory. As the fire is contained and circumscribed by its geometric oblong shape, so the poet's memory is contained and molded by the form of a work of art. The "feu oblong," like other metaphors in Apollinaire's poetry, is composed of two images, one of which suggests the order, form and plasticity of matter ("oblong") and the other of which evokes the force, freedom, chaos, and inspiration of spirit ("feu"). In juxtaposing the concepts of abstract and concrete, idea and form, it is a perfect metaphor for the work of art. Like a star that has survived the destruction of its galaxy, poetry, Apollinaire suggests, will continue to illuminate the universe long after the death of its creator. Thus, when the oblong flame grows brighter and becomes the "unique lumière," it represents the work of art that in the future will be the only vestige of and monument to its dead creator, what

---

[28] A similar interpretation of the poet's memory in "Cortège" is suggested by M. Renaud in his *Lecture d'Apollinaire* (pp. 160-61).

Mallarmé in "Le Tombeau d'Edgar Poe" called "Calme bloc ici-bas chu d'un désastre obscur." [29]

Throughout "Cortège" as a whole, and in the first three stanzas in particular, there is an unusual reversal of perspective: the movement away from things implies a movement toward light, while the movement towards things involves a movement towards darkness. Distance is associated with illumination and proximity with dullness. While from up close the earth and the material self are dull and somber (ll. 6-9), and the poet's future is drab and formless (ll. 68, 71), from a distance the opposite is true. The earth shines like the sun (l. 3), the poet's solar self, when it separates from the material self, begins to shine brightly (ll. 10-11); the past becomes more bright, the farther it recedes from the present (ll. 68-72); the work of art ("ce feu oblong") grows in brightness the farther it disappears into the future (ll. 17-18). The idea of distance, therefore, usually associated with spatial remoteness and imprecision, becomes synonymous with illumination and clarity of vision.

Proximate vision throughout "Cortège" is associated with the body, the senses, the real and the exterior world, while distant vision deals with the abstract, the imaginary, and with the inner world of the self. In the search for identity that is the focal point of Apollinaire's poetry, in general, and of "Cortège," in particular, it is distant vision that leads eventually to self-knowledge. When the poet exteriorizes himself in his works, when he projects the self onto the screen of his poems, he is externalizing the self by placing it at a certain distance from himself. Apollinaire illustrates this externalization in the poem "Zone" when he looks at himself with mockery and disdain:

> Tu te moques de toi et comme le feu de l'Enfer ton rire pétille
> Les étincelles de ton rire dorent le fond de ta vie
> C'est un tableau pendu dans un sombre musée
> Et quelquefois tu vas le regarder de près
>
> (O. P., p. 41)

or in "Merveille de la guerre," a poem from *Calligrammes*, where his being is projected onto and is integrated into the surrounding war-torn landscape:

---

[29] Stéphane Mallarmé, *Œuvres complètes* ("Bibliothèque de la Pléiade"; Paris: Gallimard, 1945), p. 70.

> Je lègue à l'avenir l'histoire de Guillaume Apollinaire
> Qui fut à la guerre et sut être partout
> Dans les villes heureuses de l'arrière
> Dans tout le reste de l'univers
> Dans ceux qui meurent en piétinant dans le barbelé
> Dans les femmes dans les canons dans les chevaux
> Au zénith au nadir aux 4 points cardinaux
> Et dans l'unique ardeur de cette veillée d'armes
>
> (*O. P.*, p. 272)

This distance gives Apollinaire the objectivity and the detachment necessary for self-analysis and eventually for self-knowledge. The self is most easily observed when it is outside the poet; to see it from afar is to become enlightened.

Apollinaire's use of self-exteriorization is paradoxically a form of introspection. It is a technique that enables the poet to explore and to discover the nature of his mysterious self. Apollinaire places a real and visible form of himself in the space around him like a thing among other things and thereafter he sees himself objectively and subjectively — from inside the self and from outside — simultaneously.

The movement away from things and into the self, the movement towards introspection, is established in the three opening stanzas of "Cortège" and gives direction to the entire poem. While the first part of "Cortège" emphasizes the movement away from the world and the withdrawal into the self, it is the second part that records the different stages of introspection by means of which the poet discovers his identity.

The second part of "Cortège" (ll. 19-65) is the most prosaic and the most lyrical part of the poem. It begins with an excellent example of Apollinaire's often used technique of self-fragmentation (ll. 19-23). "Je," "me," "moi," "tu," "Guillaume," "celui-là," these are the names the Apollinarian self answers to; and the fragmented, disjointed nature of this self along with the poet's hope that his long awaited identity will soon appear (l. 22) point to his strong desire for self-knowledge. In the lines that follow, Apollinaire describes two different types of cortege that parade by: a procession of his sense impressions and perceptions (ll. 23-47) and a cortege composed of his hallucinations, dreams, and the creations of his imagination (ll. 50-65). In each he searches for the revelation of his identity, for "celui-là que je suis."

In the first procession Apollinaire's five senses lead a parade composed of disconnected bits and pieces of reality and of fragments of sense perceptions which march in disorderly, helter-skelter fashion. The sensations described are taken from every imaginable aspect of reality: feet, hair, hands; children, blind men, mutes; rivers, churches, gardens, cities; clothes, footsteps, ships, a letter, and a dog. Moreover, the procession is not confined to the present or the quotidian; it also includes the historical past (ll. 36-39). A cortege of such disjointed sense impressions bears a certain resemblance to cubist collages where, for example, newspaper clippings, fragments of advertisements, and other disparate *bric à brac* of reality are integrated into an abstract composition. Furthermore, the enumerative quality of the poetry resembles the dismembering of reality and the cataloguing of its fragments undertaken by the cubists. Apollinaire's description of Picasso in *Les Peintres cubistes* (1913), for example, could also be applied to his own enumeration of sensations in "Cortège":

> Nouvel homme, le monde est sa nouvelle représentation. Il en dénombre les éléments, les détails avec une brutalité qui sait aussi être gracieuse.... Ce dénombrement, a la grandeur de l'épopée, et, avec l'ordre, éclatera le drame. On peut contester un système, une idée, une date, une ressemblance, mais je ne vois pas comment on pourrait contester la simple action du numérateur.[30]

The first cortege, then, is an enumeration of the poet's sense perceptions. But the poet is more than an enumerator of sensations; he is a creator. His sense impressions are only a *point de départ* for a creative act that involves his entire being. Starting with the most minute fragment of reality and with the meanest sensation, the sight of a piece of hair or of a tongue, for example, the poet can reconstruct the world or recreate the person to whom the hair or the tongue belongs (ll. 25ff). Or, making use of the most insignificant sensation, the odor of a small dog, Apollinaire is able to resuscitate the noble history of the city of Cologne, describe the citizens who lived there some four centuries earlier and evoke the legendary slaughter of Saint Ursula and her retinue of virgins (ll. 36-39). The magic that enables the poet to reconstruct what he sees only in part and to

---

[30] p. 67.

span the centuries in order to recreate the past is located in the unlimited creative power of his imagination. It is a power that enables the poet to "refaire ces gens à milliers."

In "Cortège" the poet's awareness of things comes initially from his five senses. But soon after, other senses, cerebral and not sensual ones, take control. These superior, creative, sixth "senses," what Apollinaire calls "quelques autres" (l. 24), refashion, elaborate and organize ("refaire") the disjointed, fragmentary sensations experienced by the other five senses. Like the elements used in a collage — newspaper clippings, letters, advertisements — the poet's real sensations are rearranged, reordered, and juxtaposed in new and different patterns. The result is a new conception of reality created in part by the power of the poet's imagination. With regard to his conceptual power to reconstruct reality, the poet is very much like the cubist painter who, by giving considerable thought to what constitutes reality, arrives at a reordering of his sense impressions according to the dictates of his conceptions. As the cubist painters Albert Gleizes and Jean Metzinger wrote in their essay of 1912, *Du Cubisme*, the first study entirely devoted to the subject:

> "... the visible world can become the real world only by the operation of the intellect.... There is nothing real outside ourselves; there is nothing real except the coincidence of a sensation and an individual mental tendency. Be it far from us to throw any doubts upon the existence of the objects which impress our senses; but, rationally speaking, we can only experience certitude in respect of the images which they produce in the mind." [31]

Seeing an object, then, is not merely enough; the painter has to think it. Cubism, as defined by Apollinaire in his study of a year later, is, above all, an art of the mind:

---

[31] *Cubism*, English translation (London: Unwin, 1913), rpt. in *Theories of Modern Art. A Source Book by Artists and Critics*, ed. Herschel Chipp (Berkeley: University of California Press, 1968), pp. 208 and 214. In addition, there is the statement made by Braque in 1917 that "'the senses deform, the mind forms. Work to perfect the mind. There is no certitude but in what the mind conceives.'" (Georges Braque, "Thoughts and Reflections on Art," English translation in *Artists on Art*, eds. Robert Goldwater and Marco Treves [New York: Pantheon Books, 1945]; rpt. in Chipp, p. 260.)

> Ce qui différencie le cubisme de l'ancienne peinture, c'est qu'il n'est pas un art d'imitation, mais un art de conception qui tend à s'élever jusqu'à la création.[32]
>
> Voulant atteindre aux proportions de l'idéal, ne se bornant pas à l'humanité, les jeunes peintres nous offrent des œuvres plus cérébrales que sensuelles. Ils s'éloignent de plus en plus de l'ancien art des illusions d'optique et des proportions locales pour exprimer la grandeur des formes métaphysiques.[33]

From the opening of "Cortège" there has been a movement inward, towards introspection, which has expressed the poet's search for self-knowledge. In the first cortege — the procession of the poet's sensations — there is contact between the exterior and the interior worlds, between reality and its sensations and the poet's imagination that reorders and transforms this reality. However, in the second cortege — the procession of the poet's dreams — all contact with the exterior world is ended, and the poet totally encloses himself in an interior landscape (ll. 48-65). Here a long train of fantastic, hallucinatory creatures, all born from the poet's imagination, parades by: giants covered with algae, underwater cities whose towers form islands, a sea of blood, thousands of white tribesmen who carry roses and speak a language they have invented. In both the sense-cortege and the dream-cortege the poet's imagination is at work, either organizing sensations or creating fantasies; but the difference between them is that while the former has its point of origin in the outside world, the latter begins completely within the poet's mind. In the first instance, the poetic imagination *recreates* and reorders sensations of the external world; in the second, it *creates* pure creations that have no counterparts in the exterior world, since they exist only within the poet's mind. The landscape through which this dream-cortege proceeds, at a lyrical pace, is an interior one; for, although the cortege of giants traverses an underwater world (ll. 52-55) and the cortege of "mille peuplades blanches" (ll. 56-59) walks on the earth, the environment is always that of the poet's self. The sea, for example, is his own blood and his own life force: "Et cette mer avec les clartés de ses profondeurs/Coulait sang de mes veines et fait battre mon cœur."

---

[32] *Les Peintres cubistes*, p. 56.
[33] *Ibid.*, p. 53.

Already the poet is nearing the center of the interior universe and the goal of his journey. Already he can perceive the light of self-knowledge ("clartés") shining through the depths ("profondeurs") of the sea. Yet, despite all the evidence to the contrary, Apollinaire states that he is not a member of this cortege (ll. 50-51, 60-61). These are other people ("ceux que j'aime") who march here, not himself. But, how, one might ask, can a cortege of the poet's dreams and hallucinations, a procession that literally marches right out of his imagination, not belong to him? How can he separate and dissociate himself from a cortege that he has created and that symbolizes him? How can he say that these are others marching here, when they are undoubtedly parts of his own self?

From the beginning of the poem's second part Apollinaire has mentioned his relationship with "les autres;" he has stated that he does not know himself but that he knows "les autres" (ll. 21-24); and he has boasted of his power to "ressusciter les autres" (ll. 46-47). In each case, a strong bond exists between the poet and the others he knows. But this notion of "les autres" is left equivocal; Apollinaire does not define who the others are or what their relationships are to him. Even more surprising is the fact that each time Apollinaire speaks of awaiting the arrival of himself a procession of others suddenly appears (ll. 19-24, 48-50). And for good reason, for these others are an image or a *persona* for the self that the poet has been seeking. The dream-cortege composed of "ceux que j'aime/Parmi lesquels je n'étais pas" is in fact a representation, a portrait, of the poet's *moi*:

>Le cortège passait et j'y cherchais mon corps
>Tous ceux qui survenaient et n'étaient pas moi-même
>Amenaient un à un les morceaux de moi-même
>On me bâtit peu à peu comme on élève une tour
>Les peuples s'entassaient et je parus moi-même
>Qu'ont formé tous les corps et les choses humaines

The poet's *moi* and "les autres," therefore, are the same thing seen from two different perspectives, one from inside the self and the other from outside. When Apollinaire fragments himself and calls the parts "je" and "tu" as in the line "Je me disais Guillaume il est temps que tu viennes," or in the poem "Zone" when he writes:

>Tu as fait de douloureux et de joyeux voyages
>Avant de t'apercevoir du mensonge et de l'âge

> Tu as souffert de l'amour à vingt et à trente ans
> J'ai vécu comme un fou et j'ai perdu mon temps
> Tu n'oses plus regarder tes mains et à tous moments
>   je voudrais sangloter
> Sur toi sur celle que j'aime sur tout ce qui t'a épouvanté
>   (O. P., pp. 42-43)

he is looking at himself from a double point-of-view, where self and other are experienced simultaneously as *I* and *you*. The technique of self-fragmentation in Apollinaire's poetry, therefore, involves the projection of the poet's *moi* onto an exterior object (a fine example is the "tableau pendu dans un sombre musée" of "Zone"). In its new objectified form the self becomes the other, the non-self. Thus, in "Cortège" the opposing forces of fragmentation and fusion work in concert to bring about the revelation of the poet's self-identity. The fragmentation of the *moi* creates "les autres," and the accumulation of these others, in turn, creates the self: "Les peuples s'entassaient et je parus moi-même/Qu'ont formé tous les corps et les choses humaines." The amassing of fragments adds up to self-knowledge, for the process of accumulation, according to Apollinaire, is the poet's means of attaining truth:

> Ce sont des matériaux qu'amasse le poète, qu'amasse l'esprit nouveau, et ces matériaux formeront un fond de vérité dont la simplicité, la modestie ne doit point rebuter, car les conséquences, les résultats peuvent être de grandes, de bien grandes choses. [34]

The dialectic between fragmentation and fusion in Apollinaire's poems points to the important role played by poetry in Apollinaire's search for self-identity. Each poem is an isolated, externalized form

---

[34] "L'Esprit nouveau et les poètes," p. 390. M. Chevalier points out that Apollinaire's tendency towards the creating of inventories constitutes one of the fundamental structures of his poetry. Apollinaire is "un actuaire fantastique" (p. 248), who,

> interroge tous les systèmes de signes que la caravane humaine a élaborés, le langage et les mythes, il les fait parler — et en ce sens, il est bien 'prophète,' 'celui qui parle à la place de' —, il les organise en cortège; ... (p. 92)

The poem "Cortège," observes M. Chevalier, can be considered "comme l'Art proclamé le plus clair de la grande poétique d'Apollinaire,..." (*Ibid.*)

of the self, a moment in the perpetually on-going life of the self, a fragment; the poet's *œuvre*, then, being an accumulation of these moments and of these fragments, constitutes "un fond de vérité," a tentative definition of self, which becomes definitive upon the poet's death.

The poet's journey toward self-knowledge, the subject of "Cortège," is finally realized in the third and final part of the poem (ll. 66-73). Here the poet's self is seen as the only eternal reality in a world that is constantly changing and whose temporality is defined by a meaningless sequence of past, present, and future; it is a world characterized by "Temps passés Trépassés," where "Les dieux qui me formâtes / Je ne vis que passant ainsi que vous passâtes," a world distinguished by emptiness ("vide"), dullness ("incolore"), formlessness ("informe"), and death ("mort"). The poet turns away from this vision of his temporal future, from this "vide avenir" (ll. 68-69), and looks into himself where he discovers a past that has been preserved by memory. The poet's *moi*, in which the resuscitated past — the *durée* — grows larger and larger until it finally shines with creative light ("le passé luisant") becomes a refuge against the empire of time and death symbolized by the "demain...incolore" (l. 71).[35] The poet's self and the creative memories stored therein offer him the only possibility of immortality. Self-knowledge attained through knowledge of one's past and the expression of this knowledge in poetry remain the only means open to the poet for eternalizing himself. In Apollinaire one goes from memory of the facts ("le passé luisant") to a poetic recreation ("ce qui parfait / Présente tout ensemble et l'effort et l'effet"). The "passé luisant," because of its creative energy, permits the poet to produce an immortal work of art that contains an exteriorized form of the poet's self. This work will have a future quite distinct from that of the mortal poet; it will be a unified verbal structure

---

[35] The image of the expanding past ("le passé luisant") and the image earlier in the poem (ll. 17-18) of the "feu oblong," whose intensity increases as it moves through time, like a rolling snowball, both have a distinct Bergsonian tone; they would appear to be images of Bergson's *durée*:

> Duration is the continuous progress of the past which gnaws into the future and which swells as it advances. And as the past grows without ceasing, so also there is no limit to its preservation.

(Henri Bergson, *Creative Evolution*, trans. Arthur Mitchell [New York: The Modern Library, 1944], p. 7)

bearing witness simultaneously ("tout ensemble") first to the poet's act of creation ("l'effort") and second to a content that he has imparted to that structure at the moment of its creation and that will be contained within it for all time ("l'effet"). "Cortège" ends with an aesthetic statement that declares the poet's faith in the immortality of the poetic work of art.[36]

In the concluding stanzas of "Cortège" the introspective movement of the entire poem comes to rest upon a prophetic vision of Apollinaire's poetic future. Now that the desire for inner vision and the search for self-identity have been realized through the appearance of the "passé luisant," the poet looks to the future, to "le temps de la grâce ardente" ("Les Collines," *O. P.*, p. 174), where the perfect works of art that he leaves as his legacy will become his "unique lumière." Death for Apollinaire is a question of losing in order ultimately to win:

> Perdre
> Mais perdre vraiment
> Pour laisser place à la trouvaille
> Perdre
> La vie pour trouver la Victoire
> ("Toujours," *O. P.*, p. 237)

The drama of fragmentation enacted in "Palais" and "Cortège" involves the separation of the poet from his own self. Either as a diner served a meal made from fragments of his externalized self or as a spectator watching parts of himself parade by, the poet becomes distanced from his own being. Fragmentation of the self in Apollinaire's poetry involves a movement of separation and of objectification. Only when the self is made into an object found among other objects, only when it becomes a concrete, tangible entity existing outside of the poet and at a distance from him, only, that is, when it is cast into the form of a poem, can the self be known and the poet's identity defined.

---

[36] For a similar interpretation of the last stanza of "Cortège," see Renaud, pp. 156-57. M. Renaud observes that the entire poem functions as a kind of cortege, for by marching with a *"lyrique* pas," which is to say according to the rhythms of poetry, it brings together and constructs a poeticized past, the "passé luisant."

CORTÈGE

A. M. Léon Bailby.

1 Oiseau tranquille au vol inverse oiseau
   Qui nidifie en l'air
   A la limite où notre sol brille déjà
   Baisse ta deuxième paupière la terre t'éblouit
5 Quand tu lèves la tête

   Et moi aussi de près je suis sombre et terne
   Une brume qui vient d'obscurcir les lanternes
   Une main qui tout à coup se pose devant les yeux
   Une voûte entre vous et toutes les lumières
10 Et je m'éloignerai m'illuminant au milieu d'ombres
   Et d'alignements d'yeux des astres bien-aimés

   Oiseau tranquille au vol inverse oiseau
   Qui nidifie en l'air
   A la limite où brille déjà ma mémoire
15 Baisse ta deuxième paupière
   Ni à cause du soleil ni à cause de la terre
   Mais pour ce feu oblong dont l'intensité ira s'augmentant
   Au point qu'il deviendra un jour l'unique lumière

   Un jour
20 Un jour je m'attendais moi-même
   Je me disais Guillaume il est temps que tu viennes
   Pour que je sache enfin celui-là que je suis
   Moi qui connais les autres
   Je les connais par les cinq sens et quelques autres
25 Il me suffit de voir leurs pieds pour pouvoir refaire ces gens
       à milliers
   De voir leurs pieds paniques un seul de leurs cheveux
   Ou leur langue quand il me plaît de faire le médecin
   Ou leurs enfants quand il me plaît de faire le prophète
   Les vaisseaux des armateurs la plume de mes confrères
30 La monnaie des aveugles les mains des muets
   Ou bien encore à cause du vocabulaire et non de l'écriture
   Une lettre écrite par ceux qui ont plus de vingt ans
   Il me suffit de sentir l'odeur de leurs églises
   L'odeur des fleuves dans leurs villes
35 Le parfum des fleurs dans les jardins publics
   O Corneille Agrippa l'odeur d'un petit chien m'eût suffi

Pour décrire exactement tes concitoyens de Cologne
Leurs rois-mages et la ribambelle ursuline
Qui t'inspirait l'erreur touchant toutes les femmes
40 Il me suffit de goûter la saveur du laurier qu'on cultive pour que j'aime ou que je bafoue
Et de toucher les vêtements
Pour ne pas douter si l'on est frileux ou non
O gens que je connais
Il me suffit d'entendre le bruit de leurs pas
45 Pour pouvoir indiquer à jamais la direction qu'ils ont prise
Il me suffit de tous ceux-là pour me croire le droit
De ressusciter les autres
Un jour je m'attendais moi-même
Je me disais Guillaume il est temps que tu viennes
50 Et d'un lyrique pas s'avançaient ceux que j'aime
Parmi lesquels je n'étais pas
Les géants couverts d'algues passaient dans leurs villes
Sous-marines où les tours seules étaient des îles
Et cette mer avec les clartés de ses profondeurs
55 Coulait sang de mes veines et fait battre mon cœur
Puis sur terre il venait mille peuplades blanches
Dont chaque homme tenait une rose à la main
Et le langage qu'ils inventaient en chemin
Je l'appris de leur bouche et je le parle encore
60 Le cortège passait et j'y cherchais mon corps
Tous ceux qui survenaient et n'étaient pas moi-même
Amenaient un à un les morceaux de moi-même
On me bâtit peu à peu comme on élève une tour
Les peuples s'entassaient et je parus moi-même
65 Qu'ont formé tous les corps et les choses humaines

Temps passés Trépassés Les dieux qui me formâtes
Je ne vis que passant ainsi que vous passâtes
Et détournant mes yeux de ce vide avenir
En moi-même je vois tout le passé grandir

70 Rien n'est mort que ce qui n'existe pas encore
Près du passé luisant demain est incolore
Il est informe aussi près de ce qui parfait
Présente tout ensemble et l'effort et l'effet

(O. P., pp. 74-76)

Chapter II

THE DRAMA OF DISPERSION

"NUIT RHÉNANE"

Not only is the self in Apollinaire's poetry divided into pieces and dissected into fragments, but these parts are often dispersed throughout the world like seeds. If in "Palais" and "Cortège" we found the poet meticulously performing an autopsy on the self, in "Nuit rhénane" he has forsaken his scapel for a lyre. Instead of cutting away at the self, he serenades its multiple presence in the universe. "Nuit rhénane" expresses a cosmic, almost orphic experience.[1]

The organizing image of "Nuit rhénane" is the song. Each stanza has its own tune and its own singer. From the boatman's slow, lyric melody to the magical incantation of the *ondines* to the final peal of cynical laughter, "Nuit rhénane" is a crescendo that expresses the power of song and of poetry as well. Accompanying the musical crescendo, moreover, is a succession of different selves, who succeed one another without warning, from the passive self of the opening stanza to the mocking self of the last. These disparate selves are scattered throughout the Rhenish countryside, and they participate in the different songs that fill the intoxicating night air.

In the opening stanza a state of complete passivity exists:

> Mon verre est plein d'un vin trembleur comme une flamme
> Ecoutez la chanson lente d'un batelier

---

[1] "Nuit rhénane" was written at Honnef in May, 1902 and belongs to the group of Apollinaire's poems called "Rhénanes." Like them it reflects the influence of German folklore and the power of the supernatural on Apollinaire's imagination. See below, pp. 64-69.

Qui raconte avoir vu sous la lune sept femmes
Tordre leurs cheveux verts et longs jusqu'à leurs pieds
(*O. P.*, p. 111)

The passive self listens to the boatman's song and hears a tale of mystery; but he does not participate in the song or in its telling. Another image of passivity is the wine that trembles like a flame inside the poet's glass. The comparison of wine and flame is a striking one, for they both contain a great store of potential, unexploded energy. This energy lies trapped inside them awaiting release, and, like Poe's imp in the bottle, its restlessness makes the wine tremble, sparkle, and glow mysteriously. Until their power can be released, however, wine and flame remain inactive and passive. But when that release occurs their unleashed power explodes, transforming whatever it touches.

The second stanza introduces a new self, who, unlike his predecessor, participates vigorously in an immediate and sensual experience:

> Debout chantez plus haut en dansant une ronde
> Que je n'entende plus le chant du batelier
> Et mettez près de moi toutes les filles blondes
> Au regard immobile aux nattes repliées

The *I* is in command from the start, barking out orders — "Debout chantez," "que je n'entende plus," "mettez" — calling on his companions to sing and dance, and participating actively in the life of the moment. While the passive self of the first strophe insisted on listening to the boatman's song, the active, robust self of the second rejects the former's passive way of singing and dancing: "Chantez plus haut en dansant une ronde." He also rejects the boatman's song about mystery and the supernatural ("Que je n'entende plus le chant du batelier") preferring instead to sing of the present and the familiar. He is attracted by earthy, blond, unmysterious fräuleins, whose neatly braided hair and cool, emotionless faces ("Au regard immobile aux nattes repliées") are in striking contrast to the magical water *nixes* with their green, disheveled hair.

The power of song evolves from stanza to stanza in "Nuit rhénane." In the first stanza, it is a potential and untapped force waiting to be released. In the second stanza it becomes an expression of the sensual enjoyment and physical pleasure found in the real world. In the third stanza, however, song becomes incantation, a power that can sing of the cosmic events existing far beyond the real world:

> Le Rhin le Rhin est ivre où les vignes se mirent
> Tout l'or des nuits tombe en tremblant s'y refléter
> La voix chante toujours à en râle-mourir
> Ces fées aux cheveux verts qui incantent l'été

The scene described in the third stanza closely resembles the setting of the opening strophe. The same phenomena are visible — wine, glass, flame, and song — but there is an important difference. In the third stanza these phenomena are expanded and magnified by the wine's power of intoxication and enchantment. Wine has expanded the real, transformed the familiar, and extended consciousness.

Instead of the glass filled with wine, we find a river that is filled with the reflections of the vineyards and as a result has become drunk: "Le Rhin le Rhin est ivre où les vignes se mirent." The fusion of fire and wine in the first strophe is recreated more intensely here in the reflection of the golden stars on the reddened surface of the river: "Tout l'or des nuits tombe en tremblant s'y refléter"; the same uncertain trembling is present. The "chanson lente" sung by the boatman is transformed into a mysterious, otherworldly voice that sounds like a death rattle, and the seven women of his song become "ces fées aux cheveux verts qui incantent l'été." Direct participation in the universe and in the supernatural replaces the poet's passive role of the opening stanza. There, he listened to a song about the fantastic; here, he experiences it for himself.

What the poet does experience is rather unusual. The universe is reflected in the drunken Rhine, and a spell like a heavy fog hangs over the Rhine valley. There is a confluence of all things; the river, the stars, the vines blend and fuse. The earth mixes with the sky, the real with the sur-real, the familiar with the fantastic. Channels are opened between the real world and the supernatural, and out of the latter comes a voice singing a song of death ("La voix chante toujours à en râle-mourir"). It belongs to the malefic water sprites ("ces fées aux cheveux verts") who are chanting their words of incantation in order to lure the spellbound poet into their world of non-being and death. He turns an attentive ear to their song and begins to surrender to their magic until the last line of the poem breaks the spell:

Mon verre s'est brisé comme un éclat de rire.

With the enchantment shattered, the cosmic self comes crashing to the ground from its flight into the supernatural, and so joins company with the other deposed selves, the passive and the active. A new self succeeds to power, and since it is the final spokesman of the poem, it will stay in power. This is the mocking self, who appears frequently in Apollinaire's poetry.

The final, one-line stanza of "Nuit rhénane" ends the supernatural experience of the third strophe. But the meaning of this concluding line depends entirely on its position in the poem; it is separated from the preceding stanza by a blank space. Its detachment from the rest of the poem and its isolation in high relief give it an impersonal, condescending, and somewhat ironic tone. If, however, we were to change the position of the last strophe and make it the final line of the previous stanza, with which it appears to rime ("se mirent"-"mourir"-"rire"), then we would change the entire meaning of the poem. The line would no longer arrest the poet's supernatural experience, but, rather, would intensify it. In this hypothetical situation, the water fairies would continue their incantation, until the poet finally succumbed. As the tempo of their chanting increased, the poet's consciousness would join in the quickening song, and would begin to expand. The incantation would become more feverish, the chanting louder, the song more frenzied, until, in a final, piercing note of hysterical laughter, it would break the poet's body into fragments, liberating his consciousness. At the same moment, the piercing vibrations would also shatter the wine glass, unleashing its dionysian powers ("Mon verre s'est brisé comme un éclat de rire"). Matter would be disintegrated, and the poet, as pure spirit, would pour into the universe in a mystical experience of transcendence. The hysterical laughter, at the end of the poem, therefore, would show that incantation leads to madness. The poem would suggest that the poet, who has wandered too far into the dream world and the supernatural in his search for the pure song, may lose his sanity.[2]

---

[2] This hypothetical interpretation of "Nuit rhénane" closely resembles certain lines of "Poème lu au mariage d'André Salmon" (1909); the association of laughter and breaking glass, the power of wine to transform the universe, the presence of song, and the theme of angelism — the poet damned to madness — find expression in this later poem:

The poem, however, does not end on a tragic note of madness but on a note of comic relief. Not only does the mocking self interrupt the poem's crescendo at its very peak, but it ridicules the whole idea of transcendence and incantation. It has, figuratively speaking, thrown cold water on the poet's poetic fire, and now that the poet's power of imagination has been suddenly subdued, the mocking self laughs sadistically.

The mocking self's deriding laughter comes from its detachment; it has not participated in the earlier stanzas of the poem, and from its point of view the cosmic self looks ridiculous. According to Henri Bergson, in his study *Le Rire* (1899), the intensity of laughter depends on the degree to which one is detached from a comic event:

> Détachez-vous maintenant, assistez à la vie en spectateur indifférent: bien des drames tourneront à la comédie. Il suffit que nous bouchions nos oreilles au son de la musique, dans un salon où l'on danse, pour que les danseurs nous paraissent aussitôt ridicules.... Le comique exige donc enfin, pour produire tout son effet, quelque chose comme une anesthésie momentanée du cœur. Il s'adresse à l'intelligence pure.[3]

The mocking self's detachment reflects the poet's own indifference to an experience in which many of his selves are actively and seriously involved. In the act of externalizing and dramatizing his selves in a poem Apollinaire becomes divorced from them and, as an indifferent spectator, looks at these, his own selves, with embarrassment, derision, and deprecation. He learns not to take them seriously, and in another poem, "Zone," he shows how bitterly mocking he can be toward his own self:

> Épris épris des mêmes paroles dont il faudra changer le sens
> Trompés trompés pauvres petits et ne sachant pas encore rire
> La table et les deux verres devinrent un mourant qui nous jeta
>   le dernier regard d'Orphée
> Les verres tombèrent se brisèrent
> Et nous apprîmes à rire
> Nous partîmes alors pèlerins de la perdition
> A travers les rues à travers les contrées à travers la raison
> Je le revis au bord du fleuve sur lequel flottait Ophélie
>   (O. P., pp. 83-84)

[3] *Le Rire, essai sur la signification du comique* (Paris: Presses Universitaires, 1962), pp. 3-4.

Tu te moques de toi et comme le feu de l'Enfer ton rire pétille
Les étincelles de ton rire dorent le fond de ta vie
C'est un tableau pendu dans un sombre musée
Et quelquefois tu vas le regarder de près

(O. P., p. 41)

A poem possesses the power to intoxicate with words and with song. In the opening strophe the wine-filled glass represents the intoxicating power that is potentially contained within a poem. In the second stanza this power is slightly released, and the result is a poetry that describes physical and sensual experience. However, in the third strophe poetic power explodes with all its magical and incantatory fury. The symbol for poetry now becomes the Rhine ("Le Rhin le Rhin est ivre où les vignes se mirent"); and the poetry of this stanza appears to have the magical power to express the mysteries of the stellar universe ("Tout l'or des nuits tombe en tremblant s'y refléter"). The poem takes on an enchanted voice, and like the voice that is approaching death ("en râle-mourir"), it begins to ascend into the unknown. Thus, at the beginning of the last line of "Nuit rhénane" poetry is in contact with the world of incantation. But, as it approaches the unknown, it loses its voice and suddenly turns into a formless, incoherent, noisy sound — a peal of laughter ("Mon verre s'est brisé comme un éclat de rire"). Reaching the frontiers of the ineffable, poetry can go no farther, without changing into something else. The last line of "Nuit rhénane" therefore mocks poetry's attempt to transcend language. It sets limits to the experiences that poetry can express. The final line seems to say that poetry can ascend into the supernatural and become incantation; but it warns that if poetry comes too close to the invisible mysteries of the universe it, like Icarus, will lose its form, its voice, and its life.

"Nuit rhénane" presents a four-dimensional view of Apollinaire's self. Scattered throughout the Rhenish countryside, fraternizing with the peasant women and also with the legendary water witches, slowly becoming drunk with wine and intoxicated by the night, the poet's selves enact the drama of dispersion. On every level of experience, from the familiar to the fantastic, from the serious to the comic, they are to be found celebrating the poet's power of ubiquity and his omnipresence in the universe.

Chapter III

THE DRAMA OF REINTEGRATION

"MAI"

Le mal-aimé, a name that has become synonymous with Guillaume Apollinaire, is perhaps a suitable description for the succession of failed loves that marked Apollinaire's life and inspired his greatest poems. But, if Apollinaire was badly loved, it was because he loved badly.[1] Suspicious, jealous, in continual fear of being betrayed, given to violent rages, Apollinaire was an unbearable lover. Yet, he could reveal great tenderness, and this opposition in him between tenderness on the one hand and violence on the other was transposed to his poems, where an air of exquisite charm, tenderness and grace is often shattered by a violent or extremely pejorative line. The suffering of love, then, was the source of his poetic furor. As M. Adéma points out,

> Sa souffrance de cœur sera la meilleure inspiratrice de sa poésie, il la recherchera dans toutes les femmes qu'il aimera, mais sans que la tristesse qui en découlera soit autre chose que sa vie même, l'expression sans amertume de sa volupté de vivre, de connaître, de voir et d'exprimer.[2]

---

[1] Marcel Adéma, *Guillaume Apollinaire, le mal-aimé* (Paris: Plon, 1952), p. 58.

[2] Adéma, p. 58. For an excellent discussion of Apollinaire's attitudes toward women in general as revealed in those passages of his writings showing Œdipal, incestuous, sado-masochistic, misogynous, and mytho-erotic overtones, see Scott Bates, *Guillaume Apollinaire* ("Twayne's World Authors Series," no. 14; New York: Twayne Publishers, 1967), pp. 40-50, 125-38.

The succession of his affairs reveals to what degree love was his natural state of being. Often, he would flee one unhappy love for the sake of beginning another. This was the case in the summer of 1901, when his advances toward Linda Molina da Silva, a Jewish girl of Spanish origins, were thwarted. This love, the second of any consequence in his nineteen year old life (the first had been for a Belgian girl named Marie Dubois, two years earlier during a stay in Stavelot), had produced many poems and letters; to these Linda had responded with warm and sincere friendship, but nothing more.[3] Apollinaire was therefore anxious to leave Paris, and so, late in the summer, he accepted a position as the tutor to the daughter of the Vicomtesse de Milhau, a German widow of considerable wealth, who owned estates along the Rhine. But what attracted him most to this position was the young and beautiful Englishwoman, named Annie Playden, who was the governess and companion to Gabrielle de Milhau. Apollinaire was considerably impressed by her, as Annie suggests in a letter to Robert Goffin:

> "Quand il me connut il me déclara que ses amis lui avaient demandé si la comtesse était charmante — il répondit: 'Non, mais la gouvernante l'est et c'est ce qui m'a décidé à accepter l'emploi.'"[4]

But another reason prompted Apollinaire's decision. His literary formation up to 1901, namely his admiration for the French symbolists, his fervent interest in Celtic and gothic mythology, and his love for the bizarre and the mysterious, had prepared him for the attraction of a romantic and legendary Germany.[5] The prospect of living near the Rhine, the heart of German romanticism, of visiting the scenes that had inspired Heine and Brentano, and of journeying through the land that had given birth to French symbolism[6] — the home of

---

[3] Adéma, pp. 40-46.

[4] L.-C. Breunig, "Apollinaire et Annie Playden," *Mercure de France*, CCCXIV (1er avril, 1952), p. 642, citing a letter of 1946 from Annie Playden to Robert Goffin, published in the latter's *Entrer en poésie* (Bruxelles: A l'enseigne du chat qui pêche, 1948), p. 37.

[5] Pierre Orecchioni, "Le Thème du Rhin dans l'inspiration de Guillaume Apollinaire," *R. L. M.*, II (mars, 1955), 169-170.

[6] *Ibid.*, pp. 168-169.

Wagner — fired his imagination. A voyage to the Rhine, in his eyes, was "comme un pèlerinage aux sources de toute poésie." [7]

Apollinaire's year stay in Germany was his most prolific period up to this time. The nine poems of *Alcools* composed between September 1901 and May 1902, that are known as the "Rhénanes," are only a part of the poems that constitute this Rhine cycle. [8] In these poems, which differ considerably in tone, style and content, Apollinaire is either a spectator, reporting the real and often comic aspects of daily life in the region ("La Synagogue," "Les Femmes"), or the narrator of an imaginary tale, embroidered by the power of his fantasy ("La Loreley," "Schinderhannes," "Les Sapins"), or again, an active participant, experiencing joy and sadness ("Nuit rhénane," "Mai," "Les Cloches," "Rhénane d'automne"). In each poem elements of fantasy, humor, and the quotidian mingle with elements of the picturesque. However, one of the marks of Apollinaire's originality was his ability to avoid the facile use of the picturesque and the hackneyed, conventional image of the Rhine, which one critic has called "le poncif rhénan." [9] Apollinaire's descriptions of the Rhenish countryside involve his own impressions and images; they are completely subjective and personal, totally "Apollinarian."

Yet, aside from their differences, the Rhenish poems have one common point of resemblance. As the traveler never loses sight of the Rhine, so the poet never forgets its presence. [10] While the Rhine

---

[7] *Ibid.*, p. 170.

[8] "Rhénanes" is also the title of nine poems published posthumously in *Le Guetteur mélancolique* (1952) and belonging to the same period as those in *Alcools*. According to M. Raymond Warnier ("Guillaume Apollinaire et l'Allemagne," *Revue de littérature comparée*, XXVIII [avril-juin, 1954], 169-174) the nine poems excluded from *Alcools* were probably considered by Apollinaire to be inferior in two areas: one, psychological, the other, aesthetic. Some poems, like "Les Bacs" and "Le Dôme de Cologne" were conceived by chance in a moment of inspiration, and therefore appeared too immediate and too close to the experience they described. "Une sorte de pudeur sentimentale les fait écarter" (p. 172). Others still, like "Mille Regrets" and "La Vierge à la fleur de haricot à Cologne" were rejected on aesthetic grounds. M. Orecchioni in his study finds the "Rhénanes" of *Le Guetteur mélancolique* closer to the popular life of the region than those in *Alcools*, and he states that "les aspects sordides de la réalité ne sont transfigurés par aucune alchimie poétique: il manque ce charme particulier aux meilleures réussites d'Apollinaire" (*R. L. M.*, II [avril, 1955], p. 258).

[9] Orecchioni, *R. L. M.*, II (avril, 1955), 263-269.

[10] Almost every poem alludes to it; for example, "Le Rhin le Rhin est ivre" ("Nuit rhénane," *O. P.*, p. 111); "Le mai le joli mai en barque sur le

is a geographic landmark, localising the experiences of the "poèmes rhénans" to the villages, meadows, and vineyards on its banks, it also, more importantly, infuses those experiences with the collective soul of the region, for, more than a river, the Rhine is a symbol. To evoke it is to stir the legends, the myths, and the folklore associated with it.

Although the Rhenish legendary past is symbolized by the Rhine, it is in the people of the region that it lives and survives.[11] They are its true inheritors, responsible for bequeathing this legacy to their sons and daughters, and thus insuring its immortality. The collective soul of the Rhineland is rooted deeply in them. Apollinaire realized this, and so he visited the Rhineland, not as a tourist, but as a poet, keenly sensitive to the customs and traditions of the people, more aware of them than of the ruins that dotted their countryside.

Through the people he became acquainted with the Rhenish tradition; through them, he perceived that the past lives in the present. To understand in a year what a people has known for generations is a herculean task, but one that Apollinaire achieved. By absorbing their local and traditional culture, by spending his evenings in their restaurants drinking and in their homes listening to ageless songs and folk tales, by his insatiable curiosity and his almost superhuman power of assimilation, Apollinaire comprehended the collective soul of the Rhineland, and finally identified himself with it. As M. Orecchioni points out, "pour devenir un véritable poète du Rhin, il lui fallait se faire une âme de Rhénan."[12]

Apollinaire's power of assimilation and identification has already been demonstrated in "Nuit rhénane," where the different fragments of his *moi* dispersed themselves throughout the Rhenish landscape and then blended with it. In "Cortège" Apollinaire gives further evidence of this power, when he says,

> Moi qui connais les autres
> Je les connais par les cinq sens et
>   quelques autres
>   (O. P., pp. 74-75)

Rhin" ("Mai," O. P., p. 112); "Le vieux Rhin soulève sa face ruisselante et se détourne pour sourire" ("La Synagogue," O. P., p. 113); "Elle se penche alors et tombe dans le Rhin" ("La Loreley," O. P., p. 116); "Le vent du Rhin ulule" ("Rhénane d'automne," O. P., p. 120); "Les bateaux qui sur le Rhin voguent" ("Les Sapins," O. P., p. 121).

[11] Orecchioni, *R. L. M.*, II (mars, 1955), 172.
[12] *Ibid.*

and again in "Vendémiaire," where he penetrates and embraces the universe:

> Mais je connus dès lors quelle saveur a l'univers
> Je suis ivre d'avoir bu tout l'univers
> ... ...
> Ecoutez-moi je suis le gosier de Paris
> Et je boirai encore s'il me plaît l'univers
> Ecoutez mes chants d'universelle ivrognerie
>
> (O. P., pp. 153-154)

In the first poem, he underlines his omniscience; in the last, he stresses his omnipresence.

It is not surprising, then, given this unique "sixth sense," which may be called intuition or genius, or simply, orphic assimilation, that Apollinaire was successful in apprehending the Rhenish soul and in transposing its essence to his "Rhénanes." This is succinctly pointed out by Mr. Breunig in his interview with Annie Playden:

> A entendre Miss Playden raconter ces souvenirs on comprend mieux l'inspiration directe et immédiate des poèmes rhénans où il n'y a presque rien de livresque, mais une authenticité simple qui résulte de la compréhension intuitive d'un peuple étranger.[13]

Slowly the Rhine integrated itself into Apollinaire's imagination, and there, like all images appropriated by him, it was personalized, mixed, that is, with his subjective impressions and fused with the self. As M. Orecchioni writes,

> ...à son insu, le génie rhénan s'insinuait bien plus profondément en lui et se mêlait à tous ses sentiments, à tous ses travaux: non seulement parce que tout ce qui faisait alors partie de sa vie, y compris le décor rhénan, se trouvait valorisé par son aventure sentimentale, mais aussi parce que le site rhénan lui-même, traditionnellement, est un 'espace sentimental': Le Rhin, fleuve idyllique et romantique où les états d'âme prennent inévitablement une tonalité particulière.[14]

---

[13] Breunig, "Apollinaire et Annie," p. 643.
[14] Orecchioni, R. L. M., II (mars, 1955), 167-168.

Yet, even more striking than Apollinaire's assimilation is the speed with which it was accomplished. In less than a month after his arrival, Apollinaire had composed "La Synagogue" (September, 1901), in which a quarrel between two Jews on their way to pray is related in terms of the silent and amused Rhine that watches them. In November, he wrote "Rhénane d'automne," describing All Souls' Day in a Rhine cemetery, and in December, "Les Femmes," which shows an intimate knowledge of the gossip and daily concerns of Rhenish women.

Apollinaire's attempt to penetrate the Rhenish character was more ambitious, according to M. Orecchioni, than any other French poet who had come to Germany before him.[15] While such poets as Hugo and Nerval had sung patriotically of the Rhine as the river frontier between two great nations, or written of their impressions as tourists, or adapted the work of Rhenish poets, Apollinaire envisioned a more difficult task for himself:

> Apollinaire lui, prétend pouvoir faire passer dans ses vers tout essentiel de l'âme rhénane, il prétend non seulement être un poète rhénan authentique, mais le poète rhénan par excellence... Apollinaire découvre une mystérieuse correspondance entre son âme et cette province, une sensibilité commune.[16]

It is M. Orecchioni's view that Apollinaire did not succeed in becoming "le poète rhénan par excellence" but that he was, nevertheless, successful in adding a new dimension to French lyrical poetry by his use of the German poetic genre, the "Rheinlieder," a word whose French translation, M. Orecchioni suggests, is "Rhénanes."[17]

If the Rhine gives the "Rhénanes" their geographical and mythical unity, it is the veiled presence of Annie Playden which gives them their sentimental orientation. Many of the poems were either directly or indirectly inspired by her, and it is one of the ironies of Apollinaire's life that she was not aware until 1946 that he was a celebrated poet.[18] The Rhenish poems trace the development of Apollinaire's

---

[15] *Ibid.*, pp. 174-175.
[16] *Ibid.*
[17] Orecchioni, *R. L. M.*, II (mars, 1955), 171.
[18] " 'Je suis fière de savoir que Kostro [Apollinaire's nickname] est devenu un des meilleurs poètes de France et je serais particulièrement heureuse de

love from the fall of 1901 through the spring of 1902. The first stage of this love was characterized by an extreme courtesy, which is reflected in the poem, "Dans le jardin d'Anna" (*Il y a*).[19] Set in the Germany of the eighteenth century the poem has a graceful, delicate charm, which one critic has aptly called "la grâce mozartienne."[20] But the beginning of 1902 saw Apollinaire's graciousness turn to violent passion, and the elegant charm of the early poems change to the lyric sadness and bitter suffering of the later ones. This second stage is best described by Mr. Breunig:

> ... à mesure que sa passion s'approfondit un côté plus sombre, plus farouche ressort, et la résistance froide de l'Anglaise provoque des accès de jalousie et des actes d'une cruauté si excessive que parfois la jeune fille craint pour sa vie.[21]

A celebrated anecdote relates how Apollinaire proposed to Annie atop the Drachenfels, the mountain where Siegfried had slain the dragon and one of the most romantic spots in the Rhineland, and how, when she refused, he threatened to push her onto the crags below. Terror-stricken she quickly consented, only to refuse again when she had reached firmer ground.

As the months of 1902 slipped by and Annie continued to resist his advances, Apollinaire began to despair and to believe that his love was poisoned, an impression he gives in the poems "Les Colchiques" and "La Tzigane." He assumed, as Mr. Breunig writes, that "cette Anglaise aux yeux ronds et nuisibles avait été déstinée par toute une suite de générations à l'anéantir."[22] During this twilight period of his love, at the very moment that the dawning spring was spreading its warmth over the renewed countryside, Apollinaire com-

---

lire ses œuvres si vous voulez me les envoyer comme vous me l'offrez.... Puis-je vous demander pourquoi vous avez essayé de me découvrir pendant ces derniers cinq ans en Amérique — et comment êtes-vous parvenu à entrer en contact avec ma famille d'Angleterre. Mais quel intérêt peut avoir ce fait pour quiconque à l'heure actuelle? Comment avez-vous été au courant de notre jeune amitié?'" Letter from Annie Playden to Robert Goffin, cited by Julia Hartwig, *Apollinaire*, trans. by Jean-Yves Erhel (Paris: Mercure de France, 1972), p. 69.

[19] Breunig, "Apollinaire et Annie," p. 646.
[20] *Ibid.*
[21] *Ibid.*, p. 647.
[22] *Ibid.*, p. 648.

posed the poem "Mai." Although he and Annie would not part until August, it is in "Mai" that he resignedly bids her farewell, and, at the same time, says adieu to the Rhenish countryside.

The drama of dispersal becomes the drama of reintegration in "Mai." The poem opens with fragments of the poet's self scattered throughout the spring countryside. As the poet bids farewell to the Rhineland, where so many of his selves are embodied, he suddenly becomes aware of the powerful reintegrating force of memory; it combines his dispersed selves and restores, although in a different form, an experience that he believed was lost forever.

> Le mai le joli mai en barque sur le Rhin
> Des dames regardaient du haut de la montagne
> Vous êtes si jolies mais la barque s'éloigne
> Qui donc a fait pleurer les saules riverains
>
> Or des vergers fleuris se figeaient en arrière
> Les pétales tombés des cerisiers de mai
> Sont les ongles de celle que j'ai tant aimée
> Les pétales flétris sont comme ses paupières
>
> Sur le chemin du bord du fleuve lentement
> Un ours un singe un chien menés par des tziganes
> Suivaient une roulotte traînée par un âne
> Tandis que s'éloignait dans les vignes rhénanes
> Sur un fifre lointain un air de régiment
>
> Le mai le joli mai a paré les ruines
> De lierre de vigne vierge et de rosiers
> Le vent du Rhin secoue sur le bord les osiers
> Et les roseaux jaseurs et les fleurs nues des vignes [23]
>
> (O. P., p. 112)

The opening stanza finds Apollinaire in a boat, slowly moving along the Rhine, while, at the same time, the May season glides along the river, spreading its spring warmth over the countryside: "Le mai le joli mai en barque sur le Rhin." From the very first line there is a strong Germanic ring. The use of the definite article in "Le mai" is unusual in French, where one would usually say "mai," but

---

[23] "Mai" was first published in *Vers et Prose*, IV (décembre, 1905-février, 1906).

not in German, where the names of the months usually take an article. But more striking still is Apollinaire's borrowing of a classic German motif, the descent of the Rhine by boat:

> Il y a un certain charme touristique du Rhin, lié à l'évocation de la classique descente du fleuve en bateau à vapeur, par une radieuse journée de printemps ou d'été....[24]

In other poems Apollinaire mentions ferries and steam boats plying their way up and down the river;[25] but here, for the first time, he is on one of them himself. He borrows this traditional German image not, as one might expect, to express the feeling of happiness, or of well-being, or of "joie de vivre," usually associated with a journey down the peaceful and scenic Rhine, but, instead, to convey a personal feeling of melancholy. Apollinaire is not on board to sightsee, or to enjoy the scenery, but rather to leave, and what he sees and describes is colored by the purpose of his voyage.

What Apollinaire does see on his journey is no different from what the other passengers might observe: women looking down at them from high up on a mountain, the weeping willows and flowering orchards of the banks, the gypsy caravan, the ivy-covered ruins and vineyards — all elements of local color that give the Rhineland its particular charm and quaintness. But Apollinaire observes these sights differently from his fellow passengers; he perceives sadness behind the picturesqueness. "Qui donc a fait pleurer les saules riverains," he asks. Using elements of the picturesque to transmit his subjective inner feelings, he succeeds in expressing less a charming description of the Rhine than an intense portrait of his melancholy soul.

"Mai" is both a folk song and a personal lyric, referring on one level to the collective past of a people, and on another to the personal past of an individual. The poem involves not one, but three images of May, all in some way associated with the poet: the conventional image of May, the season of Nature's rebirth; the Rhenish image

---

[24] Orecchioni, *R. L. M.*, II (avril, 1955), 269.
[25] He writes for example in "Plongeon" (*Le Guetteur mélancolique*): "Et des vapeurs pleins de mouchoirs descendent le Rhin" (*O. P.*, p. 535); and in "Les Bacs" (*Le Guetteur*...):

> Les bacs du Rhin s'en vont et viennent
> Au long de la belle saison
>   (*O. P.*, p. 536)

of May, the month of traditional folk and pagan festivals handed down for generations and the month celebrated in the works of such artists as Heine and Schumann; and the Apollinaire image of May, the end of an intimate love amidst the splendor of spring. Although the folkloric and the personal mingle harmoniously throughout the poem, they sometimes give rise to an unsettling ambiguity. There is no better example of this than the line, "Des dames regardaient du haut de la montagne." Is this a reference to the Lorelei and other legendary *ondines* that inhabit the Rhine country, or does it simply refer to a group of women watching his boat sail away?

The first stanza of "Mai" makes no reference to an experiencing self. The sadness that is suggested by the departing boat and by the weeping willows must remain vague and general because it is not experienced by anyone in particular. But in the second stanza the poet's subjective center is revealed. From a panoramic view of the Rhine, the poem now moves to a highly detailed and specific view, like a movie camera narrowing in for a close-up. The lens closes in first identifying an orchard ("vergers fleuris") and then the fallen petals of its trees ("Les pétales tombés des cerisiers de mai"). The camera does not stop; it continues to probe, searching for some detail to enlarge even further. It discovers that the fallen and wilted petals are more than what they appear to be:

> Les pétales tombés des cerisiers de mai
> Sont les ongles de celle que j'ai tant aimée
> Les pétales flétris sont comme ses paupières [26]

These petals represent a past experience that antecedes the experience described in the poem. A new temporal dimension is introduced as

---

[26] These lines recall similar images from "Le Printemps" (*Le Guetteur mélancolique*):

> Les pétales tombés des pêchers qui fleurissent
> Sont les ongles cruels des tendres bien-aimées
> Les cerisiers défleuriront au mois de mai
> Leurs fleurs sont des bourgs qui là-bas se rapetissent

and from the same poem:

> Les villages du vent deviennent des paupières
> Voyez voyez cligner des yeux les cerisiers

(*O. P.*, p. 557)

well as a subjective dimension. The poem gains added depth and intensity by the appearance of a self which gives it a new point of reference and by the introduction of the past. Although the "I" does not reappear, it will remain omnipresent in the poem, informing all the lines with its identity.

The opening lines of the second stanza contain elements of the ambiguity that characterizes "Mai." The image of the blossoms on the trees ("vergers fleuris") precedes the image of the same blossoms strewn on the ground ("pétales tombés," "pétales flétris"); therefore, it represents an earlier moment in the poet's experience, a time when his love was filled with the same life, freshness, and hope as these blossoms. But love, like the blossoms, dies, and the image of "pétales tombés" in the next line represents the end of his idyllic courtship. Yet, in between this thriving love of the past and the ruined love of the present appears a love which is remembered ("Les vergers fleuris *se figeaient* en arrière"). Memory preserves the past — the flowering orchards — in a changeless, almost petrified state ("se figeaient en arrière"), so that the past may continue to endure in the present.

In falling from a tree, a blossom prepares the way for the growth of the fruit. The destruction of the petal intimates the creation of the fruit. Similarly, the end of Apollinaire's love affair, expressed in the image of the fallen petals, suggests that something will be created in its place. The fruit of this unhappy experience will either be memory, which replaces the moment-in-time that is gone forever, or poetry, which will also preserve and immortalize that moment. For Apollinaire memory and poetry are invulnerable against the effects of time. After the passing away, after the dying, something does remain, whether the fruit, the memory, or the poem.

In the first moment of his recollection the poet uses a metaphor ("Les pétales tombés des cerisiers de mai/Sont les ongles de celle que j'ai tant aimée"), and in the second, a simile ("Les pétales flétris sont comme ses paupières"). This distinction, although Apollinaire may not have been consciously aware of it, is nevertheless significant because it illustrates the distance that now exists between the poet and the woman he loves. The metaphor incorporates the dissimilar terms "pétales tombés" and "ongles." These are fused together, until they lose their individual meanings and acquire one common meaning. With the simile, on the other hand, the continuity between subject and object does not exist because the terms of the simile never merge. The petals are not the beloved's eyelids, they are *like* them. The resemblance is no longer intuited; it is announced and stated explicitly. While the metaphor tries to reveal the hidden resemblance between the petals and the woman's nails through a symbolic jump in meaning from one term of the metaphor to the other, the simile functions more slowly, stopping to explain the relationship between "pétales flétris" and "paupières" by the use of the intervening word "comme."

Love itself is, by definition, a metaphor: the assimilation of two separate beings into one. "Love, by reason of its passion, destroys the in-between which relates us to and separates us from others." [27] However, the use of a metaphor and then a simile in this stanza shows to what extent the poet's love has failed. By using a figure of comparison that has its own "in-between" — the word, "like" — he remarkably illustrates, even if unconsciously, the real "in-between" that has grown between himself and "celle que j'ai tant aimée."

There is also another way of explaining this stanza. As the boat pulls away from the shore, the landscape seems to freeze, to remain motionless, a sort of *trompe-l'œil* phenomenon. The farther away the poet's boat moves, the more solid, immobile, and petrified the land appears ("... se figeaient en arrière"). Between himself and the beloved he leaves somewhere on that shore, lies a rapidly growing expanse of water. The poet is being separated from the selves that are embodied in that receding landscape. This striking image suggests, above all, that, aside from the watery distance between the boat and the shore and between the poet and his beloved, there is a larger, ever-widening expanse between the present and the past. With the exception of the distances between things which are growing larger, there are no other perceptible changes in the second stanza. Neither the boat nor the shore changes; it is only their distance from and their relationship to each other that alters, thus illustrating that nothing really changes between the present and the past except distance. The passage of time merely involves a rearrangement and readjustment of distances and relationships. The experience itself remains unchanged. In the poem, for example, the beloved returns

---

[27] Hannah Arendt, *The Human Condition* (Garden City: Doubleday Anchor Books, 1958), p. 217.

to the poet as a memory, but she reappears so alive in fact that he mistakes the memory for the past itself, reincarnated. Not only is the past experience unaltered, but it is even preserved against change and decay; the freezing of the flowering orchard, symbol of the poet's love, protects it and insures its immortality. Time does not change the essence of the poet's experience, but merely separates him from it. Memory is the preserved form of the past which recurs in the present. Its appearance here lightens the melancholy air created by the images of distance and separation; it is a spark of hope lighting the poet's sadness. [28]

An important element of the poetic ambiguity of "Mai" is the alternation between pessimism and optimism. Throughout the poem images of flux and change, expressing the poet's melancholy, vie with images of recurrence, expressing his hope. Sometimes, the same image expresses both aspects; for example, "vergers fleuris" and "pétales tombés" represent both the irretrievable past and the redeemed memory. The best example, of course, is the image of the Maytime which passes away one year only to reappear the next.

In the first strophe the poem opens on an almost joyful tone ("Le mai le joli mai"), which is quickly diminished by a touch of sadness ("Qui donc a fait pleurer les saules riverains"). The reverse occurs in the next stanza, where the feeling of melancholy is qualified by the appearance of hope in the form of a recurring memory. In the third stanza, undoubtedly the most picturesque and melancholy of the poem, images of flight and departure gain poetic power, but they are again challenged by images of recurrence. With the fourth and final stanza, the lyrical power struggle between pessimism and optimism is finally resolved.

---

[28] An interesting, and somewhat related, interpretation of these lines is made by M. Renaud, who sees in them "un processus de 'fixation' consécutif à l'éloignement et au regard *porté vers l'arrière* du narrateur" (p. 106). This backward looking glance, capable of petrifying, and therefore, eternalizing the past with a Medusa-like stare, is an important and universal theme of Apollinaire's poetry and is used particularly to structure a number of the poems of *Alcools*. M. Renaud identifies it with the myth of Orpheus,

> tentant de ramener à la vie une Eurydice dont la silhouette "se fige en arrière" au moment où Orphée se retourne — et la scène se termine par un échange de regards; Orphée continue à vivre, à descendre le cours de sa vie, et Eurydice devient regret, souvenir dont naît la mélancolique complainte. (p. 106)

In the third strophe the poet's "I" disappears, the memory of the beloved dims, and the semi-immobility of the previous stanza is broken. Instead of a close-up, the view gradually returns to a panorama. Descriptions of the poet's observations replace the memories of his past. We return to the earlier picturesqueness of the first stanza, and, as before, Apollinaire strongly identifies with the landscape he observes. Like himself, the gypsy caravan he watches is leaving one place, en route to another. Like himself, they are foreigners in the Rhineland, and their slow, yielding march suggests that like Apollinaire they are resigned to some invisible destiny that draws them away. The poet's identification, however, goes deeper. Although it is not stated in the poem, the gypsies are closely associated with his Rhenish experience, and, above all, with his love. It is a gypsy fortune teller who prophesies his doomed love in the poem, "La Tzigane":

> La tzigane savait d'avance
> Nos deux vies barrées par les nuits
> Nous lui dîmes adieu et puis
> De ce puits sortit l'Espérance
>
> (O. P., p. 99)

The departing gypsy caravan is a further reminder to him of the beloved he is now leaving.[29]

The slow procession of these vagabonds, like the flowing river and the regimental notes of the fife that disappear softly in the spring air, is an image of change and of flight. Everything in the stanza either disappears, flows away or departs. An intense melancholy pervades the landscape. Yet, in the very image of flight and passage lies the idea of recurrence. If the gypsies leave, it is only because vagabondage and emigration have always been their way of life, the one constant, recurring element of their otherwise uncertain, changing

---

[29] Victor Hugo also expressed the end of love using the image of departing gypsies in his "Tristesse d'Olympio":

> "Toutes les passions s'éloignent avec l'âge
> L'une emportant son masque et l'autre son couteau
> Comme un essaim chantant d'histrions en voyage
> Dont le groupe décroît derrière le coteau."
>
> (Œuvres poétiques, I ["Bibliothèque de la Pléiade"; Paris: Gallimard, 1964], p. 1097)

lives. Similarly, if the river continually flows, it is in the act of flowing that is found its recurrence. No matter how much water passes downstream, it is still the same river that flows and that will continue to flow. Like the image of May and the images of the poet's love ("vergers fleuris," "pétales tombés") the image of the gypsy caravan and that of the river express the two *leitmotivs* of optimism and pessimism that are found in the poem. And these two themes form an ensemble; optimism and pessimism, recurrence and flux, are two sides of the same coin. All that passes away also recurs.

In contrast to the rest of the poem the final stanza has a lively tone. Its movement differs greatly from the slow speed of the boat in the opening strophe, from the semi-immobility of the second stanza and from the sluggish, unresisting procession of gypsies in the penultimate strophe. Here, the wind, sweeping in from the Rhine ("Le vent du Rhin") and the lively, fertile May ("Le mai le joli mai a paré les ruines") animate and enliven the countryside. Reeds, which once divulged King Midas's well guarded secret, chatter and gossip indiscretely ("roseaux jaseurs"), perhaps about the poet's broken love affair. Willows ("les osiers") do arabesques in the wind. Ruins of old castles are adorned with lush vegetation.

The ruins, one would assume, are the remains of old castles that once bordered the Rhine, and a symbol of the poet's ruined love. They represent both the collective past of the region and the personal past of the poet. As ruins, they bear witness to the destruction caused by time, and yet they also affirm their own permanence, their resistance to time. Associated with these ruined castles, furthermore, are the myths and legends of the Rhineland. Like the ruins themselves these myths have suffered changes down through the centuries, but they still continue to endure. As an image of the poet's love affair the ruins refer both to the beloved who is gone forever and to her memory which still remains. The only change, therefore, which the passage of time has brought to the ruins, the myths, and the poet's love is a change of form.

The ruins, which were stones long before they were used to build castles, have almost returned to their original form. The same change of forms is equally true of the Rhine myths. Traditionally associated with the May, they reappear every year, unaltered except for certain changes in the forms by which they are expressed or narrated by poets, writers, and storytellers. Finally, the poet's love, which as present, living experience disappeared into the past, changes its form and returns as memory. In *essence*, the ruins, the myths, and the poet's love have been preserved against time's decay; it is only their *forms* that have changed. This is the significance of the line, "Le mai le joli mai a paré les ruines." May does not essentially change the stones of these ruined castles: it merely embellishes their outward appearance giving them a floral covering that will wear off by winter.

The castle ruins, like the earlier image of the petrified orchards, are an image of the past made indestructible and eternal through the recurrence of memory. Since the ruins are redecorated by nature and blended into the May countryside, they symbolize the way in which the past is embellished with new forms and assimilated into the present. The image of the May creatively embellishing and then assimilating the ruins of the past represents the creative act in which the poet uses the power of memory and song to express his past selves and experiences in different forms and through various *personae*. Nature produces a May spectacle containing the ruins of the collective past, while the poet creates a poem which incorporates the ruins of a personal past.

One of the striking qualities of "Mai" is that the same images express both pessimism and optimism. Such images as the river, the wind, May, and the gypsies represent the passing away of life and at the same time its recurrence. The oscillation between death and recurrence reflects a greater rhythm, one that characterizes all of life; it is what Apollinaire in "Merlin et la vieille femme" calls "l'éternelle cause/Qui fait mourir et puis renaître l'univers" (*O. P.*, p. 88). This rhythm of life supposes that every event inherently implies its opposite, which identifies it and eventually will replace it, and that the event and its antithesis are nothing more than different forms or stages of the same recurring cycle. This is illustrated throughout "Mai," where a blossom intimates coming death and yet a dying petal promises future life; where the wind scatters blossoms, but also spreads the seeds for future blossoms; where a river flows away and yet never ceases to flow; and where the present replaces the past but continually recalls that past. Each image suggests two antithetical states that replace one another and then continue to alternate in seesaw fashion. Recurrence, as it appears in "Mai," is distinguished by this rhythmic alternation between all the possibilities of existence, between life and death, change and permanence, hope and melancholy, present and past.

In "Mai" the poet's selves, and there are many of them — the self involved with the Rhine's collective past, the self identified with the poet's personal past (which, in turn, is divided into the *I* that has experienced the love affair and the *I* that remembers it), the self associated with the homeless gypsies, and finally the self that is leaving the Rhine — all these different selves are given diverse forms which are integrated together to create a unified and total portrait of the Rhenish self. Now that the poet is leaving, these selves, once widely dispersed and scattered throughout the countryside, as they were, for example, in "Nuit rhénane," are recalled from their hiding places and haunts along the Rhine, in order to be packed together with his baggage for the voyage home. As they answer his call, reappearing from villages, fields, roads, vineyards, and inns, they carry with them the experiences that have already become part of the poet's cherished memory, a priceless legacy that will be one of Apollinaire's greatest sources of poetic inspiration.

"MERLIN ET LA VIEILLE FEMME"

Merlin, the celebrated magician of Celtic myth and Arthurian legend, according to the twelfth century *Le Roman de Merlin* by Robert de Boron, was born from the union of a virgin and a demon who had cohabited with her while she slept. Merlin was supposed to be the Anti-Christ, Satan's vengeance for the Harrowing of Hell. But his mother's infinite goodness and the efforts of her confessor toward God thwarted the devil's plan. Merlin inherited his mother's goodness and his father's demonic powers, but he escaped the latter's penchant for evil. Moreover, the grace of God endowed Merlin with a power even demons like his father did not possess: the power to know the future and to foretell it. [30]

This prophetic power explains, perhaps, why Apollinaire was greatly attracted to the character of Merlin, not only in "Merlin et la vieille femme" (1899), but also in other works of the same period:

---

[30] E. Sydnor Ownbey, "Merlin and Arthur. A Study of Merlin's Character and Function in the Romances Dealing With the Early Life of Arthur. [Condensation of a thesis]," *Dissertation Collection Ph. D. Vanderbilt University*, IV, no. 5 (1932), 9.

"La Maison de Cristal" (1896) and l'*Enchanteur pourrissant* (1898-1899).[31] Apollinaire often likened himself to a twentieth-century prophet. For example, in l'*Esprit nouveau et les poètes*, a manifesto delivered as a lecture in 1917, he equates poetry with prophecy and calls upon all poets to take up the prophetic task of creating new fables for the twentieth century:

> L'esprit nouveau exige qu'on se donne de ces tâches prophétiques. C'est pourquoi vous trouverez trace de prophétie dans la plupart des ouvrages conçus d'après l'esprit nouveau. Les jeux divins de la vie et de l'imagination donnent carrière à une activité poétique toute nouvelle.[32]

Further on, he adds: "Les poètes modernes sont donc des créateurs, des inventeurs, et des prophètes."[33]

Another of Merlin's powers with which Apollinaire identified strongly was the power of ubiquity and simultaneity. As sheer intelligences demons were not circumscribed by physical limits; they could come and go freely from one place to another, and they were able to assume any shape they desired.[34] Similarly, in such poems as "Nuit rhénane," "Zone," "Cortège," "Vendémiaire," and "Le Brasier" the Apollinarian self possesses these supernatural powers of cosmic identification, ubiquity, and simultaneity and the demonic ability to alter its forms and shapes.

---

[31] For the role played by Merlin in *L'Enchanteur pourrissant* and other works by Apollinaire, see Durry, I, 208-13. See also Jean Burgos's fine introduction to his annotated edition of *L'Enchanteur pourrissant* (Coll. "Paralogue," no. 5; Paris: Minard, 1972), pp. v-clxii. M. Burgos discusses at length Apollinaire's identification with Merlin in *L'Enchanteur*:

> Comment ne pas voir que, derrière le Merlin... c'est son propre visage que découvre Apollinaire, plus ou moins tragique, plus ou moins grotesque ou grimaçant, mais toujours inquiet et solitaire? (pp. lxxii-lxxiii)

By adopting the *persona* of Merlin, Apollinaire attributes to himself the magician's prophetic powers and also transfers to the story of his own life the mythic and legendary qualities that have always been associated with Merlin's adventures (pp. xcv, cxxv-cxxvi). Thus *L'Enchanteur* presents "une construction mythique de l'être du poète" (p. xcix). (M. Burgos also devotes detailed study to the sources, genesis, composition, themes, structures, language, and influence of *L'Enchanteur*.)

[32] p. 392.
[33] *Ibid.*, p. 394.
[34] Ownbey, p. 10.

A further resemblance between the poet and the magician is found in their respective love affairs. Merlin, like Apollinaire was a "mal-aimé." He fell madly in love with Vivien, or as she is sometimes called, Niniane, god-child of Diana, who, according to one story, bespelled Merlin into an eternal sleep and kept him prisoner in a tower of air deep in the forest of Broceliande, and who, according to another version of the story, hated him so intensely that she put him to sleep by enchantment and then sealed him in a tomb to die.[35] Unrequited love did not prevent Merlin from becoming totally enchanted and helplessly victimized by the woman he loved, as it did not prevent Apollinaire from passionately loving Annie.[36]

"Merlin et la vieille femme" (O. P., pp. 88-89), first published in Les Rubriques nouvelles of June 1912, is one of the oldest poems in Alcools.[37] It is typical of Apollinaire's early symbolist period and resembles two other of his poems, "L'Ermite" and "Le Larron," both written about the same time.[38] Apollinaire's early symbolist poetry, which is characterized by long, allegorical, and dramatic poems containing obscure fin de siècle imagery, has been treated somewhat harshly by modern critics, who prefer to dismiss it as the youthful exuberance of an unripened poet.[39] Although this criticism is to a

---

[35] The first story belongs to the Lestoire de Merlin or the Vulgate Merlin, as it is called, and the second version to the Huth Merlin, written in 1225 or 1230. Lucy Allen Paton, Studies in the Fairy Mythology of Arthurian Romance, 2nd ed. (1903; rpt. New York: Burt Franklin, 1960), pp. 205, 219, 221, 234, 245-47.

[36] Although it is true that Apollinaire was completely enchanted by Annie Playden, he was not her victim; in all probability he victimized her. However, in the poem "La Loreley" Apollinaire does portray Annie as a beautiful, but fatal sorceress, with many victims under her spell:

    A Bacharach il y avait une sorcière blonde
    Qui laissait mourir d'amour tous les hommes à la ronde
                                      (O. P., p. 115)

[37] Breunig, "Chronology," p. 909.

[38] For a comparison of these three poems, see Renaud, pp. 46-53 and Chevalier, pp. 73-149. The former offers a thematic comparison, while the latter gives a formalist analysis of the three poems.

[39] S. I. Lockerbie states that this group of poems "... ne vaut pas la peine qu'on s'y arrête longtemps." They seem to fail today, he continues, because they illustrate the weaknesses of a too facile, overly obscure fin de siècle poetry, characterized by "l'atmosphère légendaire ou moyenâgeuse trop appuyée, la sensualité exaspérée, le décor qui n'évite pas le poncif." ("Alcools et le Symbolisme," R. L. M., nos. 85-89 [automne, 1963], p. 9.) Mr. Breunig in his article ("Chronology," p. 920) states that Apollinaire did himself a

certain degree justified, it fails to consider that, despite their weaknesses, these poems contain the first *essais* of many themes and images that appear in *Alcools*. Already at this early stage in his poetry Apollinaire's search for self-knowledge and identity is fully developed, as are the poetic techniques he uses throughout his poetry to dramatize this search. As in many poems throughout *Alcools*, *personae* are used to represent the poet and his myriad selves. In addition, "Merlin et la vieille femme" testifies to the use of the disguised *art poétique*, a technique by which Apollinaire subtly weaves personal statements on the art of poetry into the fabric of narrative or allegorical poems, thus creating a poem that is in fact a commentary on the nature of poetry. "Nuit rhénane," "Le Brasier," and "Crépuscule" are other examples of this type of poem.

"Merlin et la vieille femme" is an allegory about the union of fragmented selves. Both Merlin, who represents a sterile, passive self, and Morgane, who represents memory, are *personae* for the poet. From their sexual union in the poem, comes a child, the fruit of love; but their union also dramatizes the creation of poetry, the fruit created from the union of the poet and his memory. In "Merlin et la vieille femme," as in "Mai," the drama of reintegration not only combines fragmented selves into a complete self, but also stresses the creative power of this union.

Three voices are heard in "Merlin et la vieille femme": a narrator, Merlin, and Morgane. Except for one line in the opening stanza, where the mask of impersonality momentarily drops off ("La lumière est ma mère ô lumière sanglante"), the narrator gives an objective, dispassionate narration throughout the poem. In contrast to this objectivity are the impassioned and violent soliloquies of Merlin and Morgane, who have been separated for so long that their words are charged with thwarted desire and frustrated emotion. Each of their speaking parts begins with an interjection of feeling: "O mon être glacé" (Merlin); "Ah! qu'il fait doux danser" (Morgane); "Qu'il monte/Le fils de la Mémoire" (Merlin). Yet, despite the physical union they finally achieve, there is no real dialogue between them.

---

great disservice by scattering the eight poems composed during his symbolist period (between 1898 and 1901) throughout *Alcools*. "The erudite artificiality for which *Alcools* as a whole has been strongly criticized is confined in large part, we discover, to this youthful period, after which it becomes greatly attenuated."

In classical, dramatic style, they walk to the center of the stage and deliver their *tirades*. The only link between their passionate soliloquies is the narrator's dispassionate descriptions.

The theatrical quality of the poem is reinforced by its division into three distinct "moments" or "acts," each dominated by one character in particular. In the opening "act" (sts. 1-6), Merlin stands at an unworldly, desolate crossroads, surrounded by a blood-red sky, where he seeks to discover the principle of life and death ("l'éternelle cause/Qui fait mourir et puis renaître l'univers"). He observes an old woman on a donkey and is moved to cry out a challenge which changes the season and renews the universe. The second "act" (sts. 7-12) is no less symbolic. Morgane descends from her donkey, approaches Merlin, joins hands with him, and, while she dances, tells the story of her sterile life spent waiting for him. The third "act" (sts. 13-15) begins with a sexual union and ends with Merlin's journey eastward, resigned to a fate he already foresees, but nevertheless joyful at the immortality he has achieved through the creation of a son ("il sera bien mon fils mon ouvrage immortel"). Although Merlin and Morgane are reunited in the poem's final moment, it is the presence of their unborn child that dominates the scene.

I. *Merlin, the frozen self.*

As the poem begins, Merlin stands at the crossroads of a cold, windswept expanse of space and at a crossroads in his life:

> Le soleil ce jour-là s'étalait comme un ventre
> Maternel qui saignait lentement sur le ciel
> La lumière est ma mère ô lumière sanglante
> Les nuages coulaient comme un flux menstruel [40]

---

[40] This stanza bears a certain resemblance to the opening stanza of Rimbaud's "Soleil et Chair" (1870):

> Le Soleil, le foyer de tendresse et de vie,
> Verse l'amour brûlant à la terre ravie,
> Et, quand on est couché sur la vallée, on sent
> Que la terre est nubile et déborde de sang;
> Que son immense sein, soulevé par une âme,
> Est d'amour comme Dieu, de chair comme la femme,
> Et qu'il renferme, gros de sève et de rayons,
> Le grand fourmillement de tous les embryons!
>
> (*Œuvres complètes*, pp. 46-47)

> Au carrefour où nulle fleur sinon la rose
> Des vents mais sans épine n'a fleuri l'hiver
> Merlin guettait la vie et l'éternelle cause
> Qui fait mourir et puis renaître l'univers

The opening stanzas are as different from each other as fertility is from sterility, as spring from winter. A world of plenitude in a continual state of process and renewal is suggested in the first stanza. In contrast, however, is the following strophe with its suggestion of a lifeless, barren world (an impression triply reinforced by the negative expressions in the first two lines) where Merlin, unable to feel any sensation, lies in wait for life like some destitute highway robber.

At this otherworldly crossroads East meets West and North meets South; night encounters day, past meets future, and death joins with life. It is a point where all opposites converge and where, therefore, the eternal cause, which governs the rhythm of life and death in the universe, should be found. Yet the eternal cause is not found at the crossroads because here nothing lives and nothing dies. It is an unworldly void, a barren frozen wasteland, a neutral, cheerless region in limbo between all the antitheses of change in the universe. If it does possess any one characteristic, it is nothingness. Here, in this vacuum, from which all life and feeling have been removed, Merlin leads a sterile existence within a timeless and eternally present moment.[41]

The otherworldly quality of the crossroads is best expressed by the image of "la rose/Des vents." This "wind-rose," or, as it has been called for centuries, the *Rosa ventorum*, does not refer to any species of rose, nor does it grow in any garden or nursery. Instead, it is found in the pilot room of a ship. It refers to that part of a mariner's

---

[41] In this respect, Merlin resembles the heroes of two other poems by Apollinaire. Like the hermit in "L'Ermite" and the thief in "Le Larron" Merlin is a solitary figure, an exile, wandering through a wilderness. In addition, all three characters possess the same magical and supernatural powers. Moreover, according to M. Burgos, loneliness is the central theme of Apollinaire's *L'Enchanteur pourrissant* (p. cxxi). From beginning to end, the work is a "chant de solitude," expressed by a prophet-poet (Merlin-Apollinaire) "qui ne se sent pas tout à fait de la même race que les autres [hommes], et qui cherche à se faire adopter; mais en même temps qu'il se trouve quelque parenté avec ceux qui l'entourent, il se trouve aussi différent. C'est tout le drame d'Apollinaire que celui-là, et *L'Enchanteur* de ce point de vue préfigure admirablement l'œuvre ultérieure..." (p. cx).

compass, called the compass card — a circular card or dial attached to the compass needle and on which the thirty-two divisions of the horizon, corresponding to the thirty-two winds (N, NNE, NE, E, etc.) and the 360 degrees of the circle are so marked, as to take the shape of a rose. As the petals of a rose form a cluster around the flower's pistil, so the thirty-two compass points form a corolla around the concentric circle that is drawn at the center of the compass card (see illustration).

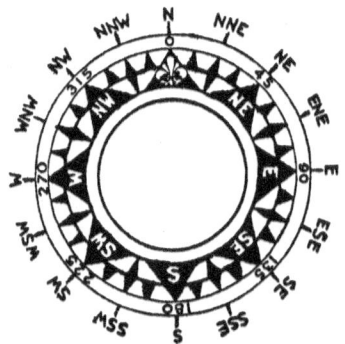

Compass card (from *Webster's Third International Dictionary*)

This inner circle, to which the different compass points converge and around which they are arranged, circumscribes an empty space, a void. Thus, the compass card, the "rose/Des vents," has the same geometric form as the "carrefour" which is also an axis, enclosing a void, and around which the contradictory forces of the universe are arranged like petals on a rose. Not only does the "rose/Des vents" bloom here, but it is the very symbol of the crossroads. [42]

---

[42] The image of "la rose/Des vents" also occurs in the poem "Clair de lune" (1901):

> J'ai peur du dard de feu de cette abeille Arcture
> Qui posa dans mes mains des rayons décevants
> Et prit son miel lunaire à la rose des vents
>
> (*O. P.*, p. 137)

In an original version of the poem, entitled "Lunaire," an additional line with the same pun appeared: " 'O rose à peine rose en des livres savants' " (cited by Durry, I, 220).

There is a further play on words in this image. If we were to take the meaning of "la rose/Des vents" literally and acknowledge that, aside from being a compass card, it is also a rose, and the only flower that can grow in this wasteland environment ("Au carrefour où nulle fleur sinon la rose/Des vents mais sans épine n'a fleuri l'hiver"), then we would soon discover that it is an unusual variety of rose. This crossroads species is thornless, and no rose under the sun grows without thorns.

There is, however, a logical explanation for the thornless rose. Birth and death, past and future and all other contradictory forces in the universe are barred from entering the crossroads. A rose with thorns symbolizes many of these antitheses. Its petals represent the freshness of life; its thorns, the prick of death. It also represents other basic antimonies of life such as hope and despair, pleasure and pain, beauty and ugliness. The thorned rose, therefore, is a symbol of the changing, antithetical nature of life; it is an image of the rhythm of birth and death which defines all existence and an example as well of the "éternelle cause/Qui fait mourir et puis renaître l'univers." Most importantly, however, it represents those forces that have been banished from the crossroads. If the thorned rose symbolizes life in all its multiple contradictions, rhythms, and antitheses, then the thornless rose represents a life without change, without death, and without contradiction. It is an image of the non-life, the nothingness, and the monotony that characterizes eternity. The rose without thorns, then, is the perfect symbol for the lifeless, eternal void where Merlin stands.

The sun, as it is portrayed in the opening stanza of the poem, resembles a large celestial rose; its darting rays of light form a corolla around it, as they do in medieval solar representations. (The rosette and the disc with radial beams are two of the ornamental shapes that represent the sun in medieval popular art.) [43] Like the thorned rose, the sun is a symbol of life and death and, because of its daily death and resurrection, an example of the eternal cause. The "rose/Des vents," then, can also refer to the sun.

But in the second stanza the "rose/Des vents" is thornless, which means that the sun, whose piercing, sharp, darting rays resemble

---

[43] *The Sun in Art*, ed. by Walter Herdeg (Zurich: Amstutz and Herdeg, Graphis Press, 1962), p. 47.

thorns, is without these beams of light. It becomes a sun without light or creative power. Like Merlin's frozen heart ("ce soleil de chair grelotte") the sun shivers. The image of "la rose/Des vents mais sans épine," therefore, has three meanings: it refers to a compass card, a thornless rose and a heatless sun, all of which illustrate the desolation and sterility of Merlin's crossroads world.[44]

Already this poem, one of the oldest in *Alcools*, prefigures the image "Soleil cou coupé," which concludes "Zone," the last poem to be written by Apollinaire for the collection. The difference between these images, however, is sharp. While "Zone" announces the destruction and assassination of the solar body, "Merlin et la vieille femme" praises the sun's powers of creation and birth.

> Une vieille sur une mule à chape verte
> S'en vint suivant la berge du fleuve en aval
> Et l'antique Merlin dans la plaine déserte
> Se frappait la poitrine en s'écriant Rival
>
> O mon être glacé dont le destin m'accable
> Dont ce soleil de chair grelotte veux-tu voir
> Ma Mémoire venir et m'aimer ma semblable
> Et quel fils malheureux et beau je veux avoir
>
> Son geste fit crouler l'orgueil des cataclysmes
> Le soleil en dansant remuait son nombril
> Et soudain le printemps d'amour et d'héroïsme
> Amena par la main un jeune jour d'avril

Merlin addresses a frozen self that has lost the ability to feel and experience life ("O mon être glacé"). As the sun is the center of the cosmos, sustaining all life in the universe, so the heart is the center of the microcosm, man. It is a sun of flesh and blood ("ce soleil de chair"), not unlike the bloodied sun that opens the poem. The outpourings of the heart through feeling, passion, and love resemble the warm light of the sun that bathes the earth. But in Merlin this sun is frozen; its fires have been banked and its rays extinguished by old age. His inner world is without sunlight, his heart shivers with

---

[44] Mme Durry finds another meaning for the image of the thornless rose. She considers it a symbol of the pre-Christian world: "La rose sans épine est antérieure à la couronne d'épines, au christianisme, et figure le monde d'avant le christianisme" (I, 220).

cold, and his feelings and passions are iced over. As a *persona* for the poet Merlin's plight represents the terrible sterility (so common to Mallarmé's poetry) which afflicts the poet when his heart, the source and well-spring of poetry freezes. He can no longer feel nor create.[45]

While Merlin is surrounded by a frozen no man's land, a similar no man's land lies within him. His sterility is total. Both the exterior and the interior worlds — nature and the heart, landscape and the self, object and subject — are frozen wastelands that mirror each other's desolation. The creative rapport that sometimes exists between the poet and nature is unknown to Merlin. Instead, a frozen stalemate prevails. Merlin's sterility prevents him from experiencing his environment, and the barren landscape is without power to inspire him.

Thus, incapable of feeling and helpless against his sterility, Merlin is forced to steal in order to survive; and what he tries to steal is life itself: "Merlin guettait la vie et l'éternelle cause." Forced to become a metaphysical highwayman, Merlin waits in ambush, ready to take by surprise the life he can no longer experience for himself. The irony of his predicament is that he waits in vain. Neither life nor the eternal principle of death and resurrection are to be found anywhere at the crossroads.

If the image of Merlin's frozen heart represents a present self, then the old woman, who approaches him riding a donkey represents the return of a past self, the return of memory ("O mon être glacé... /... veux-tu voir/Ma Mémoire venir et m'aimer ma semblable"). With the appearance of Morgane a heavy gust of warm, life-giving air rushes into the airless crossroads and into Merlin's icy heart. Her arrival starts a thaw that melts away the crossroads' frozen immobility and warms the shivering Merlin. With the appearance of Morgane, the past is resurrected, the "éternelle cause" reappears, the rhythm of birth and death is resumed, and feeling and desire are renewed.

---

[45] Merlin's description of his "être glacé" recalls these lines from Baudelaire's "Chant d'automne":

> Tout l'hiver va rentrer dans mon être: colère,
> Haine, frissons, horreur, labeur dur et forcé,
> Et, comme le soleil dans son enfer polaire
> Mon cœur ne sera plus qu'un bloc rouge et glacé!

(*Œuvres complètes* ["Bibliothèque de la Pléiade"; Paris: Gallimard, 1961], p. 54)

Like "Mai," "Merlin et la vieille femme" illustrates the power of memory to transform the present and the power of the woman to reanimate the poet.[46]

The old woman inspires a primitive masculine instinct in Merlin, who "Se frappait la poitrine en s'écriant Rival." Morgane fills him with emotion, passion, and the desire for procreation: "Et quel fils malheureux et beau je veux avoir." The desire for creation pulses through his veins and inspires the challenge he hurls at Morgane and at the universe: "Rival." Merlin intends to possess Morgane sexually and also at the same time to resist by means of the sexual act the forces of destruction in the universe. Such acts of rebellion will, he hopes, satisfy his desire for creation and his desire for immortality. Almost immediately after his defiant cry of revolt, the universe is transformed. The proud, unchallenged, cataclysmic forces of nature that play havoc with human achievement are humbled: "Son geste fit crouler l'orgueil des cataclysmes." And the sun, at his command, performs a celestial belly dance, which transforms the frozen crossroads into spring:

> Le soleil en dansant remuait son nombril
> Et soudain le printemps d'amour et d'héroïsme
> Amena par la main un jeune jour d'avril

The renewal of the universe, like Merlin's own reawakening, involves the return of a past, only now it is a romantic, historical past, that of medieval legend and courtly romance ("le printemps d'amour et d'héroïsme").

Merlin declares himself a rival of time, of age, of nature, of death, in short, of all the elements of mortality that interfere with man's efforts to immortalize himself. He wishes to create something that will survive after he is gone. If his cry of revolt changes the universe, it is only because it is inspired by the two creative forces by which he can possess immortality: love and memory. Love produces the child, and memory creates the poem: two ways by which man en-

---

[46] M. Chevalier has demonstrated how in this stanza Merlin, by the repetition of the initial consonant of his name in eight of the words in the stanza, and especially in the first person possessive adjectives, "mon" and "ma," which are themselves repeated as both semantic and phonemic units, becomes identified with the old woman and with his past (p. 115).

sures that his name, at least, will not be forgotten. Merlin's challenge echoes throughout the poem, but it is only the first step toward the immortality that he seeks and will eventually find.

Although Merlin succeeds briefly in humbling the universe, he is reminded of its infinite power of destruction in the last strophe of the poem's first "act." A constant reminder to him of the magnitude of his revolt is the sight of those roads that come to the crossroads from the West:

> Les voies qui viennent de l'ouest étaient couvertes
> D'ossements d'herbes drues de destins et de fleurs
> Des monuments tremblants près des charognes vertes
> Quand les vents apportaient des poils et des malheurs

The smell of putrefying flesh, the sight of dried bones and crumbling grave monuments, and the touch of infected winds make up a ghastly spectacle of death, forcing Merlin to realize that all life, like the sun, moves relentlessly westward towards death and oblivion.

Thus, at the end of the poem's first "act" Merlin's frozen self has begun to thaw, his desires and feelings have reawakened, and the barren crossroads have been transformed into a world alive with the promise of spring. This miraculous regeneration, occasioned by the appearance of Morgane, demonstrates the power of memory to transform the present.

II. *Morgane, the sterile dancer.*

Despite the pronounced effect Morgane has had on Merlin and on the character of his crossroads habitat, she is as impotent, although in a different way, as he was before her arrival. Unlike Merlin, Morgane is capable of artistic creation because she is a dancer; but, unfortunately, what she creates are irrelevant, shadowy fantasies. While she may have accidentally awakened Merlin from a comatose state, she herself still slumbers in a dream world of illusions as different from the world of rhythmic change and regeneration as was Merlin's crossroads.

As the second "act" of the poem begins, Morgane awkwardly approaches Merlin:

> Laissant sa mule à petits pas s'en vint l'amante
> A petits coups le vent défripait ses atours

> Puis les pâles amants joignant leurs mains démentes
> L'entrelacs de leurs doigts fut leur seul laps
>   d'amour

In joining their hands together, their first physical contact of the poem, Merlin and Morgane prefigure the sexual act they will later accomplish. The stylized, artificial nature of this first encounter is emphasized by the image of the "entrelacs," an ornament composed of intertwined floral designs, lines, leaves, and vines. In the poem the "entrelacs" describes the design formed by Merlin's and Morgane's joined hands, whose interlaced fingers imitate the intertwining of legs and arms of the sexual embrace. Their brief moment of contact ("leur seul laps d'amour") amounts to no more than an intricate ballet of dancing, interlocking fingers. More emphasis is placed on the form and artistry of their union than on the union itself. This awkward, fumbling encounter is therefore a sterile and uncreative imitation. Afflicted by a sterility they have not yet overcome, both Merlin and Morgane are incapable of sexual union, and so, are forced to express their violent passion through their hands ("leurs mains démentes"). And yet, their encounter is an important step toward the creative sexual union to come. Once Merlin and Morgane have overcome their individual sterilities, they will be capable of creating a child.

This finally occurs in the third "moment" of the poem:

> Et leurs mains s'élevaient comme un vol de colombes
> Clarté sur qui la nuit fondit comme un vautour

In these lines, images of illumination, spirituality, and mystical union replace the earlier stylized image of the "entrelacs." For a brief moment, Merlin and Morgane are fused together in an explosion of light that is similar to the creative light of the sun at the beginning of the poem. But before this union can take place Morgane, who has just joined hands with Merlin, must deliver her soliloquy:

> Elle balla mimant un rythme d'existence
> Criant Depuis cent ans j'espérais ton appel
> Les astres de ta vie influaient sur ma danse
> Morgane regardait du haut du mont Gibel
>
> Ah! qu'il fait doux danser quand pour vous se déclare
> Un mirage où tout chante et que les vents d'horreur

> Feignent d'être le rire de la lune hilare
> Et d'effrayer les fantômes avant-coureurs
>
> J'ai fait des gestes blancs parmi les solitudes
> Des lémures couraient peupler les cauchemars
> Mes tournoiements exprimaient les béatitudes
> Qui toutes ne sont rien qu'un pur effet de l'Art
>
> Je n'ai jamais cueilli que la fleur d'aubépine
> Aux printemps finissants qui voulaient défleurir
> Quand les oiseaux de proie proclamaient leurs rapines
> D'agneaux morts-nés et d'enfants-dieux qui vont mourir
>
> Et j'ai vieilli vois-tu pendant ta vie je danse
> Mais j'eusse été tôt lasse et l'aubépine en fleurs
> Cet avril aurait eu la pauvre confidence
> D'un corps de vieille morte en mimant la douleur

Throughout her speech the emphasis is on dance and on the subtle gestures of mime. Morgane pantomimes life itself, enacts the rhythm of existence with her hands and body, fills her solitude with illusory gestures ("gestes blancs") and whirls furiously ("mes tournoiements"). The suggestive art of her body punctuates her soliloquy, and the allusions to "mimant," "feindre," "chante," "mirage," and "pur effet de l'Art" illustrate the illusory and stylized qualities of her art. Morgane's dance and pantomime are more artifice than art, more imitation than creation.

The "rythme d'existence" that Morgane imitates is, like the "éternelle cause," the rhythm that governs the diastole and the systole of the universe: the ebb and flood of the sea, the death and rebirth of life, the beating of the heart. But Morgane is insensitive to this rhythm. As Merlin earlier in the poem had to lie in ambush for the eternal cause he could no longer experience, so Morgane pantomimes the rhythm of life that she can no longer feel. The "rythme d'existence," moreover, has another meaning, an erotic one. Since "baller" means to oscillate and sway, as well as to dance, Morgane seems to pantomime the sex act. Like the image of the "entrelacs" her dance and mime are surrogates for sexual union — artistic imitations of the rhythmical act that creates life.

Since "Merlin et la vieille femme" was composed at a moment when the dancer enjoyed great popularity in Europe and when poets and painters, especially those in the Symbolist camp, as a result of their having discovered that the art of the dance contained a power of evocation and a purity of expression reserved until then for music, were beginning to make the dancer a symbol of their art, it is not surprising that Morgane should bear a resemblance to the Salomé, Hérodiade, and other dancer images of the time. It is perhaps worthwhile, in order to understand Apollinaire's portrait of Morgane, to consider briefly the *fin de siècle* phenomenon of the dancer.

The dancer, not the ballerina but the music-hall dancer, enjoyed an immense popularity among the artistic élites of Paris and London. Jane Avril and La Goulue, their skirts pulled up and their kicking legs frozen in a mid-air arabesque, were painted by Toulouse-Lautrec in his *affiches*. Loïe Fuller, waving the long folds of her silk skirt about her in an evocative incarnation of a butterfly or a lily or gliding across the boards in her famed Serpentine Dance, while varicolored lights played about her and optical effects heightened the magic of her dance, hypnotized Stéphane Mallarmé so greatly that he found in her living proof of what he had always believed the dancer to be: "poème dégagé de tout appareil du scribe."[47] In "Ballets" (1886) Mallarmé remarked that the dancer is not a woman who dances, but "une métaphore résumant un des aspects élémentaires de notre forme...."[48] Moreover, she does not even dance, but rather suggests "par le prodige de raccourcis ou d'élans, avec une écriture corporelle ce qu'il faudrait des paragraphes en prose dialoguée autant que descriptive, pour exprimer dans la rédaction...."[49] The dance illustrates "le caprice à l'essor rythmique" and is the "incorporation visuelle de l'idée."[50] The dancer is a poem; or, as he wrote in "Les Fonds dans le ballet" (1893) — an article describing the performances of Loïe Fuller — the dancer is "la forme théâtrale de poésie par excellence."[51] Moreover, she creates around herself an air of exquisite purity:

> ...la danseuse: le plancher évité par bonds ou dur aux pointes, acquiert une virginité de site pas songé, qu'isole, bâtira, fleurira, la figure.[52]

---

[47] *Œuvres complètes*, p. 304.
[48] *Ibid.*
[49] *Ibid.*
[50] *Ibid.*, p. 306.
[51] *Ibid.*, p. 308.
[52] *Ibid.*

Across the Channel in England, Arthur Symons, the poet and critic, shared a similar conception. The dancer, he wrote in 1898, has "the intellectual as well as sensuous appeal of a living symbol," and, he continued,

> A world rises before one, the picture lasts only long enough to have been there: and the dancer, with her gesture, all pure symbol, evokes, from her mere beautiful motion, idea, sensation, all that one need ever know of event. There, before you, she exists, in harmonious life; and her rhythm reveals to you the soul of her imagined being.[53]

Thus, the dancer — autotelic, free of the limitations of time and space, possessing all that is relevant to herself, "une fontaine intarissable d'elle-même,"[54] according to Mallarmé — suggested to Symbolist and *fin de siècle* poets that most perfect and virtual of all poems, the "page blanche." Her movements, provoked by an inner creative force, imposed themselves on the unorganized space she danced through making the air around her palpable. Like a ship, the dancer stirred behind her a wake that continued long after she had passed on. She concretized the invisible, not with words, not with description, but with the evocative movements of her body, which spoke a mute language perfectly described by Mallarmé as "une écriture corporelle." The motions of her body constituted an exquisite language of silence, and she and her dance were one:

> O body swayed to music, O brightening glance,
> How can we know the dancer from the dance?[55]

Morgane appears at first glance to be a dancer in the Symbolist tradition. She evokes by her movements an imaginary world of bliss and harmony, where ugliness and horror are transformed into laughter and joy ("Ah! qu'il fait doux danser quand pour vous se déclare / Un mirage où tout chante et que les vents d'horreur / Feignent d'être le rire de la lune hilare"). She carves from empty space ("les soli-

---

[53] "The World as Ballet," in his *Studies in Seven Arts* (London: Martin Secker, 1924), p. 246.
[54] "Le seul, il le fallait fluide...," *Œuvres complètes*, p. 311.
[55] W. B. Yeats, "Among School Children," *The Collected Poems* (Definitive Edition; New York: Macmillan, 1956), p. 214.

tudes") and by means of a pantomime of pure gestures ("gestes blancs") an atmosphere, a *milieu* (what Mallarmé called "une virginité de site pas songé").

Morgane's pantomime of "gestes blancs" appears to illustrate Mallarmé's notion that art must attempt to express the purity of silence, the ultimate form of expression, through the creation of pure fictions. As he had done with the dance, Mallarmé regards the art of pantomime in terms of its "poetic" aspects. The mime, "le fantôme blanc," [56] is like "une page pas encore écrite." [57] The mime creates a fictive world through the suggestive power of his art: "il installe, ainsi, un milieu, pur, de fiction." [58] In addition, Morgane's whirling dance, which enables her to reach a state of bliss, beatitude, and harmony — a state that she recognizes as being "un pur effet de l'Art" — suggests the Symbolists' attempts to regain an ideal, pre-original world through poetic creation.

Morgane would appear therefore to illustrate the Symbolists' conception of the dancer and of the mime. And yet behind Apollinaire's portrait lies a subtle criticism of Symbolism. Morgane's choreography, although artistically perfect and appealing, is a failure. It creates an artificial, fictive world as unreal and as sterile in its way as was Merlin's "carrefour." Her creation fails to recognize the dominion of change, the necessity of impermanence, and the presence of flux. Nothing illustrates this better than her attempt to create "gestes blancs," which indicates the desire to free herself from the constraints of time and space and to attain a world of purity and being from which change and chance would be excluded. But a victory over chance or change is also a victory over life. It is a negation of the "éternelle cause / Qui fait mourir et puis renaître l'univers"; it negates the world of becoming for a world of being. Like Merlin's crossroads, it is a world of permanence rather than of flux, of product rather than of process, of death rather than of life. Apollinaire's portrait of Morgane as dancer may coincide in some respects with the Symbolist model, but within the context of the poem she represents the sterility of the Symbolist aesthetic. She has become the symbol for an art that has lost touch with life, for an art that, in renouncing

---

[56] "Mimique" (1886), *Œuvres complètes*, p. 310.
[57] *Ibid.*
[58] *Ibid.*

the world of change, has opted for a barren, unchanging world of uniform purity. This world is, as Morgane says, *nothing but* "un pur effet de l'Art." [59]

Morgane's sterility and her ignorance of the rhythms of life are clearly evident when she states, "Je n'ai jamais cueilli que la fleur d'aubépine / Aux printemps finissants qui voulaient défleurir." It is ironical that, when she does decide to pick a flower, she waits until it is about to die. Her contact with the real world comes at the moment when the air is filled with death, pillage and horror, when "... les oiseaux de proie proclamaient leurs rapines / D'agneaux mort-nés et d'enfants-dieux qui vont mourir." [60]

---

[59] Apollinaire's anti-Symbolist attitude appears to have been shared by other poets of the period, as is evident from the following statement made a year after "Merlin et la vieille femme" was written:

> "Le meilleur moyen de savoir ce que veulent les poètes de demain est encore de savoir ce qu'ils reprochent à la Poésie qui est déjà pour eux la Poésie d'hier. Or, le reproche général que l'on fait au symbolisme et qui les résume tous en un mot: c'est d'avoir négligé la *vie*. Nous avons rêvé; ils [les poètes de demain] veulent vivre et dire ce qu'ils ont vécu, directement, simplement, intimement, lyriquement. Ils ne veulent pas chanter l'homme en ses symboles, ils veulent l'exprimer en ses pensées, en ses sensations, en ses sentiments."

(Henri de Régnier, "Poètes d'aujourd'hui et poésie de demain," *Mercure de France* (août, 1900), p. 349; cited by Léon Somville, *Devanciers du surréalisme. Les groupes d'avant-garde et le mouvement poétique 1912-1925* ("Histoire des idées et critique littéraire," vol. 116; Geneva: Droz, 1971), p. 13, n. 3.

[60] M. Renaud sees in all three poems of Apollinaire's symbolist period ("Le Larron," "L'Ermite," and "Merlin et la vieille femme") a possible satire of symbolist poetry in general:

> On sent assez bien dans ces poèmes qu'Apollinaire, en se servant de la poésie symboliste, souligne ses défauts, notamment celui qu'elle a de faire du langage une scintillante barrière entre la conscience et l'expérience directe de la vie (p. 52).

But, rather than severely criticizing Symbolism for having caused an ever widening divorce between life and art, these three poems, according to M. Renaud, express a fundamental ambivalence on Apollinaire's part towards the symbolist poetry of the *fin de siècle* period and reflect his desire to reduce the gap separating experience and poetry:

> Il s'agissait de ne pas abandonner les conquêtes du symbolisme, mais de rendre vie à son univers de plus en plus exsangue. Car c'est un fait que ces poèmes vivent — même si ce qui les anime violemment est un effort qui se reconnaît vain de rejoindre la Vie (*Ibid.*).

The meeting of Morgane and Merlin has a profound effect. Had they never met, Merlin would have remained sterile, continuing to inhabit the cold reaches of the crossroads; as for Morgane, she would have died an old woman, continuing to the very end her pantomime of life ("l'aubépine en fleurs / Cet avril aurait eu la pauvre confidence / D'un corps de vieille morte en mimant la douleur"). But their meeting saves each of them from a death of one sort or another, and in the final "act" of the poem it will renew their powers of feeling, their desire for creation, and their taste for life.

III. *The Son, the immortal creation.*

The third "act" of "Merlin et la vieille femme" opens with the sexual union of Merlin and Morgane and ends with Merlin's hope for immortality:

> Et leurs mains s'élevaient comme un vol de colombes
> Clarté sur qui la nuit fondit comme un vautour
> Puis Merlin s'en alla vers l'est disant Qu'il monte
> Le fils de la Mémoire égale de l'Amour
>
> Qu'il monte de la fange ou soit une ombre d'homme
> Il sera bien mon fils mon ouvrage immortel
> Le front nimbé de feu sur le chemin de Rome
> Il marchera tout seul en regardant le ciel
>
> La dame qui m'attend se nomme Viviane
> Et vienne le printemps des nouvelles douleurs
> Couché parmi la marjolaine et les pas-d'âne
> Je m'éterniserai sous l'aubépine en fleurs

Throughout these stanzas Merlin speaks of his son in equivocal terms: "Le fils de la Mémoire égale de l'Amour," "Qu'il monte de la fange ou soit une ombre d'homme," "mon fils mon ouvrage immortel." Merlin is the father of two different offspring, and his words reveal this double paternity. In mating with Morgane, the woman, he has conceived a child. In his union with Morgane, the memory, he has

---

Although M. Renaud's arguments are compelling, it seems to me (as the interpretation of the dancer figure attempted to show) that the failure of Symbolism is emphasized in "Merlin et la vieille femme" to a greater degree than M. Renaud appears willing to recognize.

created a work of art. In both cases, because of the equally creative powers of memory and love, Merlin has succeeded in creating life out of undifferentiated matter, out of mud ("fange"). Moreover, both creations assure him the immortality he desires.

Merlin refers to his son as "une ombre d'homme." A shadow is formed when rays of light are blocked by an opaque object; the intercepted light takes the form of the object it strikes and projects an image of that object onto a space. The shadow, therefore, is an object expressed through the medium of light. When Merlin speaks of his son as "une ombre d'homme," he is referring to this union between light and matter that the shadow represents. Both of his offspring (the child, the poem) are conceived in pure light ("Clarté"), and both will appear in a material form. The child will be a shadow of a man because it will be pure light incarnated in a human body. Similarly, the poem will be a shadow because it will be poetic light or inspiration expressed in the material form of words. [61]

At the crossroads Merlin could neither feel nor create; as for Morgane, since she was a dancer, she was capable of creating, but her creations were meaningless fictions. Unlike either of his parents, however, the son will be capable of both feeling and creation. He carries the mark of these powers on his forehead: "le front nimbé de feu." He walks alone with Promethean confidence, completely self-sufficient and independant ("il marchera tout seul"), his halo of fire representing poetic inspiration. If he looks to the sky, it is not for divine aid, but to pay homage to the sun, the source of his being. Moreover, he is an image not only of the solitary, godlike poet, but also of the perfectly self-contained work of art.

But why does Merlin's son walk toward Rome with his eyes turned skyward:

> Le front nimbé de feu sur le chemin de Rome
> Il marchera tout seul en regardant le ciel

---

[61] In the poem "Ombre" (*Calligrammes*) Apollinaire refers to his shadow as a kind of poem:

> Ombre encre du soleil
> Ecriture de ma lumière
>
> (*O. P.*, p. 217)

See below, pp. 174ff.

Mme Durry admits that these lines have given her considerable difficulty and asks:

> Mais n'avancera-t-il pas vers Rome en regardant le ciel, par un défi au ciel, et à la religion dont Rome possède le chef suprême? Regardera-t-il le ciel comme le ferait un ange obscur opposé aux anges chrétiens, ou bien s'avancera-t-il vers la religion pour se fondre en elle, pour lui apporter et incliner devant elle les puissances féeriques et magiques d'un surnaturel différent qui était l'apanage de Merlin? Je ne puis trancher avec certitude. [62]

But as a possible explanation, she suggests that, while Merlin felt certain ties to Christianity, he possessed nevertheless demonic and pagan powers which prevented him from travelling to Rome, from adopting Christianity, by the beaten path taken by all converts. To support this, Mme Durry cites a passage from *L'Enchanteur pourrissant,* where Merlin tells Isaac Laquedem:

> "O riche voyageur, je suis incirconcis et baptisé, et pourtant j'ai été à Jérusalem, mais par d'autres chemins que le chemin de la croix, et j'ai été à Rome par d'autres chemins que tous ceux qui y menent." [63]

Merlin's son, on the other hand, may make the trip to Rome; he can travel by the beaten path.

Once his act of creation with Morgane has ended Merlin sets off toward the East, in the direction of the rising sun. Fully aware of the fate that awaits him at the hands of Vivien, he is, nevertheless, filled with hope; he realizes that new misfortunes and suffering also bring the possibility of new poems. As the sun is resurrected each morning, as spring reappears after winter, and as things die only to be reborn — all in accord with the eternal cause and the rhythm of existence that govern the universe — so Merlin will suffer new misfortunes in order to create poetry: "Et vienne le printemps des nouvelles douleurs / Couché parmi la marjolaine et les pas-d'âne / Je m'éterniserai sous l'aubépine en fleurs." And yet, although Merlin will immortalize himself through the creation of poetry, he does not claim to live

---

[62] I, 222.
[63] *Ibid.*

forever. Indeed, his words indicate that death is close by. During spring the hawthorne's blossoms give off a decaying, fish-like odor that is regarded, superstitiously, as a portent of death. Moreover, when Vivien captures Merlin in her tower, it will be surrounded, ironically enough, by white hawthorne bushes. [64]

Merlin's original cry of revolt, "Rival," is amplified at the poem's conclusion into a more defiant and enduring challenge. He opposes the cycle of life and death in the universe by creating immortal works of art. At the same time, however, he yields to this same cycle. Merlin knows from experience that without the rhythm of existence, the world would be as barren as the crossroads, and feeling and poetry would be extinct. He has learned that in order to create something immortal the poet must first understand his own mortality. He must suffer sadness, feel misfortune, and participate, above all, in the rhythm of life. Birth and pain, creation and suffering, are inseparable. In order to shine the sun must die; in order to give birth the maternal belly ("ventre/Maternel") must bleed; in order to return, spring must have its winter, day its night, and the sun its moon. Only through life is life conquered.

The allegory of "Merlin et la vieille femme" not only dramatizes the creation of poetry, it also dramatizes the integration of the poet's different selves into a coherent and undifferentiated self. When the poet remembers and then turns that memory into a work of art, he succeeds in joining two previously separated selves. A past self, represented in the poem by Morgane, and a present self, represented by Merlin, are united, forming a third self which is embodied in the poem. The birth of Merlin's and Morgane's son symbolizes the birth of a poem and, above all, the creation of a united and unfragmented self. Poetic creation acts as the catalyst in this dramatic reintegration of self.

Although "Merlin et la vieille femme" is compromised poetically by its erudite, turn-of-the-century imagery [65] and by its belabored,

---

[64] Ownbey, p. 15.

[65] Many *fin de siècle* images are scattered throughout the poem. For example, the flowing organic forms and the interlaced tendrils of *art nouveau* are suggested by such words as, "s'étalait," "coulaient," "flux," "joignant," "l'entrelacs," "influaient," while the passion of the decadents for the macabre is seen in the words, "ossements," "mirage," "fantômes," "lune hilare," "rapines," "mort-nés," and "printemps finissants."

allegorical style, still it is an important poem in the canon of Apollinaire's work. In the fourteen years that separate it from "Zone," such poetic devices as *personae* and the concealed *art poétique*, such themes as recurrence, the creative power of memory, and the wanderer in the wilderness, such images as the Christ-like poet, the bloodied sun, and the gesturing hands — all of which are found in "Merlin et la vieille femme" — appear again and again in both the traditional and the more experimental poems of *Alcools*. Although the poet's presence is not felt as strongly here as in his later poems, "Merlin et la vieille femme" succeeds, nevertheless, in revealing the drama of self that characterizes all of Apollinaire's poetry.

PART 2

THE METAPHORS OF SELF

> Nulle des nymphes, nulle amie, me m'attire
> Comme tu fais sur l'onde, inépuisable Moi!...
> (Paul Valéry, "Fragments du Narcisse," *Charmes*)

CHAPTER IV

HARLEQUIN: THE PROTEAN SELF

From the commedia dell'arte, the comedy of histrionic skill and improvisation established in Italy around 1550,[1] sprang a group of stock characters and burlesque masked types of which Harlequin is perhaps the most famous and the most durable. Harlequin, or as he is often called, Arlecchino, was one of four principal masked characters known as the "four masks."[2] These included two old men or "vecchi" (Pantalone and Il Dottore) and two servants or "zanni" (Brighella and Arlecchino),[3] and from them the other masked characters of the commedia dell'arte were created.[4]

Although in the four centuries since the founding of the commedia dell'arte Arlecchino has undergone changes in style, dress and sophistication, these have been changes of detail only, refinements and embellishments rather than major transformations.[5] Originally, Harlequin's costume was marked with irregularly placed patches of color.[6] But by the second half of the seventeenth century these irregular patches were replaced by geometric forms,[7] and the costume of evenly placed, brightly colored triangles, with which we are familiar today, was created. Such uniformity in costume and acting have made

---

[1] Allardyce Nicoll, *The World of Harlequin: A Critical Study of the Commedia dell'Arte* (Cambridge: The University Press, 1963), p. 9.
[2] *Ibid.*, p. 40.
[3] *Ibid.*
[4] Thelma Niklaus, *Harlequin Phoenix: or The Rise and Fall of a Bergamask Rogue* (London: The Bodley Head, 1956), p. 38.
[5] Nicoll, pp. 69-70.
[6] *Ibid.*, p. 69.
[7] *Ibid.*

Harlequin one of the most easily recognized characters in the theatre.[8] Yet his popularity has not been limited to the stage alone. In our own century he has infiltrated almost every art form.[9]

Aside from his familiar patchwork costume and his black half-mask, Harlequin is identified by his agility and skill at acrobatics[10] and by certain inner qualities. He is unable to think of more than one thing at a time, and he never considers the future consequences of his acts.[11] As he moves from one embarrassing situation to another, constantly creating new lies and gestures to cover up previous ones that have failed, Harlequin demonstrates a clever wit, a quick mind and a sense of fun which enable him to wriggle out of all imbroglios.[12] Although he loves to impersonate other characters, his disguises are rarely successful, partly because of his clumsiness and partly because he always says something to give himself away.[13]

Harlequin, like a chameleon, is always assuming different colors. From one situation to another and from one moment to the next he changes his mind, adopting opinions that are convenient for him and views that excuse or justify his actions. In the harlequinade, *La figlia disubbediente*, for example, Harlequin tries to beg for money by claiming that he is dumb. The man to whom he speaks asks how a dumb beggar can speak so well, and Harlequin answers that he is not

---

[8] *Ibid.*, p. 2.
[9] In the art of the dance Harlequin has been portrayed, for example, in *Arlequinade* performed by Anna Pavlova and Michel Fokine in 1900, in Fokine's 1910 ballet *Carnaval*, and more recently in *Harlequin in April* (1951) (Niklaus, pp. 179-180). In operatic works Harlequin and four other characters of the commedia dell'arte appeared in Richard Strauss's and Hugo von Hofmannsthal's work *Ariadne auf Naxos*, first performed in 1916 (Nicoll, p. 219). Harlequin has also been a favorite subject for painters such as Degas, Cézanne, Derain, and most importantly, Picasso, who painted him in different acrobatic and family groups during his rose period. In the youngest of the arts, the cinema, Harlequin has appeared less frequently. A celebrated sequence from *Les Enfants du paradis* (1944) showed a Harlequin (played by Pierre Brasseur) and a pierrot (played by Jean-Louis Barrault) performing before a beautiful statue (played by Arletty). Jean Renoir's *La Carrozza d'Oro (The Golden Coach*, 1952) starred Anna Magnani as the leader and Harlequina of a band of actors travelling in South America in the last century. In the same year Harlequin was seen again in a ballet sequence from Charlie Chaplin's *Limelight* (Niklaus, p. 181).
[10] Nicoll, p. 70.
[11] *Ibid.*
[12] *Ibid.*, p. 72.
[13] *Ibid.*, p. 73.

dumb after all but only deaf; when pressed again to explain how he can hear so well if he is deaf, he hastens to add that he is neither dumb nor deaf but really blind.[14] Harlequin is never at rest long enough to be caught by his own mistakes; he is so clever as to be never at a loss for words.

His love of disguise, his complex self-contradictions, and his protean nature make harlequin a flesh and blood facsimile of Apollinaire's self. If the self could have human form, it would look, speak, and act like Harlequin. Harlequin loves to wear disguise and impersonate others, as does Apollinaire's self, which hides its identity behind different masks and *personae*. Harlequin contradicts himself continually, as does the poet's self, which is a network of contradictory selves. Harlequin is a fleeting character never at rest long enough to be caught, as is the self, which will never be grasped in its entirety because it resembles an unfinished jigsaw puzzle from which pieces will always be missing. Harlequin's costume is a series of unrelated, brightly colored triangles like the series of disjointed selves that compose the self. Harlequin and the self resemble each other in that they are continually moving and always in the process of becoming something else. Any definition of them fails to take into consideration the very form they have assumed while the definition is being made. They are, therefore, indefinable. Their protean natures defeat all attempts at classification.

Harlequin is a key metaphor for Apollinaire's self in *Alcools*. Although he makes his appearance in only one poem, "Crépuscule," he is present throughout the collection in the other images and characters Apollinaire uses to represent the self. As a member of an itinerant group of actors who once toured the countryside performing commedia dell'arte, Harlequin has much in common with the sad group of acrobats in the poem, "Saltimbanques." As a wanderer he resembles the nomadic hermit in "L'Ermite" and the outcast thief in "Le Larron." Like Merlin ("Merlin et la vieille femme") he is a magician and a demon, who at the end of "Crépuscule" grows to three times his size. Like the mythic Loreley ("La Loreley") he contemplates his reflection in a pond. Like all these characters Harlequin is a *persona*, a mask assumed by the poet to hide his identity and at the same time to reveal the self. But because he is actor, clown, pariah,

---

[14] Nicoll, p. 72.

magician, and Narcissus all in one, he is Apollinaire's most important *persona*.

The harlequin that appears in "Crépuscule" is a more serious and less boisterous character than his forefather, Arlecchino. He is even more respectable than the harlequin that Verlaine describes in "Colombine":

> Cet aigrefin si
> Fantasque
> Aux costumes fous
> Ses yeux luisants sous
> Son masque [15]

In Apollinaire's poem Harlequin becomes a serious artist. But his new sobriety and respectability do not prevent him from exuberantly playing all the roles in the poem.

Published in February 1909 in *Les Argonautes*, along with its companion poem, "Saltimbanques," [16] "Crépuscule" is dedicated to Marie Laurencin, Apollinaire's mistress and a celebrated painter in her own right. [17] The five stanzas of "Crépuscule" are filled with a charming air of fantasy that recalls Verlaine's poems in *Fêtes Galantes*. The great resemblance between Apollinaire and Verlaine is their use of the sad, melancholic *chant*; they have, according to Mme Durry, "une façon de sentir qui a besoin des mêmes harmoniques musicales." [18] But while Verlaine's harlequins live in the eighteenth century, Apollinaire's are totally modern; they are harlequins, *saltimbanques*, and acrobats he has seen at fairs, along roads, and on street corners. [19] And yet in his poetry they acquire a vague unreality, as the poem "Crépuscule" shows:

---

[15] *Œuvres poétiques complètes* ("Bibliothèque de la Pléiade"; Paris: Gallimard, 1938), pp. 94-95.

[16] "Crépuscule" and "Saltimbanques" are, so to speak, two branches of the same tree. An incomplete, untitled manuscript, published by Jeanine Moulin in her *Apollinaire: Textes inédits* (Geneva: Droz, 1952), pp. 174-176, contains together in the same poem an early version of "Saltimbanques" and an even earlier and more crude version of "Crépuscule."

[17] In all probability, M. Décaudin observes, the poem was not inspired by Marie, but had already been written when she met Apollinaire in 1908 (*Le Dossier*, p. 115).

[18] II, 68.

[19] *Ibid.*

> Frôlée par les ombres des morts
> Sur l'herbe où le jour s'exténue
> L'arlequine s'est mise nue
> Et dans l'étang mire son corps
>
> Un charlatan crépusculaire
> Vante les tours que l'on va faire
> Le ciel sans teinte est constellé
> D'astres pâles comme du lait
>
> Sur les tréteaux l'arlequin blême
> Salue d'abord les spectateurs
> Des sorciers venus de Bohême
> Quelques fées et les enchanteurs
>
> Ayant décroché une étoile
> Il la manie à bras tendu
> Tandis que des pieds un pendu
> Sonne en mesure les cymbales
>
> L'aveugle berce un bel enfant
> La biche passe avec ses faons
> Le nain regarde d'un air triste
> Grandir l'arlequin trismégiste
>
> (*O. P.*, p. 64)

From out of the half-light of evening, at the beginning of the poem, strange things begin to emerge. The scene is marked by a motley of light and dark colors similar to Harlequin's costume. Columbine's ("L'arlequine") naked body, for example, is touched by shadows, and the stars that emerge are pale white dots surrounded by an immense black sky:

> Le ciel sans teinte est constellé
> Des astres pâles comme du lait [20]

As the poem moves from a nebulous twilight to night, elements of purity and whiteness are uncovered. Columbine's body is revealed

---

[20] Mme Durry underlines the similarity between this sky and the one painted by Verlaine in *Sagesse*:

> "L'onde, roulée en volutes,
> De cloches comme des flûtes
> Dans le ciel comme du lait"
> (II, 61-62)

from under its mask of clothing and then further purified when it becomes a reflection on the surface of the pond, a reflection which is answered across the infinite and darkening world by the milk-white purity of the night-locked stars.[21] At twilight, an expectant, unsettled universe stands pure and naked, ready to receive the fantastic, supernatural world which Harlequin will create with his magic.

In "Crépuscule" a succession of extraordinary and fantastic characters appears and disappears without warning. The first to appear is Columbine, but she soon becomes a reflection of herself and disappears altogether. She is followed by a charlatan-barker, who announces the wondrous tricks soon to be performed. His voice dies out in the night, and Harlequin appears on stage, first welcoming his audience of supernatural beings and then performing his act, assisted by a hanged man. Finally, they exit, and the stage becomes filled with a blind woman (or man), a doe, a dwarf and a gigantic harlequin, all of whom perform a supernatural finale.

From all signs it appears that a magical harlequinade is being performed in "Crépuscule" and that the star of the show is Harlequin. But more than the star of this spectacle he is practically the only actor in it. He plays nearly all the major roles, and those he does not perform remain characters associated or closely identified with him. Disguises, masks, and magic enable him to perform what amounts to almost a one-man harlequinade. Because he is restless and always moving Harlequin never plays one character for any considerable length of time. Instead, he impersonates a succession of characters, impressing on each one his mystery and his quicksilver temperament. He assumes the color, voice, demeanor, and appearance of each character. By the impersonations he performs and the masks he wears, Harlequin succeeds in revealing hidden aspects of himself. Each character he plays becomes a dramatization of one of his many selves. Thus, mask is used not only to disguise his identity but also to reveal the nature of his protean self.

---

[21] In "La Chanson du Mal-Aimé" a feeling of infinite purity is also suggested by a comparison between naked bodies and milk-white stars:

> Voie lactée ô sœur lumineuse
> Des blancs ruisseaux de Chanaan
> Et des corps blancs des amoureuses
> (O. P., p. 48)

The first role Harlequin plays is that of Columbine with whom he is always associated in the commedia dell'arte. Wherever Harlequin is found, there too is Columbine, the cunning and frivolous coquette he loves. In the first stanza Harlequin portrays his female counterpart with comparative ease because harlequins, according to Apollinaire's description of Picasso's paintings of them, are hermaphroditic:

> ... Des arlequins accompagnent la gloire des femmes, ils leur ressemblent, ni mâles, ni femelles.
>
> La couleur a des matités de fresques, les lignes sont fermes. Mais placés à la limite de la vie, les animaux sont humains et les sexes indécis.[22]

But Columbine is an ephemeral character, as unstable as the unsettled, ever-changing world that surrounds her and as fleeting as the ghosts ("les ombres des morts") that graze her in passing. Before disappearing, however, Columbine contemplates her reflection in a pond. Having removed her clothes, she now becomes reclothed in her own pure reflection:

> L'arlequine s'est mise nue
> Et dans l'étang mire son corps

But Columbine's floating, wavering reflection is also ephemeral. As easily as it can be broken up by a ripple on the pond's surface, so the slightest movement causes Columbine to disappear.

Now that his feminine self is gone, Harlequin, maskless, searches for a new character to portray. The self he finds comes from the dark side of his personality. Harlequin is descended, according to one legend, from Mercury,[23] god of thieves, charlatans and swindlers, and the charlatan he now portrays has a marked talent for deceit and exaggeration:

> Un charlatan crépusculaire
> Vante les tours que l'on va faire

This charlatan is another nebulous, twilight being, who emerges from the shadows like some sly, night animal and announces the magic soon to be performed. He is the herald of the fantastic world to come.

---

[22] *Les Peintres cubistes*, pp. 63-64.
[23] Niklaus, p. 22.

In the next scene Harlequin appears on stage and welcomes his extraordinary audience, which in many ways resembles himself:

> Sur les tréteaux Arlequin blême
> Salue d'abord les spectateurs
> Des sorciers venus de Bohême
> Quelques fées et les enchanteurs

According to legend, Harlequin has supernatural and magical powers, not unlike Merlin's:

> Mercury bestowed magical power upon his protégé. Arlecchino was enabled to make himself invisible at will: to transport himself from one end of the earth to another in the twinkling of an eye: to reach the heights of Olympus, or penetrate into the depths of Pluto's dark kingdom. He was, moreover, endowed with Mercury's own winged grace, and godlike inscrutability: and so that all should know that he was under the protection of the God, he wore Mercury's own livery, as the Roman clowns had done before him. So Arlecchino acquired his multi-coloured tunic, symbol of the temperamental instability and dubious slickness of Mercury's protégés: and carried a stick as Mercury carried his caduceus. [24]

Harlequin is a devil, and it is not surprising that his audience is made up of fellow demons and other supernatural companions, all trained like himself in the art of magic.

Harlequin's act finally begins in the fourth strophe. He pulls down a star from the sky and with taut arms juggles it:

> Ayant décroché une étoile [25]
> Il la manie à bras tendu

The sorcerer's magical power and the acrobat's muscular dexterity, which Harlequin possesses, work together during his performance. His

---

[24] Niklaus, p. 22.

[25] This line recalls a line from Verlaine's "Sur L'Herbe" (*Fêtes Galantes*):

> —Que je meure, Mesdames, si
> Je ne vous décroche une étoile!
> (*Œuvres poétiques complètes*, p. 84)

Verlaine uses the word "étoile," however, in its archaic sense, meaning the "extremité d'une tresse de cheveux" (Littré).

magic permits him to detach the star from the sky, and his acrobatic skill enables him to twirl it in his hands.

The act Harlequin is performing on stage is neither an exhibition of skill nor an entertaining *divertissement*. Rather, it is an act of creation similar to the one performed by the poet. Harlequin uses sorcery and witchcraft, and perhaps the magical slapstick or bâton he carries, to unhook the star. This corresponds to that mysterious first step of all creative acts which is signaled by inspiration, illumination, or revelation. Harlequin then uses his acrobatic skill and muscular dexterity to manipulate and control the star ("Il la manie"). His arms are taut and tense ("à bras tendu"), as he begins careful work on the celestial body in order to make it do exactly what he wants. A ball juggled by an acrobat, for example, ceases to be a ball and becomes instead an extension of the acrobat's body, doing exactly what he orders it to do, in the same way that his body responds to the control and discipline he exercises over it. Hence, Harlequin imposes on the star or on a ball, or on any object for that matter, his idea of what that object should do when he juggles it; this is the second step in the creative act.

Like Harlequin, the poet imposes form and control on the initial, magical inspiration that has unexpectedly dawned within him. As Harlequin gives meaning to the star and makes it comprehensible to his audience through gesture, mime, and acrobatics, the poet gives external form to the unexpressed inspiration within him. The acrobatics he uses to communicate this inspiration, however, are different from Harlequin's. They are the verbal acrobatics of poetry, the juggling and manipulation of words.

Harlequin is assisted in his act by a hanged man who rhythmically clashes cymbals together with his toes, which is quite natural in this supernatural world:

> Tandis que des pieds un pendu
> Sonne en mesure les cymbales

Like the star juggled by Harlequin, the loud, percussive sound of the cymbals is controlled ("en mesure"). Struck in cadence they create a trance-like effect, a sort of hypnosis by music, and this hypnotic accompaniment to Harlequin's act heightens the spell and magic of his juggling. The hanged musician controls the sounds of his cymbals in the same manner that the poet manipulates the words and sounds of his poems. Since he plays both the role of the magical, acrobatic juggler twirling a star, and that of the hanged musican clashing his cymbals together, Harlequin illustrates two parallel endeavors of the poet during the creative act: first, to express inspiration by the juggling of words and second, to create feeling by the rhythmical control of sounds. The poet, like Harlequin, is magician, acrobat-juggler, and musician all in one.

The hanged man, therefore, is another one of the roles played by Harlequin in "Crépuscule." However, this is not the first time he has played or considered playing the part. In a humorous scene, known as the "Scène du Desespoir," from the harlequinade, *Arlequin, L'Empereur dans la lune* (first produced in 1684), Harlequin contemplates suicide by hanging himself.[26]

In the grand finale of "Crépuscule" Harlequin's magical power increases and, surrounded by unknown figures who seem to have no relation to him or to the poem but have appeared suddenly from nowhere, he grows to three times his size:

> L'aveugle berce un bel enfant
> La biche passe avec ses faons
> Le nain regarde d'un air triste
> Grandir l'arlequin trismégiste [27]

---

[26] Columbine is to marry a farmer, and Harlequin is desolate at the prospect of losing her. He decides to hang himself, but each time he is about to leave the stage to do it, he changes his mind:

> Je m'en irai dans ma chambre j'attacherai une corde au plancher: je monterai sur une chaise: je me mettrai la corde au cou, je donnerai un coup de pied à la chaise, & me voila pendu: *Il fait la posture d'un pendu.* C'en est fait, rien ne peut m'arrêter, courons à la potence.... A la potence? Et fi donc, monsieur, vous n'y pensez pas....

(Evaristo Gherardi, *Le Théâtre Italien de Gherardi, ou le recueil général de toutes les Comédies & Scènes Françoises jouées par les Comédiens Italiens du Roi, pendant tout le temps qu'ils ont été au service* [6 vols.; Paris: Briasson, 1741], I, 129).

[27] Apollinaire's use of the word "trismégiste" echoes Baudelaire's famous lines in "Au Lecteur":

> Sur l'oreiller du mal c'est Satan Trismégiste
> Qui berce longuement notre esprit enchanté,
> ... ...
> (*Œuvres complètes*, p. 5)

From the beginning of the poem until this stanza, although there has been an unreal, fantastic air to the events described, a certain logic has, nevertheless, prevailed. Events have followed one another in a temporal, cause and effect manner. The characters have been situated in relation to each other and in relation to time. As twilight turned to night, Columbine gave way to the charlatan, who, in his turn, disappeared, leaving Harlequin and the hanged man on stage. All the characters have been related to each other because they have been played by the same actor, namely Harlequin. In the final stanza, however, logic disappears. Nothing seems to connect the lines of poetry to each other. The relationship of the blind woman and her child to the doe with her fawns, for example, is uncertain. The characters no longer seem related to each other or to Harlequin. Even their identities are ambiguous. Is it a blind man or a blind woman ("L'aveugle") who cradles the child in its arms? Although the dwarf may belong, perhaps, to Harlequin's troupe of actors and clowns, the presence of the doe is difficult to explain. Who, then, are these strange characters who appear on stage during Harlequin's act, and what do they have in common with him and with each other?

The blind figure, the doe, the dwarf and the gigantic Harlequin are associated with Harlequin's past. They are characters in a harlequinade entitled *Les Fées ou les contes de ma mère l'Oye*, first produced in 1697. In the third scene of the play, Harlequin, who is in search of Ismenie, the beautiful woman loved by his master Octave, relates to a fairy he meets along the way the story of Ismenie's birth:

> Il étoit un prince d'une coudée & demie de haut, qu'on surnommoit Croquignolet, à cause de quantité de batailles qu'il avoit gagnées à coups de croquignolles. Il avoit epousé l'infante Bichette, surnommée l'œil poché, à cause d'un coup de poing qu'il lui donna le premier jour de ses nôces. L'infante Bichette étoit heritiere presomptive d'un royaume que son pere avoit envie de conquerir. Croquignollet [sic] eut de l'infante une fille belle comme le jour, & dont il étoit si raffolé, qu'il passoit les jours & les nuits à la bercer, en

---

Apollinaire makes use of the word "trismégiste" again in "Vendémiaire," rhyming it with the word "triste," as in "Crépuscule":

> Je vivais à l'époque où finissaient les rois
> Tour à tour ils mouraient silencieux et tristes
> Et trois fois courageux devenaient trismégistes
>
> (*O. P.*, p. 149)

chantant: *Do, do, l'enfant dort.* Car c'étoit le premier prince du monde, & qui avoit les plus beaux talens pour endormir les petits enfans.[28]

Harlequin continues his story. Croquignolet had learned from a fairy that an ogre would one day deflower his daughter unless an able prince could prevent it. To protect Ismenie's chastity Croquignolet locked her in a high iron tower. But an ogre, who had fallen madly in love with her, magnetized the tower and carried it away with him. For five years, Harlequin explains, he has been searching for Ismenie. The fairy agrees to help and gives him an enchanted wand. Harlequin discovers Ismenie and uses the wand to change her into a mountain just as the ogre is about to marry her; later he changes her back to human form. Thus, he becomes the hero foretold in the prophecy. From a lowly and unappreciated servant Harlequin has risen to become Ismenie's liberator, a hero as gallant as the best of the knights of the Round Table.

The similarities between *Les Fées ou les contes de ma mère l'Oye* and the final stanza of "Crépuscule" are too striking and too numerous to be called mere coincidence. The dwarf of the poem, who sadly watches Harlequin grow, and Croquignolet, the tiny prince, no taller than "une coudée & demie," resemble each other. Croquignolet's wife, Bichette or "little doe," resembles the doe ("la biche") in the poem, if only in name alone. Like the blind woman in "Crépuscule" Bichette is blind in one eye, where her husband struck her on their wedding day. Ismenie, the beautiful daughter whom Croquignolet loved to cradle, corresponds to the "bel enfant" held by the blind woman. Finally, the gigantic harlequin ("l'arlequin trismégiste") at the end of "Crépuscule" resembles the Harlequin in the play who grows in stature and prestige from a careless and inept servant to a princely hero. Now, the extent of Apollinaire's knowledge of Italian theater and of the commedia dell'arte can only be guessed at. Whether, through his vast and erudite readings or during the long hours spent in the Bibliothèque Nationale, he came across Gherardi's plays in general or *Les Fées* in particular, is almost impossible to determine. However, in 1910, he did write a long introduction to an anthology of Italian theatre from the thirteenth century up to and including

---

[28] Gherardi, VI, 633.

D'Annunzio, entitled *Le Théâtre italien*[29] of which he was also the editor. It is quite possible, then, that during the course of his research into the subject of the Italian theater Apollinaire became acquainted with Gherardi's works and with the commedia dell'arte. But this is only an hypothesis.

When the blind woman, the doe, and the dwarf — characters identified with Harlequin's past — join him on stage, Harlequin is already thinking about the future. In his final performance of the poem, he gives a prophetic, larger-than-life impersonation of the Harlequin of the future, who will be three times larger than himself:

> Le nain regarde d'un air triste
> Grandir l'arlequin trismégiste

In his future form, Harlequin will be more than an acrobat, a clown, a juggler, or even a magician. He will become a god, a supernatural creator, not unlike the deity, Hermes Trismegistos, to whom he is compared. In this vision of himself growing in size, stature, and power Harlequin dramatizes the future destiny of the poet, as before he had dramatized the poet's creative act. Harlequin grows because he possesses the magical and skillful power of the artist, which the difformed, sterile, and ungraceful dwarf, who sadly and quite hopelessly watches his rival's creative growth, does not possess. The dwarf is a symbol of human and artistic failure, but he is not the only sterile character in the strophe. The blind woman also represents artistic failure, for she can not perceive the beauty of her own child ("un bel enfant").

That Harlequin's aggrandizement represents the growth of the poet in the future is established by the word "trismégiste." It indicates not only the extent of the growth (thrice-greatest) but also the kind of magic involved (poetic magic), since it refers to Hermes Trismegistos, the Greek name for the Egyptian deity, Thoth, inventor of writing, patron of all arts dependent on the written word, scribe to the gods, and reputed author of occult or so called "Hermetic" writings. The future Harlequin, therefore, will be three times greater in size and in his ability to write, to perform magic, and to create.[30]

---

[29] (Paris: Louis-Michaud, n. d.)
[30] It is interesting to note that harlequin's expansion in the poem is not necessarily of Apollinaire's own invention. It resembles a strange trick that

The final vision of "Crépuscule" is that of the poet's future grandeur. What the poet and Harlequin have created in the present will eventually attain glory in the future, although they may not be alive to witness it. Harlequin and the poet are like the blind woman who cradles the baby she cannot see. They, too, are blind to their young, unripened creations, too close to the works of art they have only just produced. Eventually, however, with time, the child will grow to manhood, and the poem will realize its potentiality.

The poet's creations float in a sea of days, years, and centuries, where, pounded by the relentless waves and polished by the coarse sand, they remain until thrown up by chance on some distant, future shore. Of this future event the poet sees only a faint glimmer, as Apollinaire does in "Cortège,"

> ... ce feu oblong dont l'intensité ira s'augmentant
> Au point qu'il deviendra un jour l'unique lumière;

or he foresees the absolute, indestructible, granite-like form his poem will finally acquire, as Mallarmé does in his sonnet, "Le Tombeau d'Edgar Poe":

> Calme bloc ici-bas chu d'un désastre obscur
> Que ce granit du moins montre à jamais sa borne
> Aux noirs vols du Blasphème épars dans le futur. [31]

Harlequin's future vision of himself, which he performs at the end of "Crépuscule," illustrates another of his many talents: the power of prophecy. Apollinaire belongs to a tradition of French poets and painters since Baudelaire, and including Verlaine, Toulouse-Lautrec, Laforgue, Picasso, and Rouault, who have recognized the prophetic power of clowns. Baudelaire pointed to their mysterious powers in "Bohémiens en voyage," where he describes them as "La tribu prophétique aux prunelles ardentes," [32] who gain entrance into "L'empire familier des ténèbres futures." [33] Since the clown is exiled

---

was one of harlequin's characteristic actions in the commedia dell'arte. In order to appear taller harlequin would lower his head without moving his shoulders, and then suddenly extend his neck "concertina-wise" without moving the rest of his body (Nicoll, p. 70).

[31] *Œuvres complètes*, p. 70.
[32] *Ibid.*, p. 17.
[33] *Ibid.*, p. 18.

by a hostile world to a life on the outskirts of society (like Baudelaire's "vieux saltimbanque" who is "sans amis, sans famille, sans enfants, dégradé par sa misère et par l'ingratitude publique, et dans la baraque de qui le monde oublieux ne veut plus entrer!"[34]) the clown turns to the contemplation of the future, where he beholds at least a glimmer of recognition. To dream of the future is the only luxury in his otherwise sordid life.

In addition to the Harlequin in "Crépuscule" another clown in Apollinaire's poetry dreams of the future. In "Un Fantôme de Nuées" (*Calligrammes*), Apollinaire describes a troupe of *saltimbanques* performing on a Paris street corner. The oldest performer, an organ grinder, attracts his attention:

> Vois-tu le personnage maigre et sauvage
> La cendre de ses pères lui sortait en barbe
>   grisonnante
> Il portait ainsi toute son hérédité au visage
> Il semblait rêver à l'avenir
> En tournant machinalement un orgue de Barbarie
> Dont la lente voix se lamentait merveilleusement
> Les glouglous les couacs et les sourds gémissements
>
> (*O. P.*, p. 194)

Like Harlequin, this old organ grinder, who is near death, is a creature heavily endowed with a sense of the past, but who continues to dream of the future. Unlike Harlequin, however, his vision of the future is pessimistic. Those who will descend from him will be no better off than he. Along with the costume, the clown's damnable fate is handed down from generation to generation.

In "Crépuscule" Harlequin plays a series of roles that belong to his past, his present and his future. Each one is a different self. While Columbine is his feminine self, the charlatan represents a deceitful aspect of his personality. Harlequin's impersonation of a magical juggler of stars and of the hanged man is a dramatization of his artistic and poetic selves. The dwarf and the blind woman, although not played by him, are nevertheless characters associated with a past Harlequin self. Finally, the "arlequin trismégiste" is a prophetic, future self. Harlequin, therefore, dramatizes different aspects of him-

---

[34] "Le Vieux Saltimbanque," *Œuvres complètes*, p. 249.

self in the harlequinade that he performs throughout "Crépuscule." He is, in this respect, like Apollinaire, who dramatizes his many selves in his different poems.

Like Harlequin, Apollinaire's self is the only actor in a drama where it plays all the roles. It assumes different guises, wears many costumes, speaks many voices, and has diverse faces. Each of these is a different role and a different self. Yet, the masks worn by the self are also mouthpieces by which it reveals itself. The anonymity of the mask gives the self a freedom of expression it does not otherwise have. Behind its protective covering the self can speak freely.

The mask, therefore, is a device of self-objectification. The self cannot be understood unless it is objectified, brought, as it were, out of the self, and externalized in an exterior form that is called the other or the non-self. The mask is this non-self. By assuming the face, the costume, and the appearance of the other the poet's self reveals its nature. In "Crépuscule" Harlequin is the mask behind which Apollinaire's self hides.

CHAPTER V

PARIS: THE POETIC MONTAGE OF SELF

In the twentieth century, the pedestrian or the *flâneur*, who walks aimlessly through a modern city yielding his will to the power of chance, has become the subject of many novels, poems, and films. The *flâneur* is a modern day vagabond. Instead of wandering from village to village or from region to region, he now strolls from street to street, and the extraordinary adventures that once befell him in distant lands now occur at corners, squares, and intersections. As the explorer of an enigmatic and unknown maze of streets and buildings the *flâneur* seeks what the surrealists in general called *le merveilleux* and what Louis Aragon in particular referred to as "le vertige du moderne" and "le visage de l'infini,"[1] both indigenous to the modern city.

The *flâneur* is an artist, a poet, and the art he practices is what Apollinaire, in one of the stories from *L'Hérésiarque et Cie*,[2] calls "l'amphionie," which is described as follows by the baron d'Ormesan, the protagonist of the story:

> "Désespérant de me faire un nom comme peintre, je brûlai tous mes tableaux. Renonçant aux lauriers poétiques, je déchirai cent cinquante mille vers environ. Ayant ainsi institué ma liberté dans l'esthétique, j'inventai un nouvel art, fondé sur le péripatétisme d'Aristote. Je nommai cet art: l'amphionie, en souvenir du pouvoir étrange que possédait Amphion

---

[1] *Le Paysan de Paris* (Paris: Gallimard, 1926), pp. 139 and 140.
[2] "L'Amphion faux-messie ou histoires et aventures du baron d'Ormesan," part 1: "Le Guide."

sur les mœllons et les divers matériaux en quoi consistent les villes.

"Au reste, ceux qui feront de l'amphionie seront appelés des amphions.
"
....

"L'instrument de cet art et sa matière sont une ville dont il s'agit de parcourir une partie, de façon à exciter dans l'âme de l'amphion ou du dilettante des sentiments ressortissant au beau et au sublime, comme le font la musique, la poésie, etc.

"Pour conserver les morceaux composés par l'amphion, et pour que l'on puisse les exécuter de nouveau, il les note sur un plan de la ville, par un trait indiquant très exactement le chemin à suivre. Ces morceaux, ces poèmes, ces symphonies amphioniques se nomment des antiopées, à cause d'Antiope, la mère d'Amphion.

"Pour ma part, c'est à Paris que je pratique l'amphionie." [3]

But along with novelists, poets, surrealists, and even "amphions," filmmakers have also used the aimless perambulations of an inhabitant of the modern metropolis as both the point of departure and the organizing structure for their films. In the movies of Michelangelo Antonioni and Alain Resnais, for example, the hero walks slowly and aimlessly through different quarters of a large city, either observing the color and excitement around him or withdrawing into himself in

---

[3] *Œuvres complètes*, I, 203-4. The baron then relates an "antiopée" entitled *Pro Patria* which he has created in order to inspire patriotism:

"On part de la place Saint-Augustin où se trouvent une caserne et la statue de Jeanne d'Arc. On suit ensuite la rue de la Pépinière, la rue Saint-Lazare, la rue de Châteaudun jusqu'à la rue Laffite, où l'on salue la maison Rothschild. On revient par les grands boulevards jusqu'à la Madeleine. Les grands sentiments s'exaltent à la vue de la Chambre des députés. Le ministère de la Marine, devant lequel on passe, donne une haute idée de la défense nationale, et l'on monte l'avenue des Champs-Elysées. L'émotion est extrême à voir se dresser la masse de l'Arc de Triomphe. A l'aspect du dôme des Invalides, les yeux se mouillent de larmes. On tourne vite dans l'avenue Marigny, pour conserver cet enthousiasme, qui arrive à son comble devant le palais de l'Elysée.

"Je ne vous cache point que cette antiopée serait plus lyrique, aurait plus de grandeur si on pouvait la terminer devant le palais d'un roi. Mais, que voulez-vous? Il faut prendre les choses et les villes comme elles sont." (pp. 204-5)

When Apollinaire objects that what the baron has been describing is nothing more extraordinary than the act of walking and that he, Apollinaire, does it every day, the baron replies: "Monsieur Jourdain..., vous dites vrai, vous faisiez de l'amphionie sans le savoir" (p. 205).

order to meditate. In Resnais' *Hiroshima Mon Amour*, for example, a visiting French actress strolls through the honky-tonk quarters of Hiroshima and remembers an unfortunate love affair with a German soldier that occurred twenty years earlier in France; the camera shows her recurring memories as brief flashbacks. In Antonioni's *La Notte* the lonely wife of a successful writer walks aimlessly through poor sections of Milan, thinking despairingly about her marriage and observing for the first time a way of life very different from her own. Despair is also the feeling of the young heroine of Antonioni's *Il deserto rosso* who has been unable to adjust to the pressures of a technological society. As the film begins, she is seen strolling with her son on the outskirts of Ravenna, while from a nearby refinery networks of twisted pipes spew forth clouds of steam, towers expel jets of flaming gas, and turbines roar deafeningly.

The technique of the "long walk" is by no means an invention of contemporary cinema, although in this medium it has had one of its finest expressions. Almost four decades before either *Hiroshima Mon Amour* or *Il deserto rosso* and a decade before the surrealists would make *la flânerie* one of their major preoccupations, Apollinaire used the technique of the "long walk" in his poem "Zone." Here the poet walks through Paris from the morning of one day to the dawn of the next, observing various aspects of the modern city and praising the infectious spirit of the twentieth century present in them.[4] In addition, he sees anemic immigrants and ugly prostitutes, inhabitants of the poorer sections of Paris, and is overcome by pity for them. But as he walks, the poet also withdraws into himself, lamenting the end of a love affair ("L'angoisse de l'amour te serre le gosier") and carrying on a long interior dialogue where he addresses himself as *je*, *tu*, and *vous*. His stroll through Paris, moreover, is often interrupted by the return of past memories, like the flashbacks which cut into the present action of *Hiroshima Mon Amour*. Suddenly, he is no longer in Paris but on the Mediterranean coast, or in a garden near Prague, or in Coblenz. The present moment is enriched by the return of the past, and the city of Paris expands to include all the major cities of Europe. At the end of his twenty-four hour walk,

---

[4] For a discussion of the circular structure of "Zone," see Chevalier, pp. 29-33.

alone and desperate, he ambles toward his home in Auteuil to find solace in sleep, as milkmen clink their cans, and the sun slowly begins to rise. In "Zone," therefore, Apollinaire uses cinematic techniques — devices that dislocate time and space — to represent his search for self-knowledge.[5]

Although "Zone" (*O. P.*, pp. 39-44) is the initial poem of *Alcools*, announcing the main themes of the collection as a whole, it was actually the last to be written. Completed sometime during the late summer and early autumn of 1912,[6] it was hastily added to the proofs of *Alcools* in November of that year[7] and first appeared in print a month later in *Les Soirées de Paris*.[8] Structurally, it is constructed of single lines or groups of lines, all written in a free verse of an intensely prosaic quality.

Apollinaire had originally entitled his poem "Cri," an allusion to the despair he felt after his break with his mistress Marie Laurencin in June 1912. But in November, while working on the proofs of *Alcools*, he changed the title to "Zone."[9] Much research has been devoted to explaining the meaning of the title. To some critics it refers to a duty-free frontier region near Etival in the Jura Mountains, where Apollinaire, at the invitation of Francis Picabia and his wife, spent a number of days in October 1912.[10] Picabia's wife, Gabrielle Buffet, has recalled that during his visit Apollinaire read a long and unusual poem:

> "Ma mère lui demanda le titre de ce poème. Il n'était pas encore terminé, répondit-il, et n'avait pas encore de nom...

---

[5] For a discussion of Apollinaire's attraction to the cinema and a study of his esthetic statements on the "seventh art," see Michel Décaudin's "Apollinaire et le cinéma image par image," in *Apollinaire*, ed. by M. Bonfantini (Turin: Giappichelli; Paris: Nizet, 1970), pp. 19-28. In addition, see Alain Virmaux's study of *La Bréhatine* (a conventional, undistinguished, "cinéma-drame," which Apollinaire wrote in collaboration with André Billy around 1916-1917) entitled "*La Bréhatine* et le cinéma: Apollinaire en quête d'un langage neuf," in Guillaume Apollinaire and André Billy, *La Bréhatine*, ed. by Claude Tournadre ("Archives des lettres modernes," no. 126; Paris: Minard, 1971), pp. 97-117.

[6] Décaudin, *Le Dossier*, p. 83.
[7] Durry, I, 235.
[8] Décaudin, *Le Dossier*, p. 73.
[9] *Ibid.*, p. 85.
[10] *Ibid.*

Puis, tout-à-coup, gentiment, il se tourna vers elle et lui dit: 'Je l'appellerai *Zone*,' ce qui fut fait." [11]

In a later poem entitled "Fumées" (*Calligrammes*) Apollinaire again refers to this frontier region by mentioning a duty-free tobacco he was able to buy there:

"Et je fu
    m
   e
  du
  ta
  bac
  de NE" [12]
  Zo

Another geographical allusion suggested by the title is to the squalid shantytown on the outskirts of Paris, known colloquially as "la zone." [13] Until 1935 most of the city's *clochards* lived here, and it is possible that the poet walks through this bleak district near the end of his poem. But aside from its specific geographical references the title "Zone" describes the way Apollinaire's poem is organized, for it appears to be written in a series of zones, to be composed of lines or groups of lines that are separated from each other by blank spaces. Each group or block of lines appears as a distinct poetic zone distinguished from the other zones of the poem by the particular theme or idea it treats. As the poet walks through different quarters of Paris, his poem moves, at a similarly brisk pace, from one zone of verse to another and thus from one observation, memory, or theme to the next.

There is no logical order to the succession of zones in the poem because there is no logic or direction either to the poet's wandering or to his train of thought. As anyone who has wandered aimlessly and leisurely through a bustling city will admit, the eye wanders over different objects and the mind leaps from thought to thought. A tense excitement dominates such aimless wandering; the eye and the mind are assaulted by so many sensations and thoughts that the pe-

---

[11] Gabrielle Buffet, *La Guilde du Livre* (décembre 1937), cited by Décaudin, *Le Dossier*, p. 85.
[12] Cited by Durry, I, 260.
[13] *Ibid.*, pp. 260-261.

destrian is continually forced to move his attention from one to the other without rest. The abrupt change from zone to zone in Apollinaire's poem recreates these jerky movements of eye and mind.

The brusque change from one zone to another testifies to the strong influence of the cinema on "Zone." Like a movie, "Zone" moves unexpectedly and without warning from one setting or event to another; like a film, the continuity of time and space is broken. Between scenes of a movie, as between the zones of Apollinaire's poem, there are jumps in time and space. In *Hiroshima Mon Amour*, for example, a sequence of shots of the heroine walking down a street in Hiroshima is followed by a series of shots in which the same woman, ten years earlier, walks through a small town in France. In "Zone" a scene in which the poet describes the charm of a Paris street fades out, and a "shot" of himself as a child on a street in Monaco, where Apollinaire spent his childhood, comes immediately into focus:

> J'aime la grâce de cette rue industrielle
> Située à Paris entre la rue Aumont-Thiéville et
>   l'avenue des Ternes
>
> Voilà la jeune rue et tu n'es encore qu'un
>   petit enfant
> Ta mère ne t'habille que de bleu et de blanc

This sort of montage is used extensively in "Zone."

Although there is a discontinuity of time and space between the different scenes of a film, within an individual scene itself "the time continuum must never be disturbed." [14] There can be no jumps in time; events must follow each other in the order of their occurrence. This cinematic law is respected in "Zone." The absence of continuity between the different zones of the poem — between, for example, the poet's description of an industrial street, his flashback memory of childhood, and his vision of an airplane — is compensated for by the presence of continuity within each zone. Thus, in the fantastic vision of an airplane at the end of the first part of the poem, a procession of birds comes to pay homage to the flying machine and the order of their cortege gives the passage its continuity and coherence. No bird is

---

[14] Rudolf Arnheim, *Film as Art* (Berkeley: University of California Press, 1957), p. 22.

out of formation; the time continuum is never dislocated. Every zone in "Zone," therefore, like every scene in a film, is an island of continuity and sequence in a sea of discontinuity and disorder.

When a movie is projected onto a screen in a darkened movie house, time appears to stand still. The continuity of past, present and future is temporarily suspended for the viewer. All that attracts the viewer's attention is the flickering image on the screen, which he watches in what is a continually present moment. The time that invades the blackened silence of a movie theatre may be called the expanded present. It is what Susanne Langer calls "an endless Now." [15] Similarly, for the reader of Apollinaire's "Zone," what holds his attention like the flickering screen image and what creates the expanded present moment, is the poet's long walk through Paris. "Zone," figuratively speaking, is the "film" of a long walk but in poetic form. Everything that occurs during Apollinaire's promenade, which is everything in the poem, happens entirely in the present.

More than any other poem in *Alcools*, "Zone" is concerned with the movement and force of the present moment. If the poet remembers the past, his act of remembering is in the present: "Voilà la jeune rue et tu n'es encore qu'un petit enfant / Ta mère ne t'habille que de bleu et de blanc." If he contemplates the future, he is doing so in the present: "Et tous aigle phénix et pihis de la Chine / Fraternisent avec la volante machine." If he hears cars blowing their horns, he hears them in the present: "Maintenant tu marches dans Paris tout seul parmi la foule / Des troupeaux d'autobus mugissants près de toi roulent." Memories of the past, observations of the present, visions of the future all take place as the poet's legs carry him at will and by chance down the streets, across the boulevards, and through the parks of Paris.

Despite the fact that the poet's walk gives "Zone" its coherence and organization as a poem, it is not particularly orderly or coherent; it lacks continuity, proceeding in bursts and jerks rather than continuously. By way of example, if one were to remove from the poem the digressions of the poet's mind — his memories, visions and thoughts — one still would not have a continuous picture of his promenade through Paris. At one moment he would be standing near the

---

[15] "A Note on the Film," in her *Feeling and Form* (New York: Scribner, 1953), p. 415.

Eiffel Tower and at the next between "la rue Aumont-Thiéville et l'avenue des Ternes." At one instance he would be sauntering through a business district and at the next through an immigrant quarter. The poet has not presented a minute by minute account of his walk; rather, he has selected highlights. Like a skillful film editor he filters out the superfluous details of his experience and compresses the essentials into a highly concentrated representation.

By way of example, one could say that two cameras simultaneously film the poet's walk; one focuses on his movements through Paris, the other records the impressions within the self. His promenade therefore is viewed at the same time from two different angles or perspectives, one extrospective, the other introspective. In editing his poem, the poet splices together footage from both films, so that "shots" of himself strolling beside cars, among pedestrians, and in front of churches are suddenly interrupted by dissolves to his memories, to his intimate feelings, or to his thoughts. For example,

> Maintenant tu marches dans Paris tout seul parmi la foule
> Des troupeaux d'autobus mugissants près de toi roulent
> L'angoisse de l'amour te serre le gosier
> Comme si tu ne devais jamais plus être aimé

or,

> Une famille transporte un édredon rouge comme vous transportez votre cœur
> Cet édredon et nos rêves sont aussi irréels.

In this manner Apollinaire represents the sights and sounds of the city and at the same time the memories and thoughts they suggest to him. The reader as well as the poet both have a window onto the cosmopolitan Paris of the early twentieth century and a view as well into the hidden regions of Apollinaire's self. Interestingly, this technique of presenting oneself through "exterior" and "interior" films that run sometimes simultaneously and sometimes successively has been described by Alain Robbe-Grillet, who sees in it a fundamental characteristic of the imagination:

> Que sont, en somme, toutes ces images? Ce sont des *imaginations*; une imagination, si elle est assez vive, est toujours

au présent. Les souvenirs que l'on 'revoit', les régions lointaines, les rencontres à venir, ou même les épisodes passés que chacun arrange dans sa tête en modifiant le cours tout à loisir, il y a là comme un film intérieur qui se déroule continuellement en nous-mêmes, dès que nous cessons de prêter attention à ce qui se passe autour de nous. Mais, à d'autres moments, nous enregistrons au contraire, par tous nos sens, ce monde extérieur qui se trouve bel et bien sous nos yeux. Ainsi le film total de notre esprit admet à la fois tour à tour et au même titre les fragments réels proposés à l'instant par la vue et l'ouïe, et des fragments passés, ou lointains, ou futurs, ou totalement fantasmagoriques. [16]

Apollinaire's use of poetic montage permits him to represent simultaneously not only the events that happen around him but also the aspects of himself that occur at different times and in different places; in this way it functions as an invaluable tool in his search for self-knowledge. One of the best examples in "Zone" of this montage effect is the following passage:

> Te voici à Marseille au milieu des pastèques
>
> Te voici à Coblence à l'hôtel du Géant
>
> Te voici à Rome assis sous un néflier du Japon
>
> Te voici à Amsterdam avec une jeune fille que
> tu trouves belle et qui est laide

---

[16] *L'Année dernière à Marienbad* (Paris: Editions de Minuit, 1961), p. 16. Moreover, what Robbe-Grillet describes as the problems confronting the spectator watching *L'Année dernière à Marienbad*, are also of the same order as those confronting the reader of "Zone":

> Deux attitudes sont alors possibles: ou bien le spectateur cherchera à reconstituer quelque schéma "cartésien," le plus linéaire qu'il pourra, le plus rationnel, et ce spectateur jugera sans doute le film difficile, si ce n'est incompréhensible; ou bien au contraire il se laissera porter par les extraordinaires images qu'il aura devant lui, par la voix des acteurs, par les bruits, par la musique, par le rythme du montage, par la passion des héros..., à ce spectateur-là le film semblera le plus facile qu'il ait jamais vu: un film qui ne s'adresse qu'à sa sensibilité, qu'à sa faculté de regarder, d'écouter, de sentir et de se laisser émouvoir. L'histoire racontée lui apparaîtra comme la plus réaliste, la plus vraie, celle qui correspond le mieux à sa vie affective quotidienne, aussitôt qu'il accepte de se débarrasser des idées toutes faites, de l'analyse psychologique, des schémas plus ou moins grossiers d'interprétation que les romans ou le cinéma ronronnants lui rabâchent jusqu'à la nausée, et qui sont les pires des abstractions (*Ibid.*, pp. 17-18).

Thus in one moment (the space of five lines) Apollinaire experiences life in five European cities. Moreover, to aid in the multi-representation of himself, Apollinaire calls himself by three different names; he changes his identity from *je, tu,* and *vous* as easily as an actor changes masks:

> *Tu* as fait de douleureux et de joyeux voyages
> Avant de *t*'apercevoir du mensonge et de l'âge
> *Tu* as souffert de l'amour à vingt et à trente ans
> *J*'ai vécu comme un fou et *j*'ai perdu *mon* temps
> *Tu* n'oses plus regarder *tes* mains et à tous moments
>   *je* voudrais sangloter
> Sur *toi* sur celle que *j*'aime sur tout ce qui *t*'a
>   épouvanté   [italics mine]

In this passage Apollinaire sees himself from two points of view, one personal and intimate (*je*), the other distant but still familiar (*tu*). The *je* and *tu* are both fragmented selves, the latter having been detached from the poet and objectified and the former still remaining strongly attached to him. The technique of montage, therefore, permits Apollinaire to juxtapose aspects of himself and points of view that in real time and space occur not simultaneously but in succession.[17]

During his walk through Paris, Apollinaire's emotions range from visionary hope to self-deprecating despair. While in the first part of "Zone" (ll. 1-70) he is filled with the great promise of the new century and with an optimistic faith in man's power to transform the world, in the second part (ll. 71-155) he sinks to the despair and disillusion that come from a broken love affair. Although "Zone" begins as a hymn in celebration of the twentieth century, it ends with a brutal and bloody assassination of the sun. Opposed to the poet's optimistic belief in mankind is a pessimistic lack of faith in himself as a man. Although he celebrates the birth of the new century, he also withdraws into the darkness of himself and despises what he finds there. In "Zone" there is not only a contrast between an old dying world and a new dawning one but also a conflict between the city

---

[17] In this respect, Apollinaire resembles the cubist painters, who represented the numerous angles and points of view of an object simultaneously, by juxtaposing these views on the flat surface of a canvas. A cubist's portrait of a man's head from both a full face view and a profile, for example, would correspond to Apollinaire's portrait of himself as *je* and *tu*.

outside the poet — vibrant, bustling, filled with sunlight — and the dark, brooding landscape within.

The movement in "Zone" from optimism to pessimism and from hope to despair indicates that the poet's dejection gradually dominates the poem, like a dark cloud slowly covering the sky. It also implies a change in point of view. From a panoramic view of mankind and of the history of civilization in the first part of the poem, the poet in the second part turns his glance inward and takes a long hard look at himself. The second part of "Zone," therefore, is intensely more personal than the first, which is characterized by a paucity of autobiographical detail and by a noticeable absence of self-designation. In the seventy-two lines of the first part, for example, there are only seventeen mentions of *je, tu, te,* or *vous*, in contrast to fifteen such self-designations in the first ten lines of the second part alone.

In addition to the difference in point of view, the spatial and temporal movements of each section also differ greatly. The first part of "Zone" exhibits an upward movement (the apotheosis of the airplane, the cortege of mythic birds) and a forward movement (the future promise of the new century). The second section, on the other hand, is characterized by a movement downward into the depths of the self and backward in time to the poet's past experience ("tu recules aussi dans la vie lentement").

No introduction to "Zone" would be complete without mention of the controversy surrounding the poem's originality, and before going on to study "Zone" in detail, it would perhaps be worthwhile to stop a moment and consider this question. Some critics, Robert Goffin in particular, have asserted that "Zone" owes its style, theme, and inspiration to Blaise Cendrars' "Les Pâques à New York," published the same year as "Zone" and written in couplets of similar *vers prosaïques*.[18] On the other hand, M. Décaudin and other critics see less the direct influence of one poem on the other, and more the mysterious workings of chance. Somehow, in their frequent meetings and informal conversations between 1912 and 1913 the two poets communicated to one another not the letter (or the detail) but the spirit of their poems.[19] M. Décaudin does admit, however, that a comparison of the first draft of "Zone" with a corrected version of

---

[18] Décaudin, *Le Dossier*, p. 83.
[19] *Ibid.*, p. 84.

the poem appears to indicate that "dans ses corrections Apollinaire avait voulu différencier son poème des *Pâques*" in order to attenuate any possible resemblance to Cendrars's poem.[20] While "Les Pâques à New York" describes a long walk through New York City taken by Cendrars on Easter Sunday 1912 and contains certain observations and images closely akin to those in "Zone," the major difference between it and Apollinaire's poem lies in the intensity of its religious comment. While at the heart of "Les Pâques" is Cendrars's fervent dialogue with God, in "Zone" the poet's dialogue is with himself, and the only expression of religious sentiment is a simple nostalgia for a lost faith.[21] Yet the question still remains unsolved, and it appears that it will stay that way, if one is to take the word of Marc Poupon, whose *Apollinaire et Cendrars* is perhaps the most detailed history of the friendship of the two poets and the nature of their relationship: "à l'heure actuelle rien ne permet de régler d'une façon définitive la controverse...."[22]

Whether "Les Pâques" was written prior to "Zone" and whether Apollinaire had read his friend's poem before composing his own are questions of literary history that will never want for investigation and debate. In fact, the Apollinaire-Cendrars controversy is best described by means of a question: "Apollinaire et Cendrars se sont-ils influencés mutuellement, ou n'ont-ils eu, chacun grâce à l'autre, que la révélation de ce qu'ils portaient en eux?"[23] All that can be said by way of a conclusion is what Mme Durry suggests: namely, that there are indeed similarities between the two poems, but that the differences between them, because they are of a personal nature and involve the idiosyncrasies and styles particular to each poet, far outweigh these similarities.[24]

---

[20] *Ibid.*
[21] Durry, I, 300.
[22] ("Archives des lettres modernes," no. 103; Paris: Minard, 1969), p. 6.
[23] *Ibid.*, p. 55.
[24] I, 237. For a thematic comparison of the two poems, see Robert Couffignal, *"Zone" d'Apollinaire. Structure et confrontations* ("Archives des lettres modernes," no. 118; Paris: Minard, 1970), pp. 25-30. And for a comparison based on the religious or "liturgical" qualities of each poem, see Robert Couffignal, *L'Inspiration biblique dans l'œuvre de Guillaume Apollinaire* ("Bibliothèque des lettres modernes," vol. VIII; Paris: Minard, 1966), pp. 167-68.

The opening line of "Zone" is charged with double meaning; it expresses both the feeling of hope that dominates the first part of the poem and the feeling of despair which characterizes the second:

> A la fin tu es las de ce monde ancien.

The poet is tired ("las") of the ancient world, which he later identifies as "l'antiquité grecque et romaine," for it has become outdated and meaningless in the twentieth century. Instead, he favors the hope and beauty of the modern world. But the poet is also tired and perhaps a little revolted by the world in general. Because of the anguish and lassitude brought on by his separation from Marie Laurencin, the world, even the vibrant modern world, now seems old and tedious. Later in the poem he relates how tired and filled with despair he really is:

> Et l'image qui te possède te fait survivre dans
> l'insomnie et dans l'angoisse

Thus, the first line of "Zone" can be considered as a preface not only to the poem as a whole but also to each of the poem's two sections.

Following his initial statement of lassitude, the poet continues to discuss the ancient and modern worlds:

> A la fin tu es las de ce monde ancien
>
> Bergère ô tour Eiffel le troupeau des ponts bêle
> ce matin
>
> Tu en as assez de vivre dans l'antiquité grecque
> et romaine
>
> Ici même les automobiles ont l'air d'être anciennes
> La religion seule est restée toute neuve la religion
> Est restée simple comme les hangars de Port-Aviation
>
> Seul en Europe tu n'es pas antique ô Christianisme
> L'Européen le plus moderne c'est vous Pape Pie X
> Et toi que les fenêtres observent la honte te retient
> D'entrer dans une église et de t'y confesser ce matin

What is this Greco-Roman tradition in which Apollinaire has lived all too long? It is, above all, a conception of reality, especially in the plastic arts, that perceives the visible, concrete world from a single, impersonal viewpoint and represents this point of view through fixed planes and organized space. But reality at the turn of the century was being dislocated by two new concepts foreign to the static Greco-Roman tradition, namely time and motion. The airplane had been invented; Blériot was the first to fly the English Channel in 1909. Transatlantic steamers were faster than ever before.[25] The automobile was introducing the world to speed. Marconi's invention of wireless telegraphy made possible the reporting of simultaneous events in different parts of the globe. The cinema was expanding man's knowledge of the world. The cubists were forcing art to express the "fourth dimension," time itself. At the beginning of the twentieth century, time and space were being conquered.[26] Modern reality, therefore, could no longer be explained by the outmoded Greco-Roman conception of reality. Modern man had had enough of living "dans l'antiquité grecque et romaine."

Apollinaire's rejection of the Greco-Roman tradition, moreover, may also be explained by the wave of anti-rationalism which broke on France's shores at the turn of the century. The impressive discoveries of psychology and chemistry in the latter part of the nineteenth century and in the beginning of the twentieth revealed that certain aspects of reality, long believed to be indivisible unities, were, in fact, divisible into infinite particles.[27] Man's faith in science and in his own intelligence, which up until then had taught him that the world was an ordered and logical place, was understandably shaken by these discoveries of multiple and irrational phenomena: [28]

> So the generation that grew to manhood about 1900 realized that the ground which their forbears had confidently trod was now giving way beneath their own feet; reality was everywhere breaking up into elusive, impalpable frag-

---

[25] Pär Bergman, *"Modernolatria" et "Simultaneità": Recherches sur deux tendances dans l'avant-garde littéraire en Italie et en France à la veille de la première guerre mondiale* ("Studia Litterarum Upsaliensia," Vol. II; Bonniers: Svenska Bokförlaget, 1962), p. 11.

[26] For an interesting discussion of the conquest of time and space and the development of the "Myth of the Modern" at the beginning of the twentieth century, see Bergman, pp. 1-33.

[27] Georges Lemaitre, *From Cubism to Surrealism in French Literature* (Cambridge: Harvard University Press, 1945), p. 51.

[28] *Ibid.*, p. 53.

ments.... The intellectual conceptions which for centuries had been man's stay and support in hours of doubt and trial, now suddenly collapsed encumbering the path of progress with their débris.

Then began in many eager young men an impatient desire to clear away that wreckage, to tear down the tottering remnants of the ancient, useless, outmoded structure.[29]

Apollinaire belonged to that group of young men, who in the wake of such iconoclasts as Bergson and Jarry, came to clear away the debris of the past and to start to build a new reality. Thus, in "Zone" he rejects the Greco-Roman tradition because its concept of an ordered universe is no longer valid.

But "l'antiquité grecque et romaine" refers also to an antiquated manner of speech and to an archaic rhetoric which Apollinaire has found himself using. After declaring how weary he is of the ancient world Apollinaire uses an image that belongs to that world. He represents the Eiffel Tower, example of a new architectural style, image of global communication and symbol of the modern age, in the hackneyed metaphor of a shepherdess: "Bergère ô tour Eiffel le troupeau des ponts bêle ce matin." He describes Paris at morning, when the noise of car horns fills the air with excitement, in the tranquil style of classical pastoral poetry. Since at the time "Zone" was written the painter Robert Delaunay had painted over sixty canvases of the Eiffel Tower in the process of breaking up and tumbling to earth (in an effort to depict its dynamic movement), it is practically sacrilegious for Apollinaire to describe the same monument in an image that evokes the stillness and peace of a country meadow. The Eiffel Tower was a symbol of "l'esprit nouveau." Since all attempts to represent it according to the laws of Renaissance perspective had failed, the Eiffel Tower challenged the painters and poets of Apollinaire's time to seek new solutions and to discover new answers to the spatial and philosophical problems it raised. In a lecture delivered on June 12, 1924 at São Paulo, Brazil, Blaise Cendrars described the difficult problems of representation posed by the Eiffel Tower:

> No art formula known until then could make the pretense of resolving plastically the problem of the Eiffel Tower. Realism made it smaller; the old laws of Italian perspective

---

[29] *Ibid.*, p. 55.

made it look thinner. The Tower rose above Paris, as slender as a hat pin. When we walked away from it, it dominated Paris, stiff and perpendicular; when we approached it, it bowed and leaned out over us. Seen from the first platform, it wound like a corkscrew, and seen from the top, it collapsed under its own weight, its legs spread out, its neck sunk in. Delaunay also wanted to depict Paris around it, to situate it. We tried all points of view, we looked at it from all angles, from all sides, and its sharpest profile is the one you can see from the Passy footbridge. And those thousands of tons of iron, those 35 million bolts, those 300 meters high of interlaced girders and beams, those four arcs with a spread of 100 meters, all that jellylike mass flirted with us. On certain spring days it was supple and laughing and opened its parasol of clouds under our very nose. On certain stormy days it sulked, sour and ungracious; it seemed cold. At midnight we ceased to exist, all its fires were for New York with whom it was already flirting then; and at noon it gave the time to ships on the high seas.... So many points of view to treat the problem of the Eiffel Tower. But Delaunay wanted to interpret it plastically. He finally succeeded with the famous canvas that everybody knows. He took the Tower apart to make it fit into his frame, he truncated it, and bent it to give it 300 meters of dizzying height, he adopted 10 points of view, 15 perspectives, so that one part is seen from below, another from above, the houses surrounding it are taken from the right, from the left, bird's-eye view, level with the ground. [30]

Apollinaire's image of the Eiffel Tower as a shepherdess is a sin against the cult of the modern; and Apollinaire seems to realize this. In the next line he rejects the image and the literary and cultural tradition associated with it: "Tu en as assez de vivre dans l'antiquité grecque et romaine." Apollinaire is tired of the old clichés. Words must be renewed, expressions modernized, and images reanimated in keeping with the new century. The poet must create a new idiom in poetry, as Delaunay and other painters had created one in art. The zones of language and poetry must be extended to keep pace with the ever-moving and expanding world, which changes so rapidly that automobiles, once the most modern of inventions, are becoming outmoded by the newly invented airplane:

---

[30] *Selected Writings* (New York: New Directions, 1966), pp. 238-39.

Ici même les automobiles ont l'air d'être anciennes [31]

Apollinaire then makes the startling statement that religion alone has remained completely new and simple: "La religion seule est restée toute neuve la religion/Est restée simple comme les hangars de Port-Aviation." He is not referring to any religion in particular, but rather to an eternal religious sentiment, a thirst for the divine or the sacred that lies in the heart of every man and which constitutes the source of all religion. This feeling reflects man's desire to surpass the limits of the human, and Apollinaire suggests that the new inventions of the century, like the airplane, represent and incarnate this need for transcendence. He also observes in *Les Peintres cubistes* that perhaps this same, fundamentally religious sentiment lies at the heart of the experiments then taking place in painting:

> C'est pourquoi l'art actuel, s'il n'est pas l'émanation directe de croyances religieuses déterminées, présente cependant plusieurs caractères du grand art, c'est-à-dire de l'Art religieux. [32]

Having already spoken of the newness of "la religion" Apollinaire now turns his attention to the modernity of one religion, "Christianisme":

> Seul en Europe tu n'es pas antique ô Christianisme
> L'Européen le plus moderne c'est vous Pape Pie X

The spiritual, eternal Church with its promise of salvation has always been modern, Apollinaire seems to suggest, because in every century since the birth of Christ it has responded to man's spiritual demands and satisfied his need for transcendence. As for the other Church, the temporal, historical Church led by the Pope, it too is modern but

---

[31] Apollinaire recognized quite prophetically that with the accelerated pace of modern technology would come an increased rate of obsolescence. In "La Victoire" (*Calligrammes*), he wrote:

> O mon amie hâte-toi
> Crains qu'un jour un train ne t'émeuve
>   Plus   (*O. P.*, p. 310)
>
> Songe que les chemins de fer
> Seront démodés et abandonnés dans peu
>   de temps   (*O. P.*, p. 312)

[32] p. 53.

for other reasons. Although in 1907 Pope Pius X condemned as heresy the reform movement known as Modernism, which was attempting to reinterpret the teachings of Catholicism in light of the scientific and philosophical discoveries of the late nineteenth century, Apollinaire still considers him "L'Européen le plus moderne." The reason for his modernity may be attributed to an event that took place at the Vatican in May 1911, when the Pope blessed the pilot Beaumont, winner of the Paris to Rome air race,[33] and thus symbollically gave the Church's blessing to the twentieth century, or at least to some of its machines. In Apollinaire's eyes Christianity and the Papacy had become as contemporary as the airplane.[34] Yet, one cannot help feeling that Apollinaire wishes to highlight with as much irony as possible this highly superficial association of the Church with the twentieth century.

But does Apollinaire have faith? Is there in him a spontaneous religious impulse? From the next lines of the poem it would seem not:

> Et toi que les fenêtres observent la honte te
> retient
> D'entrer dans une église et de t'y confesser
> ce matin

Because of his shame Apollinaire has personally excommunicated himself; yet, this fall from grace does not prevent him from having an intuitive sense of the divine, for later in the poem he expresses a

---

[33] Couffignal, *L'Inspiration biblique*, p. 148.

[34] Another likely source of Apollinaire's description of the Pope as a modern European, according to M. Couffignal (pp. 148-149) is *Le Monoplan du Pape*, a long futurist novel in *vers libres* by the Italian poet, Marinetti. The title of the book and the idea of a flying Pope could easily have struck Apollinaire's imagination. It seems quite conceivable that he was aware of the book's existence, for it was reviewed in the *Mercure de France* of September 1, 1912, an issue that also contained one of his own articles. The review began with the following quotation from the novel:

> "Ce fut en aéroplane, assis sur le cylindre à essence, le ventre chauffé par la tête de l'aviateur, que je sentis tout à coup l'inanité de la vieille syntaxe héritée d'Homère..." (Couffignal, *L'Inspiration biblique*, p. 149).

The same thought occurs to Apollinaire, when he asserts, "Tu en as assez de vivre dans l'antiquité grecque et romaine."

strong, wistful nostalgia for the religious ardor of his childhood and chants a litany in praise of Christ. Further evidence of this is found at the end of the poem when he looks forward to falling asleep among his collection of religious idols from Africa: "des Christ d'une autre forme et d'une autre croyance/Ce sont les Christ inférieurs des obscures espérances." Apollinaire is sensitive to the sources of religious belief in the child and in primitive man. Although "Zone" cannot be called a religious poem (like Cendrars' "Les Pâques à New York"), nevertheless it can be said to concern itself with the sacred and with man's efforts to transcend the human.

Undoubtedly, in a poem that is a hymn to the twentieth century the profane must also be included, as indeed it is. After admitting his reluctance to enter a church Apollinaire turns to the sights around him, to the poetry of street signs and the powerful grace of factories:

> Tu lis les prospectus les catalogues les affiches
>   qui chantent tout haut
> Voilà la poésie ce matin et pour la prose il y a
>   les journaux
> Il y a les livraisons à 25 centimes pleines
>   d'aventures policières
> Portraits des grands hommes et mille titres divers
> J'ai vu ce matin une jolie rue dont j'ai oublié
>   le nom
> Neuve et propre du soleil elle était le clairon
> Les directeurs les ouvriers et les belles sténo-dactylo-
>   graphes
> Du lundi matin au samedi soir quatre fois par jour
>   y passent
> Le matin par trois fois la sirène y gémit
> Une cloche rageuse y aboie vers midi
> Les inscriptions des enseignes et des murailles
> Les plaques les avis à la façon des perroquets criaillent
> J'aime la grâce de cette rue industrielle
> Située à Paris entre la rue Aumont-Thiéville
>   et l'avenue des Ternes

The city street becomes an aesthetic experience, a work of art set in motion. Its myriad aspects assault the poet's senses; posters, billboards, handbills, newspapers, pedestrians, sirens, clocks, sunlight, and reflection perform in concert for his visual and aural pleasure. He hears a symphony of sounds, follows the intricate choreography of movements on the street, and observes a chiaroscuro of sunlight and shadow. Apollinaire describes the orchestrated rhythms of the city street — its synchronous movements, its flashes of color, its bursts of noise — from the multiple viewpoints of a pedestrian who is himself in motion through the street. But his evocation of the present recalls, surprisingly enough, the past; it adds another richer dimension to the cityscape before him. The industrial street immediately recalls the memory of a street where Apollinaire had lived as a child:

>   Voilà la jeune rue et tu n'es encore qu'un petit
>   enfant
>   Ta mère ne t'habille que de bleu et de blanc
>   Tu es très pieux et avec le plus ancien de tes
>   camarades René Dalize
>   Vous n'aimez rien tant que les pompes de l'Eglise
>   Il est neuf heures le gaz est baissé tout bleu
>   vous sortez du dortoir en cachette
>   Vous priez toute la nuit dans la chapelle du
>   collège
>   Tandis qu'éternelle et adorable profondeur améthyste
>   Tourne à jamais la flamboyante gloire du Christ
>   C'est le beau lys que tous nous cultivons
>   C'est la torche aux cheveux roux que n'éteint pas
>   le vent
>   C'est le fils pâle et vermeil de la douloureuse mère
>   C'est l'arbre toujours touffu de toutes les prières
>   C'est la double potence de l'honneur et de l'éternité
>   C'est l'étoile à six branches
>   C'est Dieu qui meurt le vendredi et ressuscite le
>   dimanche
>   C'est le Christ qui monte au ciel mieux que les
>   aviateurs
>   Il détient le record du monde pour la hauteur

In describing his childhood piety Apollinaire uses an unusual image, one of the few symbolist images in "Zone":

>   Vous priez toute la nuit dans la chapelle du collège
>   Tandis qu'éternelle et adorable profondeur améthyste
>   Tourne à jamais la flamboyante gloire du Christ

As the young Apollinaire prays into the night, the sun ("profondeur améthyste") encircles ("tourne") the universe. The sun's amethyst color here prefigures the blood-red tints of the "Soleil cou coupé" at the end of the poem. But a sun of a different sort is also suggested.

Because he is the sun and light of the world it is to an omnipresent Christ, who encircles the universe ("tourne à jamais") with his shining glory ("la flamboyante gloire"), that the image makes reference. If Christ is present in the universe, then he is most certainly present in the chapel where the young poet and his friend are praying. His presence is suggested by the red vigil light over the altar ("profondeur améthyste") which encircles and bathes the chapel in amethyst light. The glory of Christ ("la flamboyante gloire du Christ"), like the flame of the vigil lamp, flickers and quivers before the two young communicants. It is never still; continually, it moves and changes form. Christ's glory, therefore, is protean, and no better proof of this is given than in the litany that follows. Christ is pictured not as one but as many things; it requires several expressions, many of them incongruous, to describe his glory: he is a lily, a torch, a tree, a double gallows, a six-pointed star, a god, an aviator. Christ is as omnifarious as he is omnipresent.

There is yet another possible meaning for the image of "profondeur améthyste." An amethyst has a deep purple color resembling that of diluted red wine. Its name is derived from the Greek word, *améthystos,* which means, literally, remedy for drunkenness. The Greeks believed that the amethyst had magical powers of preventing intoxication, and so they fashioned beakers from it, and inveterate drinkers wore amethyst amulets. The amethyst, therefore, is a charm capable of changing the essence of wine by "de-intoxicating" it, by neutralizing its dionysiac powers, which indulge the senses and confuse reason. Wine treated by an amethyst is transformed and purified in the same way that a priest's blessing sanctifies wine, thus transforming it into the blood of Christ. "Profondeur améthyste" refers, therefore, to the mystery of transsubstantiation, by which some divine catalyst ("améthyste") continually changes ("tourne à jamais") wine ("profondeur améthyste") into the blood of Christ ("la flamboyante gloire du Christ").

Apollinaire's memory of his childhood is a flashback to the past which takes place in the present. As the poet walks through Paris he sees with his mind's eye the "jeune rue" where he once lived; he re-experiences his young religious enthusiasm, and he chants once more a litany similar to one he used to sing as a child. These flashbacks, because they occur in the present, are examples of Apollinaire's attempt throughout "Zone" to describe the past in contemporary terms, so that the past would be continually renewed by direct contact with the present. It is in the litany praising Christ, therefore, that Apollinaire's modernization of the past is the most clearly illustrated. He lists the numerous, well-worn images employed since the beginning of Christianity to describe Christ; he is "le beau lys," "la torche," "le fils pâle et vermeil," "Dieu qui meurt le vendredi et ressuscite le dimanche," and so on. But to this long list of religious images he adds a new expression, which describes Christ in terms of the twentieth century:

> C'est le Christ qui monte au ciel mieux que
>   les aviateurs
> Il détient le record du monde pour la hauteur

This idea of Christ flying is not a new one. M. Décaudin suggests that Apollinaire might possibly have seen hanging in the Museum of Cologne two primitive German paintings depicting the Stigmatization of Saint-Francis, in which Christ flies on a winged Cross surrounded by angels.[35] But the expression of the idea is new. Never before has Christ been called an airplane pilot. Religion, as expressed by Apollinaire, has indeed remained "toute neuve" primarily because its language and metaphors have been renewed.

The new, as Apollinaire stated in "L'Esprit nouveau et les poètes," is characterized by surprise,[36] and nothing could surprise or startle more than the incongruous juxtapositions produced by describing the old in contemporary terms. A shock, a jarring sensation, accompanies the encounter of the old with the new. Not only is it humorous, but it is startling to hear the Pope described as "L'Européen le plus moderne," or to read that Christ "détient le record du monde pour la hauteur." The aesthetic function of surprise is to compel attention, to destroy the reader's conventional ideas, and to jolt him into an awareness of something new and different. The medium of surprise par excellence is the cinema, since

> film, which records real situations on strips of celluloid that may be joined together, has the power of placing in juxta-

---

[35] *Le Dossier,* p. 87.
[36] "Mais le nouveau existe bien, sans être un progrès. Il existe tout dans la surprise.... *La surprise est le plus grand ressort nouveau*" (p. 391).

position things that have no connection at all in real time and space.[37]

Apollinaire's poetic use of surprise resembles the cinematic technique of montage and underlines once again the similarity between "Zone" and the devices of cinema art.

Apollinaire's concern with the modernization of the past continues in the next zone of the poem, where a procession of legendary men and ancient, mythical birds flies around an ascending airplane:

> Pupille Christ de l'œil
> Vingtième pupille des siècles il sait y faire
> Et changé en oiseau ce siècle comme Jésus monte
>   dans l'air
> Les diables dans les abîmes lèvent la tête pour
>   le regarder
> Ils disent qu'il imite Simon Mage en Judée
> Ils crient s'il sait voler qu'on l'appelle voleur
> Les anges voltigent autour du joli voltigeur
> Icare Enoch Elie Apollonius de Thyane
> Flottent autour du premier aéroplane
> Ils s'écartent parfois pour laisser passer ceux
>   que transporte la Sainte-Eucharistie
> Ces prêtres qui montent éternellement élevant l'hostie
> L'avion se pose enfin sans refermer les ailes
> Le ciel s'emplit alors de millions d'hirondelles
> A tire-d'aile viennent les corbeaux les faucons
>   les hiboux
> D'Afrique arrivent les ibis les flamants les
>   marabouts
> L'oiseau Roc célébré par les conteurs et les poètes
> Plane tenant dans les serres le crâne d'Adam la
>   première tête
> L'aigle fond de l'horizon en poussant un grand cri
> Et d'Amérique vient le petit colibri
> De Chine sont venus les pihis longs et souples
> Qui n'ont qu'une seule aile et qui volent par couples
> Puis voici la colombe esprit immaculé
> Qu'escortent l'oiseau-lyre et le paon ocellé
> Le phénix ce bûcher qui soi-même s'engendre
> Un instant voile tout de son ardente cendre
> Les sirènes laissant les périlleux détroits
> Arrivent en chantant bellement toutes trois

---

[37] Arnheim, pp. 26-27.

> Et tous aigle phénix et pihis de la Chine
> Fraternisent avec la volante machine

From Apollinaire's intimate recollection of his childhood in the previous zone, the poem now moves to a panoramic view of the history of Western civilization. Figures of ancient mysticism (Simon Magus, Apollonius of Tyana), prophets of Jewish history (Enoch, Elijah), a mythical hero of Greek mythology (Icarus), and magical birds of polytheistic cultures (phoenix, sirens, pihis and the Roc) all come together to pay homage to the latest of their airborne number. Birds come hurriedly from different parts of the globe. America sends the hummingbird; China dispatches a flock of one-winged pihis; Africa is represented by ibises, flamingoes and storks. An international gathering of winged figures assembles to bear witness to the birth of human flight.

The fantastic cortege proceeds in two waves, the first made up of humans, the second of birds. What distinguishes the first wave is that its participants are either magicians or demigods who have attempted at some time to fly. Icarus, son of Daedalus, flew too close to the sun, melted the wax on his wings and fell into the sea. The Second Book of Enoch, one of three books of ancient Jewish writings preserved under the name of Enoch, the eldest son of Cain, begins with a description of a journey, undertaken by Enoch in a visionary experience, through the Kingdom of Heaven, where he observes different orders of angels and various heavenly bodies. The prophet Elijah rose to Heaven in a burning chariot of fire. The miracles of Apollonius of Tyana, a first century sage, were likened by his pagan followers to those of Christ. In order to win the favor of the Roman emperor Nero and to prove the power of his doctrines, Simon Magus, sorcerer, rival of early Christianity and first heretic, offered to ascend into the Heavens. By magic he succeeded in rising into the air, but the prayers of the apostles Peter and Paul caused him to fall and to injure himself fatally.

Following these pilots, come those for whom flight is a natural state of existence. Each bird performs an act in tribute to the plane: the eagle skydives, the phoenix bursts into flames, the sirens sing seductively. Most of the birds in the cortege are mythical, possessing occult powers and incarnating spiritual forces. Thus, the ibis is related to Thoth, the Egyptian god of wisdom, the crow symbolizes prophecy, the dove is a symbol for the Holy Ghost, the stork is dedicated to the goddess Juno, the eagle is associated with the sun, and the giant Roc is believed to have carried off elephants to feed its young.[38] The most unusual of these exotic and mythical birds, however, are the "pihis longs et souples."[39]

There is an acute sense of history in Apollinaire's spectacle of flying men and birds coming from the ends of the earth and from the beginnings of time to pay homage to the new invention of the twentieth century. The old pays tribute to the new. The first man is present at the christening of the first airplane. Adam, founder of the race, witnesses the most advanced stage of man's development.[40]

Because of the discoveries of science and technology the myths of the past are being realized. A tendency toward demythologization, a phenomenon of which Apollinaire was quite aware,[41] characterizes the twentieth century. The invention of the airplane has actualized the fable of Icarus and thus replaced the myth of flight with its reality. But in "Zone," strangely enough, the process appears to be reversed. The airplane, the very instrument of demythologization, becomes remythologized. As the angels, cherubs and seraphs that surround Christ in paintings of the Ascension lend him a divine aura, so the birds, magicians, and prophets encircling the airplane give it a mythic aspect. The plane thus appears to be receiving approval from different mythic and historical ages. The blessings of the past are given to the

---

[38] J. E. Cirlot, *Dictionary of Symbols*, trans. by Jack Sage (London: Routledge and Kegan Paul, 1962), pp. 68, 81 *et passim*.

[39] A note in one of Apollinaire's early notebooks describes them as follows:

> "Les poissons pi-mu (aux yeux accouplés) n'ont qu'un œil. Les oiseaux pi-i (aux ailes accouplées) n'ont qu'une aile. Ils vont par couple (Poème chinois) Male à dr. femelle à gauche" (Décaudin, *Le Dossier*, p. 87).

[40] It is interesting to note that the presence of Adam's skull at the resurrection of the airplane resembles a symbol found in medieval paintings of the Crucifixion, where above the Cross, which is situated between heaven and earth, flies the Holy Spirit carrying the skull of Adam (Cirlot, p. 70).

[41] "Tant que les avions ne peuplaient pas le ciel, la fable d'Icare n'était qu'une vérité supposée. Aujourd'hui, ce n'est plus une fable. Et nos inventeurs nous ont accoutumés à des prodiges plus grands que celui qui consisterait à déléguer aux hommes la fonction qu'ont les femmes de faire des enfants. Je dirai plus, les fables s'étant pour la plupart réalisées et au delà, c'est au poète d'en imaginer des nouvelles que les inventeurs puissent à leur tour réaliser" ("L'Esprit nouveau et les poètes," p. 392).

modern. But even more is bestowed on the plane than either history, blessings, or mythical qualities. Icarus, Elijah, Enoch, the phoenix, the Roc, the sirens, all these magical, spiritual figures share their divinity with the plane. It is deified by association. The airplane becomes the most modern symbol for the Absolute, for the sacred, and for the godhead in the history of mankind: "Et changé en oiseau ce siècle comme Jésus monte dans l'air." In his panoramic history of man's efforts to fly, Apollinaire represents the past and present simultaneously, so that the mythic and the modern fly, so to speak, wing to wing. Thus, he modernizes and updates the mythical past, but not without also mythologizing the unmythic present. In this manner, the past gains modernity, and the present, mythology.

Earlier in "Zone" Apollinaire had rejected the Greco-Roman concept of reality as outmoded and the image of a shepherdess as archaic. Now, he borrows myths from the same Greco-Roman antiquity and from the Judaeo-Christian past as well. What seems to be a contradiction, however, is not. If Apollinaire does borrow myths from the Greco-Roman tradition, it is not to create a representation in keeping with that ancient tradition, but rather to produce a modern, simultaneous, multiple-viewpoint portrait of the airplane. He has discarded Greco-Roman concepts and images, which are *passé*; but he does retain Greco-Roman myths, which are not. Moreover, a pastoral image like "bergère" and a myth, like the fable of Icarus, are two very different things. The image is a form of expression and a manner of speech firmly attached to the historical period in which it is used; it dates quickly. A myth, however, does not. It persists through the ages and belongs to no century in particular but to all centuries. The older it gets, the more seasoned, the more "mythical" it becomes. Even if it is finally realized, as the fable of Icarus is, the invention that actualizes it assumes mythical qualities of its own; it is recognized as the final form of a myth that stretches back to the dawn of history. It becomes the culmination of that myth, its highest development and its most perfect form.

For all his devotion to the cult of the modern, Apollinaire is unwilling to claim that the new century appeared miraculously or that the airplane was created *ex nihilo*. He acknowledges the debt owed to the past by representing the twentieth century in an historical perspective:

> Pupille Christ de l'œil
> Vingtième pupille des siècles il sait y faire

He further acknowledges the debt by juxtaposing the mythic past with the unmythic present. Thus, by painting a panoramic mural in which the history of mankind from Adam to the airplane is simultaneously represented, Apollinaire suggests that the roots of the modern are deeply embedded in the soil of the past.

A hesitation between the modern and the traditional is typical of Apollinaire. For all his modernist claims he was as much a man of the past as of the present. Unlike his cubist, futurist, and surrealist friends — iconoclasts who never looked backwards to the littered country through which they had trampled, pioneers whose eyes were fixed on what lay ahead — Apollinaire was reluctant to sever all ties with the past and unable to commit himself entirely to the present. Although some of his innovations were revolutionary, he was not. A strong sense of tradition prevented him from becoming more modern than he in fact was.[42] His double loyalty to both past and present is reflected throughout his poetry in the oscillation between traditional, lyric poems, reminiscent of Villon, and modern experimental poems, which recall the techniques of cubism and simultaneism. Thus, tradition and invention or, as he preferred to call them, "De l'Ordre et de l'Aventure,"[43] alternate in his work.

It is not surprising then, that the final image of Apollinaire's tableau of man's conquest of the air pictures the past and the present, the mythical birds and the modern airplane, flying harmoniously together:

---

[42] Apollinaire's hesitation to break completely with the past and with tradition came under heavy attack by many younger poets and painters, including Francis Picabia and André Breton. The latter has described the disappointment he felt at hearing Apollinaire's lecture on "L'Esprit nouveau et les poètes," delivered in November 1917:

> "Je me rappelle quelle fut la consternation de ces jeunes gens dont j'étais et qui ne voyaient alors que par lui, quand ils comprirent que cet esprit nouveau, il prétendait le fonder sur l'ordre, le bon sens et un prétendu 'devoir national.' Pour comble de dérision, les poètes étaient invités à modeler leurs préoccupations et leurs rêves sur ceux des mathématiciens."

(André Breton, "Ombre non pas serpent mais d'arbre, en fleurs," *Le Flâneur des Deux Rives*, no. 1 [mars, 1954], cited by Bonnet, p. 70)

[43] "La Jolie Rousse," *Calligrammes*, O. P., p. 313.

> Et tous aigle phénix et pihis de la Chine
> Fraternisent avec la volante machine

The final image also conveys Apollinaire's hope in the new century. An age that has conquered the air has also conquered distance, the distance between nations and between peoples. The world will become a global village, and the airplane will be the means to greater brotherhood among men. So suggests an optimistic Apollinaire only two years before the Great War and a quarter of a century before the saturation bombing of Guernica.

With the beginning of the second part of "Zone" the airborne procession ends and Apollinaire descends to earth:

> Maintenant tu marches dans Paris tout seul parmi
>   la foule
> Des troupeaux d'autobus mugissants près de toi
>   roulent
> L'angoisse de l'amour te serre le gosier
> Comme si tu ne devais jamais plus être aimé
> Si tu vivais dans l'ancien temps tu entrerais
>   dans un monastère
> Vous avez honte quand vous vous surprenez à dire
>   une prière

No sooner does he return to the present than he laments his solitude ("tout seul parmi la foule"), which comes as a surprise after his prophecy of brotherhood in the preceding salute to the airplane. But it is part of a general feeling of loneliness and despair which mounts like a crescendo through the entire second part of the poem. Already, the thirst for sacrificial blood, which will be satisfied in the final image of the poem, has been stimulated, first by the allusion to bleating sheep and then by the image of anguish clutching the poet's throat. His despair is further aggravated by the absence of help. Religion is unable to alleviate his trouble or calm his anxiety, for he has lost the innocent faith of his childhood ("Si tu vivais dans l'ancien temps tu entrerais dans un monastère").

Without either the love of God or the love of a woman to comfort him the poet's loneliness and despair are total. His solitude forces him to fall back on himself in the hope that at least enough self-love remains to comfort him. Like Cocteau for whom "la solitude m'oblige à être Robinson et son île, à prospecter en moi-même," [44] Apollinaire searches deep inside himself. But what he finds is cruelly disappointing. The self is seen for what it is worth, and in Apollinaire's desperate outlook it is not worth much. He turns against himself with mocking laughter and bitter irony:

> Tu te moques de toi et comme le feu de l'Enfer ton
>   rire pétille
> Les étincelles de ton rire dorent le fond de ta vie
> C'est un tableau pendu dans un sombre musée
> Et quelquefois tu vas le regarder de près

Like the fire of Hell, laughter consumes and purges what it is directed at. Laughter directed toward the self burns away the masks, the illusions, and the pretensions that constitute the self's protective covering. It brutally denudes the self, lays it bare for examination, and with irony signals out each weakness and failure. Thus the poet's crackling, seering laughter punishes and purges at the same time.

Laughter, the poet's whip of self-castigation, is also his scapel of self-dissection and thus an instrument of self-consciousness. When the poet laughs at himself, his shattering laugh fragments the self into two parts, an *I* that laughs and an *I* that is laughed at, a tormentor and a tormented. The laughing self is stripped of its selfhood, and made to assume the role and identity of the other. In this objectified form it is no longer self, since it has been removed from the universe of the self and exiled to the universe of the non-self. It becomes the sadistic, mocking outsider, the judge, jury, and executioner of whatever it regards. Laughter directed at the self, therefore, is an important technique of self-objectification and self-exteriorisation. It creates the distance, the detachment, and the objectivity necessary for self-contemplation and eventually, self-knowledge. To laugh at oneself is to contemplate the self with irony, sarcasm, and deprecation, and from the perspective of an outsider looking in.

In "Zone" Apollinaire's laughter exteriorizes the dramatic conflict within the self: "Les étincelles de ton rire dorent le fond de ta vie/ C'est un tableau pendu dans un sombre musée." It illuminates ("dorent") the depths and the darkness of the universe of self ("le

---

[44] Jean Cocteau, *La Difficulté d'être* (Montana, Switzerland: Bottinelli, 1947), p. 191.

fond de ta vie") and externalizes the self in a form ("un tableau") which the poet can contemplate and scrutinize at will: "Et quelquefois tu vas le regarder de près." The form is represented here as a painting, but any work of art may contain and preserve the self: a novel, a poem, or a film. Laughter, therefore, like memory, is a creative force that takes the drama of self out of the self and dramatizes it in an exterior form.[45]

---

[45] Bursts of laughter punctuate many poems in *Alcools*; for example: "Mon verre s'est brisé comme un éclat de rire" ("Nuit rhénane," *O. P.*, p. 111); "...le larron de gauche dans la bourrasque/Rira de toi comme hennissent les chevaux" ("Le Larron," *O. P.*, p. 94); "J'ai ri du vieil ange qui n'est point venu," "Vertuchou Riotant des vulves des papesses/De saintes sans tétons...," "Cité j'ai ri de tes palais..." ("L'Ermite," *O. P.*, pp. 101 and 102); "...et que les vents d'horreur/Feignent d'être le rire de la lune hilare" ("Merlin et la vieille femme," *O. P.*, p. 89). The tone of the laughter in *Alcools* is generally mocking, irreverent, sacrilegious, destructive, and slightly tinged with hysteria. In "L'Esprit nouveau et les poètes" Apollinaire speaks of laughter in the following terms:

> Nous avons vu aussi depuis Alfred Jarry le rire s'élever des basses régions où il se tordait et fournir au poète un lyrisme tout neuf. Où est le temps où le mouchoir de Desdémone paraissait d'un ridicule inadmissible? Aujourd'hui le ridicule même est poursuivi, on cherche à s'en emparer et il a sa place dans la poésie, parce qu'il fait partie de la vie au même titre que l'héroïsme et tout ce qui nourrissait jadis l'enthousiasme des poètes (p. 390).

Those who were friendly with Apollinaire recall his own characteristic laughter, which, according to André Breton, "'made the same noise as a first burst of hailstones on a windowpane'" (*Anthologie de l'humour noir* [Paris: Sagittaire, 1940], cited and trans. by L. C. Breunig, "The Laughter of Apollinaire," *Yale French Studies*, XXXI [May, 1964], p. 67). Jean Cocteau remembers that "le rire ne sortait pas de sa bouche. Il arrivait des quatre coins de l'organisme. Il l'envahissait, l'ébranlait, lui imprimait des saccades. Ensuite ce rire silencieux se vidait par le regard et le corps se remettait en place" (*La Difficulté d'être*, p. 171). In his article "The Laughter of Apollinaire" Mr. Breunig sees a similarity between the laughter in Apollinaire's work and the modern theater of the absurd. He concludes that the fusion of laughter and despair in Apollinaire's poetry produces a malaise that we of today are perhaps more sensitive to than were Apollinaire's contemporaries; this malaise is the sentiment of the absurd:

> And like the mask-maker of Marcel Marceau, holding the two masks of Tragedy and Comedy and putting now one, now the other on his face in rapid-fire succession, the lines of Apollinaire with their sudden shifts often convey a single sentiment, neither tragic nor comic and yet containing both, the sentiment of the absurd (p. 73).

Moreover, Henri Meschonnic has observed that laughter, "quand il est celui d'Apollinaire et non d'un de ses personnages, est la soudaine brisure où le destin devient transparent, le moment de la clairvoyance poétique" ("Apollinaire illuminé au milieu d'ombres," *Europe*, nos. 451-452 [novembre-décembre, 1966], p. 159).

Apollinaire's laughter dies away, and he returns to the city scene before him only to find it covered with blood and permeated with despair and sickness:

> Aujourd'hui tu marches dans Paris les femmes
>   sont ensanglantées
> C'était et je voudrais ne pas m'en souvenir
>   c'était au déclin de la beauté
>
> Entourée de flammes ferventes Notre-Dame m'a
>   regardé à Chartres
> Le sang de votre Sacré-Cœur m'a inondé à
>   Montmartre
> Je suis malade d'ouïr les paroles bienheureuses
> L'amour dont je souffre est une maladie honteuse
> Et l'image qui te possède te fait survivre dans
>   l'insomnie et dans l'angoisse
> C'est toujours près de toi cette image qui passe

For the first time Apollinaire speaks of his despair in terms of a physical sickness: "Je suis malade," "l'amour dont je souffre," "une maladie honteuse," "l'insomnie"; and for the first time he describes women in terms of their physiological aspects. The "belles sténo-dactylographes," who walked along the industrial street earlier in the poem, contrast sharply with the menstruating women ("les femmes sont ensanglantées") who now pass the poet.[46] An unhealthy mixture of disease and blood courses through the city.

Apollinaire's love has become a sickness, a "maladie honteuse" that is both pathological and psychological. Pathologically, Apollinaire appears to be suffering from venereal disease;[47] psychologically, he

---

[46] In an early *brouillon* of "Zone" known as the *L'Année Républicaine* version, Apollinaire wrote the following passage, which he judiciously omitted from the final poem:

> Aujourd'hui je vais dans Paris les femmes sont
>   ensanglantées
> [J'ai peur de tout leur sang]
> leurs menstrues coulent dans les ruisseaux, l'air
>   est infecté
> L'haleine des femmes est fétide et leur voix
>   est menteuse
>   (Décaudin, *Le Dossier*, p. 78)

[47] Apollinaire is more explicit in his early *brouillon*:

> L'amour dont je souffre est une maladie honteuse
> C'est une enflure ignoble dont je souhaite être
>   guéri
>   (Décaudin, *Le Dossier*, p. 78)

is suffering from the obsessive memory of his mistress, which has possessed him like some demon: "Et l'image qui te possède te fait survivre dans l'insomnie et dans l'angoisse/C'est toujours près de toi cette image qui passe." [48] Against this disease of mind and body the divine aid offered by the Virgin Mary ("Entourée de flammes ferventes Notre-Dame m'a regardé à Chartres/Le sang de votre Sacré-Cœur m'a inondé à Montmartre") [49] is powerless. Apollinaire rejects divine succor: "Je suis malade d'ouïr les paroles bienheureuses," for blessed prayers will not cure his despair. The blood that flows abundantly in this passage, a prefiguration of the poem's final image, is female blood, but of two distinct types: one, the menstrual blood of Parisian women ("les femmes sont ensanglantées") and the other, the divine blood that pours from the heart of the Virgin Mary ("Le sang de votre Sacré-Cœur"). The former is a symbol of profane love and thus refers to the blood of a temporal being like Marie Laurencin; the latter, a symbol of sacred love, refers to the blood of a holier Marie, namely the Virgin Mother. [50]

Apollinaire's break with his mistress has turned him against women in general. A vague sentiment of misogyny begins here and continues until the end of the poem. It shows itself in the poet's descriptions of the opposite sex and in his concern with female physiology. In this

---

[48] His obsession is more frankly and brutally expressed in the *L'Année Républicaine* version. The poet is speaking of his "maladie honteuse":

> Elle me tient éveillé jusqu'au matin dans mon lit
> Elle me fait mourir d'un voluptueuse angoisse [sic]
> [En songeant à la chair nue de ma maîtresse]
> [En songeant au corps de celle]
> En songeant que le corps nu de mon ancienne maîtresse je l'embrasse

(Décaudin, *Le Dossier*, p. 78)

[49] A double meaning is assigned to the expressions "Notre-Dame" and "votre Sacré-Cœur," which refer at once to the Parisian cathedrals and to the Virgin Mary (the referent for the "votre" in the expression "votre Sacré-Cœur" being the "Notre-Dame" of the preceding line).

[50] The identification of these two women is more explicitly made in "La Colombe," a poem in *Le Bestiaire*:

> Colombe, l'amour et l'esprit
> Qui engendrâtes Jésus-Christ,
> Comme vous j'aime une Marie.
> Qu'avec elle je me marie.

(O. P., p. 28)

passage, for example, women are described not in terms of their beauty or their charm, but by references to their menstrual cycle, to the venereal disease they carry and to the waning of their physical charms: "C'était et je voudrais ne pas m'en souvenir c'était au déclin de la beauté." Later in "Zone," when the poet sees immigrant Jewish women, who, in accordance with an age-old custom, wear wigs to hide what Jews believed to be the sensual power of hair, he describes them as ashen, anemic, sexless mannequins: "Il y a surtout des Juifs leurs femmes portent perruque/Elles restent assises exsangues au fond des boutiques." Near the end of the poem, as he walks through "la zone," the poet meets an ugly prostitute, and he alludes to the scars on her belly: "J'ai une pitié immense pour les coutures de son ventre." Although he pities these harlots and appreciates the misery of their lives, he still harbors a slight dislike for them, as is evident in the following passage, where his sympathy is qualified by his personal experience:

>Ces femmes ne sont pas méchantes elles ont des
>   soucis cependant
>Toutes même la plus laide a fait souffrir son
>   amant [51]

Apollinaire's despair and lovesickness are suddenly forgotten, as a series of flashback memories disengages his mind from the present and carries it swiftly back to the past:

>Maintenant tu es au bord de la Méditerranée
>Sous les citronniers qui sont en fleur toute
>   l'année

---

[51] In the more brutal *L'Année Républicaine* version Apollinaire expresses outright disgust for these women. Not all is subtlety and discretion in Apollinaire:

>Je suis avec une putain qui me paraissait
>   belle
>Ses seins ont l'air de lavettes pour laver la
>   vaisselle
>... ... ...
>Et j'ai une pitié immense pour son ventre
>C'est pour ne pas la vexer qu'avec dégoût j'y entre
>
>Et j'humilie à une pauvre fille au rire horrible
>   ma bouche
>Je baise cette sorte de plaie chevelue et rouge
>   (Décaudin, *Le Dossier*, p. 81)

> Avec tes amis tu te promènes en barque
> L'un est Nissard il y a un Mentonasque et deux Turbiasques
> Nous regardons avec effroi les poulpes des profondeurs
> Et parmi les algues nagent les poissons images du Sauveur
>
> Tu es dans le jardin d'une auberge aux environs de Prague
> Tu te sens tout heureux une rose est sur la table
> Et tu observes au lieu d'écrire ton conte en prose
> La cétoine qui dort dans le cœur de la rose
>
> Epouvanté tu te vois dessiné dans les agates de Saint-Vit
> Tu étais triste à mourir le jour où tu t'y vis
> Tu ressembles au Lazare affolé par le jour
> Les aiguilles de l'horloge du quartier juif vont à rebours
> Et tu recules aussi dans ta vie lentement
> En montant au Hradchin et le soir en écoutant
> Dans les tavernes chanter des chansons tchèques
>
> Te voici à Marseille au milieu des pastèques
>
> Te voici à Coblence à l'hôtel du Géant
>
> Te voici à Rome assis sous un néflier du Japon
>
> Te voici à Amsterdam avec une jeune fille que tu trouves belle et qui est laide
> Elle doit se marier avec un étudiant de Leyde
> On y loue des chambres en latin Cubicula locanda
> Je m'en souviens j'y ai passé trois jours et autant à Gouda
>
> Tu es à Paris chez le juge d'instruction
> Comme un criminel on te met en état d'arrestation

Apollinaire creates simultaneous poetry here by juxtaposing different events occurring at different moments in his life and enumerating them as if they occurred at the same time. The quick changes in setting, the rapid-fire enumeration of experiences, the repetition of *tu* and *te*, the scarcity of conjunctions, the absence of transitions, and the reduction of all events to a single plane, translate simultaneity into poetry.

The passage is not without its cinematic devices. Fade-ins, fade-outs, long shots ("tu es au bord de la Méditerranée"), close-ups ("La cétoine qui dort dans le cœur de la rose"), accelerated motion ("Te voici à Marseille.../Te voici à Coblence.../Te voici à Rome.../"), a mirror-image ("tu te vois dessiné dans les agates de Saint-Vit"), and montage are all effectively used. Memory renders Apollinaire simultaneously present in Prague, Marseille, Coblenz, Rome, Amsterdam, Gouda, and Paris. Within his mind the poet travels over the European continent without concern for the restrictions of real time and space, which memory easily transcends. Past moments of his life are resuscitated and return in the form of flashbacks which contain different "shots" of himself — as a child in Rome, as a grown man in a Paris jail — juxtaposed in a striking montage. When the futurist poets and painters used techniques of simultaneity, it was to express their belief in the future, their faith in the machine age, and their devotion to speed and movement. Unlike the futurists, however, Apollinaire here uses simultaneity to represent the past; his simultaneity runs backwards rather than forwards.[52]

---

[52] The truly simultaneous poem in *Alcools* is "Vendémiaire" (1912) in which long enumerations of different cities evoke a feeling of global consciousness and where the cities themselves are portrayed in continual, instantaneous communication:

> Et Rennes répondit avec Quimper et Vannes
>
> Et les villes du Nord répondirent gaîment
>   (O. P., pp. 149 and 150)

The poet is ubiquitous, embracing the universe with passion and drinking it with bacchic delight:

> J'ai soif villes de France et d'Europe et du monde
> Venez toutes couler dans ma gorge profonde
>
> Ecoutez-moi je suis le gosier de Paris
> Et je boirai encore s'il me plaît l'univers
>   (O. P., pp. 149 and 154)

Simultaneity appears often in the more modern poems of *Calligrammes*, such as "Les Fenêtres" (1913) inspired by a painting by Robert Delaunay:

> Vancouver
>   Où le train blanc de neige et de feux nocturnes
>   fuit l'hiver

Although most of the flashbacks seem to recall happier moments of the poet's life, there is in each a minute detail of unhappiness or of darkness that stains the beauty of the moment. In the first memory, the poet is sailing with friends on the Mediterranean and is suddenly overcome with fear at the sight of octopuses swimming deep in the water ("Nous regardons avec effroi les poulpes des profondeurs"). In the next flashback, the poet, seated in the garden of an inn outside Prague, is filled with happiness ("tu te sens tout heureux"); yet, instead of writing a short story, he watches a bug ("La cétoine") asleep inside a rose. The rose-beetle, like the octopuses, is a dark form that lies in the depths, or in this case, at the heart, of something larger. It resembles the stigma of despair, the mark of disenchantment, and the cancerous spot of disillusion that lie at the core of Apollinaire's self. Introspection and the search for self-knowledge have trained Apollinaire to look penetratingly into the heart and depths of things. Thus, earlier in the poem he was able to perceive the painting of himself "pendu dans un sombre musée"; and thus he notices the

> O Paris
> Du rouge au vert tout le jaune se meurt
> Paris Vancouver Hyères Maintenon New-York et
>   les Antilles
>   (O. P., p. 169)

or in a war poem, like "Merveille de la Guerre" (1915), where the poet's being flows through the universe:

> Je lègue à l'avenir l'histoire de Guillaume
>   Apollinaire
> Qui fut à la guerre et sut être partout
> Dans les villes heureuses de l'arrière
> Dans tout le reste de l'univers
> Dans ceux qui meurent en piétinant dans le barbelé
> Dans les femmes dans les canons dans les chevaux
> Au zénith au nadir aux 4 points cardinaux
> Et dans l'unique ardeur de cette veillée d'armes
>   (O. P., p. 272)

As a dynamic force in the creation of art, especially in painting, simultaneity is discussed by Apollinaire in an article, entitled "Réalité, Peinture Pure," written in 1912 and dealing with Robert Delaunay's use of "le contraste simultané." According to Apollinaire, simultaneity alone is creation:

> Le reste n'est que notation, contemplation, étude. La simultanéité, c'est la vie même et quelle que soit la succession d'éléments dans une œuvre elle mène à une fin inéluctable, la mort, tandis que le créateur ne connaît que l'éternité. L'artiste s'est trop longtemps efforcé vers la mort en assemblant des éléments stériles de l'art et il est temps qu'il arrive à la fécondité, à la trinité, à la simultanéité
> (*Chroniques d'Art* 1902-1918 [Paris: Gallimard, 1960], pp. 269-270).

octupuses in the depths, the rose-bug in the folds of the rose, and in the next flashback, an image of himself engraved on the walls of a cathedral. Later, he will make out anemic emigrants seated "au fond des boutiques."

In the next scene the poet is terror-stricken ("Epouvanté") and deadly sad ("triste à mourir") when he sees his likeness sketched in the agate walls of the Cathedral of Prague. Since the agate is composed of different colored veins or bands, called "zones," the image of Apollinaire is probably fractured by the same zones that fragment the agate. Perhaps this explains his terror; he is appalled at the ghastly, disjointed appearance these fractures and colored veins give to his portrait. Another possible explanation is found in Apollinaire's story, "Le Passant de Prague," which relates the same experience in more detail:

> Dans la chapelle où l'on couronnait les rois de Bohême, et où le saint roi Wenceslas subit le martyre, Laquedem [Apollinaire's guide] me fit remarquer que les murailles étaient de gemmes: agates et améthystes. Il m'indiqua une améthyste:
> —Voyez, au centre, les veinures dessinent une face aux yeux flamboyants et fous. On prétend que c'est le masque de Napoléon.
> —C'est mon visage, m'écriai-je, avec mes yeux sombres et jaloux!
> Et c'est vrai. Il est là, mon portrait douloureux, près de la porte de bronze où pend l'anneau que tenait saint Wenceslas quand il fut massacré. Nous dûmes sortir. J'étais pâle et malheureux de m'être vu fou, moi qui crains tant de le devenir.[53]

The final flashback of the poem refers to the poet's more recent past: "Tu es à Paris chez le juge d'instruction / Comme un criminel on te met en état d'arrestation." In September 1911 Apollinaire was falsely arrested, taken to La Santé prison and placed in solitary confinement for his suspected part in the theft of the *Mona Lisa*. Although finally released and cleared of the charges, he was humiliated; his self-respect and ego were badly shaken. In "A La Santé," written during his imprisonment, he speaks of his shame:

---

[53] *L'Hérésiarque et Cie*, in *Œuvres complètes*, I, 110.

> Avant d'entrer dans ma cellule
> Il a fallu me mettre nu
> Et quelle voix sinistre ulule
> Guillaume qu'es-tu devenu
>
> (O. P., p. 140)

Rather than alleviating his anguish the flashback memories have only intensified it. After the last of them disappears Apollinaire recapitulates his sorrowful life in a tone of self-deprecation reminiscent of Villon:

> Tu as fait de douloureux et de joyeux voyages
> Avant de t'apercevoir du mensonge et de l'âge
> Tu as souffert de l'amour à vingt et à trente ans
> J'ai vécu comme un fou et j'ai perdu mon temps
> Tu n'oses plus regarder tes mains et à tous moments
>   je voudrais sangloter
> Sur toi sur celle que j'aime sur tout ce qui t'a
>   épouvanté

Self-deprecation, shame, disenchantment, disillusion, terror, self-pity, self-disgust, these are the dimensions of Apollinaire's despair. However, in resuming the narrative of his walk where he had left off before the flashbacks began, Apollinaire forgets his own troubles and becomes involved in the plight of others. The flood-tide of self-pity that he had experienced is redirected outwards as an immense sympathy for the poor emigrants herded into the "gare Saint-Lazare":

> Tu regardes les yeux pleins de larmes ces pauvres
>   émigrants
> Ils croient en Dieu ils prient les femmes allaitent
>   des enfants
> Ils emplissent de leur odeur le hall de la gare Saint-
>   Lazare
> Ils ont foi dans leur étoile comme les rois-mages
> Ils espèrent gagner de l'argent dans l'Argentine
> Et revenir dans leur pays après avoir fait fortune
> Une famille transporte un édredon rouge comme vous
>   transportez votre cœur
> Cet édredon et nos rêves sont aussi irréels
> Quelques-uns de ces émigrants restent ici et se
>   logent
> Rue des Rosiers ou rue des Ecouffes dans des bouges
> Je les ai vus souvent le soir ils prennent l'air
>   dans la rue

Et se déplacent rarement comme les pièces aux échecs
Il y a surtout des Juifs leurs femmes portent perruque
Elles restent assises exsangues au fond des boutiques

Part of Apollinaire's pity for these foreigners is a feeling of identification, for he associates these uprooted emigrants with his own Polish ancestors, the Kostrowicki family which was forced to flee Poland for its part in an insurrection against the Russians.[54] A red eiderdown carried by one emigrant family attracts his attention. As a blanket for the newly born, a cover for the dying, a comforter for the sick, handed down from generation to generation, the quilt has been a silent witness to the long history of his particular family. More than a piece of cloth stuffed with down, it is probably the only vestige of the homeland that the emigrants possess. Wherever they travel, the past will always be present through the suggestive power of the quilt. Moreover, like any object which has been imbued with symbolic meaning, the comforter has a magical, talismanic value. During its long history in the family, it may have been associated with some happy occasion and thus may have become a symbol of good luck. Perhaps, this explains the hope the emigrants feel. Although they believe in God and have faith in the stars, they also have the quilt with them; for this reason, they can be hopeful about striking it rich in Argentina.

The red eiderdown resembles the human heart: "Une famille transporte un édredon rouge comme vous transportez votre cœur," for the heart is heavy with the burdens of the past and overflowing with the dreams of the future. Apollinaire was himself an immigrant from Italy brought to Monaco by his mother when he was only five; but he is also an emigrant of love, forced to abandon the woman he cherishes. He carries with him a heavy heart, which, like the eiderdown, evokes sad memories and creates wishful dreams. The poet, like the emigrants, would believe these fictions and would let his hopes leap high, if his despair were not so absolute; it prevents him from being drugged by such pipe-dreams and fantasies: "Cet édredon

---

[54] Adéma, p. 2. For a discussion of the role played by immigrants, gypsies, *saltimbanques,* and other "gens de voyage" in Apollinaire's poems, see Roger Navarri, "Apollinaire poète du déracinement," *Europe,* nos. 451-452 (novembre-décembre, 1966), pp. 133-141.

et nos rêves sont aussi irréels." Despair permits Apollinaire neither the luxury of dreams nor the opiate of hope.

Although Apollinaire describes the human aspects of these emigrants (the women nursing their babies, the odor of the crowd), there is something mechanical, almost unreal, about his description. By repeating the pronoun "ils," for example, he transforms them into puppets:

> Ils croient en Dieu ils prient...
> Ils emplissent...
> Ils ont foi...
> Ils espèrent gagner...

Another group of immigrants are Jews who live in the heart of the Jewish quarter of Paris, the "rue des Rosiers." They are pictured as immobile chessmen ("les pièces aux échecs") and as unmoving figures seated in the back of their shops ("Elles restent assises exsangues au fond des boutiques"). The women are the most dehumanized: lifeless, bloodless mannequins, who deny their sexuality by wearing wigs.

Apollinaire takes leave of these sexless women and strolls into a seamy quarter of Paris where he meets women of a different sort; rather than hiding their sexuality these women exhibit it; and yet, they are no happier than their sexless sisters:

> Tu es debout devant le zinc d'un bar crapuleux
> Tu prends un café à deux sous parmi les malheureux
>
> Tu es la nuit dans un grand restaurant
>
> Ces femmes ne sont pas méchantes elles ont des soucis cependant
> Toutes même la plus laide a fait souffrir son amant
>
> Elle est la fille d'un sergent de ville de Jersey
>
> Ses mains que je n'avais pas vues sont dures et gercées
>
> J'ai une pitié immense pour les coutures de son ventre
>
> J'humilie maintenant à une pauvre fille au rire horrible ma bouche

The "shot" of the poet kissing the prostitute fades and dissolves to one of him walking alone toward home at dawn:

> Tu es seul le matin va venir
> Les laitiers font tinter leurs bidons dans les rues
> La nuit s'éloigne ainsi qu'une belle Métive
> C'est Ferdine la fausse ou Léa l'attentive
>
> Et tu bois cet alcool brûlant comme ta vie
> Ta vie que tu bois comme une eau-de-vie
>
> Tu marches vers Auteuil tu veux aller chez toi à pied
> Dormir parmi les fétiches d'Océanie et de Guinée
> Ils sont des Christ d'une autre forme et d'une autre croyance
> Ce sont les Christ inférieurs des obscures espérances
>
> Adieu Adieu
>
> Soleil cou coupé

The fading night, which the poet discretely compares to his dark, Creole-blooded mistress, Marie Laurencin ("une belle Métive"), finds Apollinaire drinking a liqueur which burns as much and is as difficult to swallow as the painful memories and thoughts of his life ("cet alcool brûlant comme ta vie"). Unlike the communion wine that calmed and refreshed his young soul, the "alcool brûlant" excites and warms him. There are no transcendent powers in this burning liquid because alcohol is the water of life ("une eau-de-vie") and not of after-life. It represents human life ("Ta vie que tu bois") at its rawest, most abject level. As dawn approaches, Apollinaire nears the rock bottom of despair, and he tries to drown his suffering in alcohol. With one swallow he drains a cheap *eau-de-vie*, symbol of his unfortunate life, which, after settling in the pit of his stomach, causes him to experience a physical, as well as spiritual, malaise. Brandy and life both leave a bad taste in his mouth.[55]

---

[55] Images of alcohol and wine create a *leitmotiv* that runs through *Alcools*, from its title, which was originally "*Eau de Vie*" (Décaudin, *Le Dossier*, p. 35), to its final poem, "Vendémiaire." In "La Chanson du Mal-Aimé," for example, evenings in Paris are pictured as "ivres du gin" (*O. P.*, p. 59). The

The African idols that decorate Apollinaire's apartment are primitive works of art, which at the beginning of the twentieth century enjoyed considerable popularity in France. As early as 1902 wooden statuettes were brought from the Ivory Coast and the Congo.[56] But Negro art was more than a curiosity, and it created more than a general stir among the fashions of the day. It played a significant role in the formation of cubism. When Picasso's *Les Demoiselles d'Avignon*, the first cubist painting, appeared in 1907, it contained portraits of women whose exaggerated eyes and noses, angular features, and oversized heads resembled African masks.

Generally speaking, African art is religious. Its extraordinary, stylized forms are charged with an intense spirituality. By exteriorizing their deepest, most primitive fears and hopes (their "obscures espérances") in masks, idols, and statues, some primitive peoples attempt to placate, invoke, or ward off the spirits, gods, and demons who control their fate and govern their world. Their art, thus, is the spontaneous incarnation of that primitive, irrational fear of the unknown, which is the source of both superstition and religious belief. Apollinaire recognized this:

> Ces fétiches qui n'ont pas été sans influencer les arts modernes ressortissent tous à la passion religieuse qui est la source d'art la plus pure.[57]

---

guests in the poem "Palais" are served "le vin de Chypre" (O. P., p. 61), while the thief in "Le Larron" is given "le vin blanc" (O. P., p. 92). The poet's glass in "Nuit rhénane" is "plein d'un vin trembleur comme une flamme" (O. P., p. 111), and the bandit Schinderhannes and his gang enjoy "le vin de mai" and the "vin de Moselle" (O. P., p. 117) before going out to kill a rich Jew. Undertakers in "Les Fiançailles" clink their steins of beer together, while the poet and his friend, André Salmon, drink until "La table et les deux verres devinrent un mourant qui nous jeta le dernier regard d'Orphée" (O. P., p. 83) in "Poème lu au mariage d'André Salmon." In "Vendémiaire," wine is a means to orphic participation in the universe, and the poet's drunkenness creates "chants d'universelle ivrognerie":

> Actions belles journées sommeils terribles
> Végétation Accouplements musiques éternelles
> Mouvements Adorations douleur divine
> Mondes qui vous ressemblez et qui nous ressemblez
> Je vous ai bus et ne fus pas désaltéré

> Mais je connus dès lors quelle saveur a l'univers
> Je suis ivre d'avoir bu tout l'univers
> (O. P., pp. 153-154)

[56] Lemaitre, p. 76.

[57] In an article, entitled "Sculptures d'Afrique et d'Océanie" (1918), *Chroniques d'Art*, p. 442.

Unlike the Greco-Roman tradition, African art has never grown antiquated. Since it expresses those archetypal fears and hopes that have belonged to man since Adam, and since its source is the intuitive religious feeling at the heart of every man, African art has always been modern. Along with the airplane, it is completely new: "La religion seule est restée toute neuve la religion / Est restée simple comme les hangars de Port-Aviation." Moreover, African idols and masks are just one of many religious symbols, icons, and forms venerated throughout history; thus, Apollinaire considers them,

> ... des Christ d'une autre forme et d'une autre croyance
> Ce sont les Christ inférieurs des obscures espérances

At the beginning of "Zone" Apollinaire declares that he is weary of the Greco-Roman tradition, a conception based on reason and intellect which perceives the universe as being static and ordered. At the end of the poem, he finally finds rest but among the art forms of another tradition, one that perceives the universe in terms of man's primitive and brutal instincts. Apollinaire, therefore, rejects the rational for the irrational, the intellectual for the passionate, and the ordered for the chaotic. The change from Greco-Roman to African conceptions is strikingly illustrated by the first and last images of the poem. While beginning "Zone" with a classical pastoral image of peace and tranquility ("Bergère ô tour Eiffel") Apollinaire concludes with a primitive image of ritual sacrifice, filled with brutality and violence: "Soleil cou coupé." African primitivism slaughters Greco-Roman pastoralism.

By the end of "Zone," Apollinaire's despair is complete. With prostitutes and alcohol unable to help him, he withdraws into the darkest regions of himself, where his primitive instincts and impulses lie, and from this mysterious, irrational part of the self he destroys the universe. His assassination of the rising sun is a symbolic murder of everything that exists outside of himself, which includes all men and God. Despair is the executioner, and in one slash of the knife, one blow of the axe, one fall of the guillotine, the poet is severed from the universe of the non-self, of the other. Hope, love, and faith lie bloody and mutilated on the block. All that remains after the decapitation is the dark desolate world of the self.

The assassination of the dawning sun tolls the end of hope and of love. Neither can exist in a world where misery and despair are, as Apollinaire has seen during his walk, so widespread. Of what good are the inventions and the hopeful promise of the twentieth century, if men are not made happier, if they continue to suffer from exile, hunger, poverty, and love? The future, according to the early *brouillon* of "Zone," will not bring greater fraternal love, but rather more suffering:

> Le soleil est là [avec sa tête coupée] c'est
>   un cou tranché
> Comme l'auront peut-être un jour quelques-uns des
>   pauvres que j'ai rencontrés [58]

But greater than the poet's denial of fraternal love is his rejection of divine love. The assassination of the sun signals the end of faith and the suppression of whatever intuitive religious feeling was in the poet. No salvation, hope, or love can come from or go to heaven because the lines of communication have been severed. The rays of light between sun and earth have been cut. Transcendence is at an end. Inherent, therefore, in the decapitation of the sun is the murder of Christ, the light of the world, whose "profondeur améthyste" is now amethyst with blood. [59]

---

[58] Décaudin, *Le Dossier*, p. 81.

[59] The image of a bloodied sun is found in a number of Apollinaire's poems and frequently associated with Christ:

> Le soleil ce jour-là s'étalait comme un ventre
> Maternel qui saignait lentement sur le ciel
>   ("Merlin et la vieille femme," *O. P.*, p. 88)

> En rentrant [ils] tourneront leurs faces au couchant
> Embaumé par les foins d'occidental cinname
> Au couchant où sanglant et rond comme mon âme
> Le grand soleil païen fait mourir en mourant
> Avec les bourgs lointains le Christ indifférent
>   ("Passion," *Le Guetteur mélancolique*, *O. P.*, p. 532)

> Pourtant par tes vitraux chaque couchant tu saignes
> Jusqu'au Rhin ivre d'or et sous le vent fréquent
> Le sang du Christ-soleil et du bon pélican
>   ("Le Dôme de Cologne," *Le Guetteur mélancolique*,
>   *O. P.*, p. 538)

The "Soleil cou coupé" is also an image of decollation, of which there are many in *Alcools*: "O chef de morte O vieil ivoire Orbites Trous / Des narines

The final image of "Zone," which is a striking example of Apollinaire's use of surprise, has a chilling effect that is heightened by the abruptness of the line. By concentrating so much violence into so few words, only five syllables, the brutality of the image becomes more savage, the massacre more complete. There is also a grim, macabre suggestion of dripping blood in the alliteration of hard *c* sounds and in the repetition of "cou" in "*coupé*." In the image of the decapitated sun, moreover, there is a free association, a "jump," between the elements that create the image, between the sun ("Soleil") and the slit throat ("cou coupé"). This dislocation is an example of poetic montage, and it resembles in form a famous sequence of shots at the beginning of Salvador Dalí's and Louis Buñuel's surrealist film, Un Chien andalou (1928). The film shows a young girl's eyes being held open by two fingers of a hand. The camera closes in on the eye, as a razor approaches the eyeball. The razor slits the eyeball in two, and abruptly the film switches to a shot of the moon surrounded by clouds. The jerk with which the camera switches from the slit eye to the moon corresponds to the abrupt shift in "Zone" from the sun to the slit throat.

The decollation of the sun in "Zone" recalls the decapitation of St. John the Baptist in Mallarmé's Cantique de Saint Jean and anticipates the brutal, dislocated images of the surrealists. Unlike the *Cantique*, however, there is no suggestion of salvation in Apollinaire's act of decapitation. Rather, it represents the power of destruction that the irrational forces within the self possess when they are freed from the control of the intellect. In this respect, the image prefigures the surrealists' attempt to transform the world through the liberation of the imagination and the subconscious.

If, as the poet Wallace Stevens remarked, "the poem is the cry of its occasion," [60] then two cries rend the air in "Zone." One, the cry of hope and of jubilant joy, celebrates the birth of the twentieth century in a voice that evokes the groaning of factory sirens ("la sirène y gémit"), the twittering of street posters ("Les plaques les avis à la

---

rongées..." ("L'Ermite," *O. P.*, p. 100); "Les têtes coupées qui m'acclament / Et les astres qui ont saigné / Ne sont que des têtes de femmes" ("Le Brasier," *O. P.*, p. 108); "Pendez vos têtes aux patères par les tresses" ("Palais," *O. P.*, p. 62); "Il vit décapité sa tête est le soleil / Et la lune son cou tranché" ("Les Fiançailles," *O. P.*, p. 133).

[60] "An Ordinary Evening in New Haven," *Collected Poems*, p. 473.

façon des perroquets criaillent"), the whirr of plane engines, the barking of clocks ("une cloche rageuse y aboie"), and the honking of car horns. The other, the cry of despair and despondency, mourns the death of love in a voice that cries out with sobs of self-pity, with peals of mocking laughter, with groans of disgust and with the terrifying swish and chop of the guillotine.

CHAPTER VI

SONG: THE CATHARSIS OF SELF

In 1903, at the "Soleil d'or," a café on the Place Saint-Michel, the literary review *La Plume* resumed its series of Saturday evening gatherings, known as "Les Soirées de *La Plume*," which had been suspended for several years.[1] Here, both renowned and neophyte poets read their works to the acclaim or derision of such awesome literary figures of the day as Stuart Merrill, René Ghil, Paul Fort, Charles Henry Hirsch, and Alfred Jarry.[2] At one such gathering in April Guillaume Apollinaire made his literary début.

Introduced by the chairman of the meeting, Apollinaire rose with dignity, removed a pipe from his mouth, and with a somber, almost angry, expression walked determinedly to the piano at the front of the room, where he began to recite the lines of his Rhenish poem, "Schinderhannes," in a voice that was both cavernous and tense.[3] Filling the already colorful lines with the magnetic charm of his personality, Apollinaire read this "German" poem with the histrionic skill of a Latin, lingering on the sound of a word here, chanting certain words there, whispering, shouting, declaiming.[4] His performance was magnificent and the applause that followed was immediate and furious. Encouraged by such an enthusiastic reaction Apollinaire read a second poem, "L'Ermite," which once again brought the house

---

[1] Adéma, p. 63.
[2] Margaret Davies, *Apollinaire* (New York: St. Martin's Press, 1964), pp. 89-90.
[3] André Salmon, *Souvenirs sans fin*, I (Paris: Gallimard, 1955), p. 53.
[4] *Ibid.*

down.[5] Immediately following his performance André Salmon and Jean Mollet, two young poets who had heard the poems and had applauded wildly, rushed up to congratulate Apollinaire, and thus began a long and fruitful friendship.[6] In November of the same year, with their collaboration and after months of hard work and planning, Apollinaire founded a new literary review, *Le Festin d'Esope*.[7] Yet, in the midst of this burgeoning literary activity Apollinaire suddenly decided to leave Paris and visit the English governess with whom he had fallen in love more than a year and a half earlier, and whose memory still haunted him. His recent literary successes, one biographer has observed,[8] probably gave him that vital injection of confidence he needed in order to ask Annie Playden for her hand in marriage. But Apollinaire's visit to Annie in London in November 1903 was but a repetition of his love affair with her in Germany, for once again he frightened the prim Englishwoman with violent displays of rage and passion;[9] and once again, she rejected his entreaties and demands. Only now their already strained relationship was made worse by the presence of Annie's family, strict Anglicans who did not approve of their daughter associating with a Roman Catholic poet of uncertain birth.[10] Poor Annie, caught between her feeling for Apollinaire and her deep love for and devotion to her family,[11] was at a loss what to do with the unpredictable poet. The situation resolved itself, however, when at the end of the month Apollinaire departed from London. On his return to Paris he began to compose one of his greatest and most beautiful poems, "La Chanson du Mal-Aimé."[12] For Apollinaire, then, 1903 was a year of literary triumph and amorous defeat.

But on the field of love Apollinaire would not surrender. In May 1904 he made a second trip to London, this time to insist that Annie marry him. The Playdens refused him entrance, and one time when they tried to close the door in his face, Apollinaire attempted phys-

---

[5] *Ibid.*, p. 54.
[6] Davies, p. 91.
[7] *Ibid.*, pp. 92-99.
[8] *Ibid.*, p. 100.
[9] " 'Nous [Annie and her family] vivions dans une peur constante de ses accès de rage' " (Breunig, "Apollinaire et Annie," p. 650).
[10] Davies, p. 101.
[11] *Ibid.*
[12] First published in the *Mercure de France*, no. 285 (1er mai, 1909).

ically to force his way in, uttering threats of physical violence which terrified them all.[13] Apollinaire was becoming so embarrassing a nuisance that finally, as Annie Playden told Leroy Breunig, " 'je lui dis que je devais partir pour l'Amérique où un fiancé m'attendait. C'était la seule façon de me débarrasser de lui.' "[14] The next day, through an employment agency, she found a job as a governess in the United States and ten days later departed from London. The *mal-aimé* would never see her again.

"La Chanson du Mal-Aimé" (O. P., pp. 46-59) is a composite poem, what M. Décaudin has called a "marquetterie [sic] de pièces et d'ensembles."[15] Although Apollinaire dated it from 1903, after his first trip to London in November of that year, the accepted hypothesis today is that he made changes following his second and final visit to Annie in May 1904.[16] The poem appears to support this theory. It opens with a foggy, autumnal London evening and ends with a sunny June day in Paris. "La Chanson" is also composed of distinct sections or interludes that appear to have been written at earlier periods. The first interlude, for example, with its own title, "Aubade," probably dates from Apollinaire's stay in Germany, when his love for Annie was at its peak; the second interlude, entitled, "Réponse des Cosaques Zaporogues au Sultan de Constantinople," existe as a separate *brouillon* in the Jacques Doucet collection, suggesting that it too was written at an earlier time.[17] Yet, despite these fragments, which are skillfully pieced together like a beautiful mosaic, "La Chanson du Mal-Aimé" has an extraordinary unity, a lyric con-

---

[13] Davies, p. 102.

[14] Breunig, "Apollinaire et Annie," p. 650.

[15] *Le Dossier*, p. 100.

[16] M. Décaudin believes that "La Chanson" was composed in its initial movement after Apollinaire's first trip to London and that "elle se présente dès ce moment comme un tout achevé" (*Ibid.*). In June, Apollinaire "la compléta par quelques additions d'un ton plus mélancolique qui n'en modifièrent pas la texture" (*Ibid.*). Mr. Breunig is in agreement, although he doubts that Apollinaire wrote the poem "d'une seule haleine continue," considering it rather as "un enchaînement de plusieurs chansons octosyllabiques, écrites à des moments différents mais adroitement réunies en un tout" (L. C. Breunig, "Le Roman du Mal-Aimé," *La Table Ronde*, LVII [septembre, 1952], p. 117).

[17] Breunig, "Le Roman," p. 118. Other stanzas also appear to have been composed separately, according to Mr. Breunig, especially stanzas 6-9, concerning Ulysses and the husband of Sacontale, and stanzas 51-54, which describe the insanity of King Louis of Baveria (pp. 118-119).

tinuity created by the endless song of lamentation that flows from the poet's wounded self.

The poem also has a unity of structure.[18] From beginning to end it is constructed of rhymed and assonanced octosyllabic quintains. Moreover, as Mr. Breunig has observed, "La Chanson" is characterized by an unusual degree of parallelism between its opening (1-5) and closing (55-59) stanzas.[19] But most striking of all is the alternation throughout "La Chanson" between *dramatization* and *confession*. Passages where the self, hidden behind the masks of *personae*, speaks through the voices of others alternate with passages where the self discarding its disguises, speaks frankly and unashamedly with its own sad voice. Sometimes the self appears costumed and shielded; other times, it is naked and vulnerable. In "La Chanson du Mal-Aimé" dramatization and confession both serve as techniques of self-scrutiny.

Dramatization places the self in a dramatic situation where it is masked and disguised so that it is no longer recognizable as self but as the other; in this manner, the poet can better contemplate himself. The most obvious examples of this kind of self-dramatization in "La Chanson" are the three interludes, which are distinguished from the rest of the poem by their separate titles and by the Roman type in which they are printed (the rest of the poem being in italics). Each interlude dramatizes a different aspect of Apollinaire's self. In "Aubade," for example, his memory is dramatized in the form of a medieval lyric; in "Réponse des Cosaques Zaporogues au Sultan de Constantinople" his anger and frustration are subtly expressed through dramatic *personae*; and in the final interlude, "Les Sept Epées," intimate aspects of his love affair with Annie are concealed in hermetic symbols. Such dramatizations contain hidden confessions. Yet,

---

[18] "... si Apollinaire, après ses retours de Londres, souffrait tout le desespoir d'un mal-aimé il n'en restait pas moins artiste conscient et maître-maçon accompli, et *la Chanson* possède une unité de structure et une symétrie d'autant plus agréable qu'elle n'est ni trop froidement mathématique ni conçue selon un ordre préétabli" (*Ibid.*, p. 119).

[19] "... deux villes, deux saisons; d'une part le 'brouillard sanguinolent' de Londres, d'autre part le 'soleil ardente lyre' de Paris. Dans les deux cas c'est la rue qui se déroule, c'est le petit peuple de la rue qui passe devant les yeux du poète solitaire. Mais dans ces cadres parallèles quelle différence d'atmosphère et quelle progression depuis le début jusqu'à la fin!" And of the final stanzas Mr. Breunig writes: "On voit bien qu'Apollinaire, s'il n'a suivi aucun plan préalablement arrêté, a sûrement composé ce chapitre final en se rappelant les détails précis de son introduction" (*Ibid.*).

dramatization is not limited to the interludes alone. Dramatic episodes, such as the opening and closing scenes in London and Paris, and the episodes describing the "rois heureux" (sts. 6-7) and the "Rois secoués par la folie" (sts. 51-54), are also woven into those parts of the poem that are confessions. [20]

While the dramatizations externalize the drama of self by using *personae* and narration, the confessions externalize it through song, in such lyric forms as the elegy and the plaint. The barriers between the inner world of the self and the outer world crumble under the pressure of the poet's sadness. The dam collapses and the self flows out in a flood of lamentation and melancholy. [21] The poet's *moi*, un-

---

[20] In the finest, most exhaustive study to date of "La Chanson du Mal-Aimé" (*"La Chanson du Mal-Aimé" d'Apollinaire: essai d'analyse structurale et stylistique* ["Bibliothèque des lettres modernes," vol. XVIII; Paris: Minard, 1970]), Mme Claude Morhange-Bégué gives a penetrating, stanza by stanza, analysis of the structures which inform the poem, and in so doing, reveals the complex system of *liaison* and *rupture* which characterizes "La Chanson." The alternation between dramatization and confession which I discuss is treated in a different way by Mme Morhange-Bégué. For a discussion of the deep structures inherent in "La Chanson," see pp. 19-21, 233-34, 246-47, 268-70, 285, 289-93, *et passim*. For an analysis of the patterns of liaison and interruption which operate on both thematic and structural levels to join and divide various parts of the poem, see pp. 20, 54-6, 125, 151, 201, 208, 210, 264, 274-75, 278-79, 285-93, *et passim*.

[21] The quality of liquid expansiveness, which in "La Chanson du Mal-Aimé" is caused by sadness, is common to the nature of Apollinaire's self, although it is often the product of an overflowing joy or ecstasy inspired by the desire to become one with the universe, as in the war poem "Chant de l'Horizon en Champagne" (*Calligrammes*). Apollinaire sees himself and the horizon as one; he has become all the space between himself and the farthest point of the horizon: "Moi l'horizon invisible je chante" (*O. P.*, p. 265). He perceives himself as flooding the entire landscape:

> Je suis l'invisible qui ne peut disparaître
> Je suis comme l'onde
> Allons ouvrez les écluses que je me précipite et renverse
>   tout   (*O. P.*, p. 267)

The same expansive, horizontal flowing is evident in another war poem, "Merveille de la guerre" (*Calligrammes*):

> Mais j'ai coulé dans la douceur de cette guerre avec toute
>   ma compagnie au long des longs boyaux
> Quelques cris de flamme annoncent sans cesse ma présence
> J'ai creusé le lit où je coule en me ramifiant en mille
>   petits fleuves qui vont partout
> Je suis dans la tranchée de première ligne et cependant
>   je suis partout ou plutôt je commence à être partout
>   (*O. P.*, p. 272)

masked and naked, reveals its contradictory feelings and confesses its secrets. Its confessions are filled with unconstrained spontaneity and candor; it speaks without the help of an intermediary. But, there are some things which the self cannot bring itself to reveal directly, so these are uttered by *personae* in the dramatized passages. In "La Chanson du Mal-Aimé," therefore, the poet's *moi*, like a pendulum, swings back and forth from self-confession to self-dramatization.

One of the interesting features of "La Chanson du Mal-Aimé" is the occurrence of *dédoublement,* the splitting or division of things into two. Throughout the poem doubles appear, as if to testify to the truth of the poet's assertion: "Douleur qui doubles les destins." Images of shadow, the body's double, and of the couple (Penelope and Ulysses, Mars and Venus, Mausolus and his wife) occur frequently. Even an element of hermaphroditism creeps in. The *personae* and the dramatized episodes of the poem are described mostly in terms of two's: there is the poet and the *voyou* he follows, Pharaoh and the Hebrews, the Cossacks and the Sultan, Luitpold and Louis, happy kings and insane kings, London and Paris, winter and spring, fog and sun. One finds, moreover, a dialectic between certain ideas: acceptance or rejection of memory, sincere or false love, paganism or Christianity. Stylistically, *dédoublement* also plays a role, although a minor one, in the poem: the meaning of words is doubled by the use of erudite synonyms;[22] words are invented by joining two synonyms together;[23] sounds are doubled by repetition.[24]

Nothing appears therefore in "La Chanson" that does not also cast its own shadow. In the uninhibited, cathartic flow of self, ego and alter ego, selves and their contraries, all pour out. The struggle between contradictory selves moves from the battleground of the self

---

[22] For example, "pyraustes" and "feux follets," "satyres" and "égypans," "damnés" and "faustes" in stanza 33 (see below, pp. 193-94); "argyraspides" and "boucliers d'argent," "dendrophores" and "printemps" in stanza 39 (see below, pp. 195-96).

[23] For example, the name of the first sword in "Les Sept Epées" is "Pâline," a word composed of *pâle* and *câline* (James Lawler, "Les Sept Epées," *Le Flâneur des deux Rives. Bulletin d'études apollinariennes,* no. 3 [septembre, 1954], p. 11). The name of the third sword is "Lul de Faltenin," composed of the words *Lul* and *Faltenin,* both of which refer to the male sexual organ (Décaudin, *Le Dossier,* p. 161). In the same stanza is found the word, "chibriape," forged by Apollinaire from the words *chibre* and *priape* (Lawler, p. 12) (see below, pp. 198ff).

[24] "...un cul de *dame dama*scène" (st. 40).

to the poem. Here, carried along by the continuous river of song and melancholy, they often collide in midstream. The poem is filled with the bumps and shocks of these colliding selves; yet, such collisions never block the flow of the river nor disrupt the music of the poem.

The opening stanzas of "La Chanson du Mal-Aimé" recall the narrative form of medieval *chansons* and suggest the diffused light and shadow of Monet's paintings of London:

> *Un soir de demi-brume à Londres*
> *Un voyou qui ressemblait à*
> *Mon amour vint à ma rencontre*
> *Et le regard qu'il me jeta*
> *Me fit baisser les yeux de honte* (st. 1)

In the unsettled evening atmosphere the poet encounters a flesh and blood image of himself in the form of a *voyou*.[25] This young teddy boy incarnates a destructive aspect of the poet's amorous self, one that fills the poet with shame (l. 5) because it reminds him, perhaps, of that uncontrollable behavior which his passion for Annie has caused. He can no more control his actions than he can his passion, and what is particularly difficult for Apollinaire to acknowledge is that both his behavior and his love have been colored, tainted even, by a feeling of deep humiliation. He can not look at an image of himself or an image of his love, namely the *voyou*, without painfully cringing and casting his eyes down to the ground. And yet, the ambivalence Apollinaire feels towards himself and towards his love, the conflict in him between burning passion on the one hand and frustrated desire on the other, which makes him lose self-control thus causing him to humiliate himself, is reflected in his fascination with the *voyou*, whom he follows:

---

[25] Wallace Fowlie also identifies this *voyou* with Apollinaire (p. 92), for he sees the *voyou* as the brother and soul mate of all poets:

> The voyou has a brother who never remains very far away from him. This brother is called at times clown or acrobat or fool. Once he was called a juggler. He has even been called by the polite name of Harlequin. And from time to time fate lends him the pretentious name of poet.

(*Love in Literature. Studies in Symbolic Expression* [Bloomington: Indiana University Press, 1965], p. 80)

> *Je suivis ce mauvais garçon*
> *Qui sifflotait mains dans les poches*
> *Nous semblions entre les maisons*
> *Onde ouverte de la mer Rouge*
> *Lui les Hébreux moi Pharaon* (2)

But as the poet follows his indifferent and nonchalant guide through the misty inferno of London, the city changes appearance. What began as a foggy London evening quickly expands into a surrealistic scene, where time and space are fluid and the poet's self amorphous (ll. 3-5). The street becomes the parted Red Sea (l. 4), and the flight from Egypt is suddenly reenacted. Reality is expanded in a manner reminiscent of Baudelaire's "Les Sept Vieillards."[26] The self is no longer just the prosaic *je* of everyday experience but the legendary Pharaoh of Biblical times, and the *voyou* has become one of the children of Israel. With this expansion of reality come two new masks for the self to wear: that of Pharaoh, the tyrannical ruler of Egypt, and that of the Hebrews, a people in frantic flight. The poet's self therefore is represented as both persecutor and persecuted, as "la victime et le bourreau,"[27] a *dédoublement* of self that covertly dramatizes Apollinaire's attitude toward his love affair with Annie. He sees himself as the victim of her puritanical upbringing, suffering from her aloofness and repeated refusals; but he also sees himself as her tormentor, frightening her with outbursts of jealousy and rage and with threats of physical violence. It is this monster, lying deep within himself and exteriorized in the *voyou*, that makes the poet lower his eyes with shame.

The poet now swears to the beloved, at the risk of his own life if he is lying, that he has loved her sincerely:

---

[26] Baudelaire's poem has other affinities with the beginning of "La Chanson." It too opens with a foggy city street, lined with houses that are like banks of a river:

> Un matin, cependant que dans la triste rue
> Les maisons, dont la brume allongeait la hauteur,
> Simulaient les deux quais d'une rivière accrue,
> Et que, décor semblable à l'âme de l'acteur,
>
> Un brouillard sale et jaune inondait tout l'espace,
> Je suivais, roidissant mes nerfs comme un héros
> Et discutant avec mon âme déjà lasse,
> Le faubourg secoué par les lourds tombereaux.
>
> (*Œuvres complètes*, p. 83)

[27] Baudelaire, "L'Héautontimorouménos," *Œuvres complètes*, p. 74.

SONG: THE CATHARSIS OF SELF

> *Que tombent ces vagues de briques*
> *Si tu ne fus pas bien aimée*
> *Je suis le souverain d'Egypte*
> *Sa sœur-épouse son armée*
> *Si tu n'es pas l'amour unique* (3)

After using the subjunctive in the first two lines, one critic has observed,[28] the poet changes to the present, thus making his avowal of love more striking by replacing a hypothetical event with its reality, and acting as if the bricks were already falling on him.

As the fog thickens to almost the consistency of blood, the poet meets another of society's rejects:

> *Au tournant d'une rue brûlant*
> *De tous les feux de ses façades*
> *Plaies du brouillard sanguinolent*
> *Où se lamentaient les façades*
> *Une femme lui ressemblant* (4)

> *C'était son regard d'inhumaine*
> *La cicatrice à son cou nu*
> *Sortit saoule d'une taverne*
> *Au moment où je reconnus*
> *La fausseté de l'amour même* (5)

The red brick buildings that line the street appear to weep and to sweat blood in the humid and moist, evening air (l. 4), thus giving the fog its reddish tint.[29] The theme of the Exodus from Egypt continues in the allusion to the ten plagues ("Plaies") visited upon Pharaoh and his people. But the word also refers to wounds, openings in the skin, from which blood pours freely. It suggests not only personal suffering, the poet's, but collective suffering as well, that of

---

[28] Maurice Piron, "Sur quelques passages de *La Chanson du Mal-Aimé*," *R. L. M.*, nos. 85-89 (automne, 1963), p. 92.

[29] Mallarmé, during his visit to London, also observed how the fog appeared to make bricks bleed:

> A travers l'humidité lumineuse, inséparable même d'une matinée d'été, à Londres, voyez se détacher, à droite, à gauche, au fond surtout, *de vastes panneaux d'une brique sanguine et vivante* et des arêtes d'édifice, à la fois imprégnées de vapeur et resplendissantes.... [italics mine]
>
> ("Exposition de Londres," *Œuvres complètes*, p. 681)

the Egyptians and Hebrews. By associating his pain with theirs Apollinaire magnifies and perhaps exaggerates the effect of his own misfortune.

The London street has become a fog enshrouded Red Sea. Light from windows ("les feux de ses façades") pours out and penetrates the fog ("brouillard sanguinolent") like blood pouring from an open wound ("Plaies"). But another sort of wound is suggested, namely that experienced by the poet's ego. Out of this wound the poet's liquefying self flows and mixes with the diffuse forms of the fog. The barriers between the outer world of the city and the inner world of the self are penetrated; inscape becomes landscape. The self flows over the objects of the street, imprinting each with its mark, like a shadow darkening whatever falls in its path.

Since the reddish fog that rolls over the London street is filled with uncertain forms and diffuse shapes, it is a highly concentrated form of the shadow, an image that occurs frequently in "La Chanson du Mal-Aimé." As the faithful companion, always no more than two or three feet away, the shadow is an externalized form of the self, a twin created by the self for life in the outer world. A double like the shadow allows the self to be both inside and outside itself at the same time. As the objectified and externalized form of the self, the shadow creates the distance necessary for self-contemplation and self-knowledge. Thus, when it looks at the shadow, the self contemplates a form of itself disguised as the other. In Apollinaire's poem, the shadow functions as a metaphor for the fragmentation and exteriorization of the self.

Apollinaire's attitude toward his shadow resembles certain magical beliefs, still strongly held to this day by different peoples the world over, which regard a person's shadow as his soul. It is believed, for example, that if a man's shadow is struck, trampled, or stabbed, injury will surely come to him or that if his shadow is detached from him, he will certainly die soon afterwards. In Lower Austria, on the last day of the year, a group of men would customarily seat themselves around a table and mark whose shadow was not cast on the wall, believing that the shadowless person would die within the next year.[30]

---

[30] Sir James George Frazer, *The New Golden Bough. A New Abridgment of the Classic Work*, ed. by Theodor H. Gaster (New York: Criterion Books, 1959), p. 158.

Similarly, Apollinaire believes that the shadow is an integral part of a man and that its loss or diminution signals the automatic loss of selfhood. In "Les Fiançailles," for example, he is not willing to sacrifice it for anything in the world:

> J'ai tout donné au soleil
> Tout sauf mon ombre
> (*O. P.*, p. 135)

The shadow can be regarded as a somewhat diffuse, undifferentiated form of the mirror image. Like a reflection in a mirror or on the surface of water, a shadow owes its existence to light. It is the reflection of an object, expressed through the medium of light. Unlike a mirror image, however, the shadow is a dark, undifferentiated mass that does not render a sharp, clear image of the thing it reflects but instead reveals only the object's outlines and contours.

A shadow, moreover, can be seen as the self spatialized. It is projected onto the ground, and, wherever it lands, it takes possession in the name of the self. In this manner, the inner self extends its empire over the outside world; it infiltrates and darkens the universe. In many ways, the shadow becomes a signature of the self that is projected onto a space, a kind of writing very much like the words and the images of self that Apollinaire projects onto the screen of his poems, onto the white page of paper; in a poem addressed to his shadow ("Ombre," *Calligrammes*) Apollinaire writes:

> Ombre encre du soleil
> Ecriture de ma lumière
> (*O. P.*, p. 217)

And in the poem "La Victoire" (*Calligrammes*) he identifies his shadow with his poetic voice:

> Ma voix fidèle comme l'ombre
> Veut être enfin l'ombre de la vie
> (*O. P.*, p. 311)

The shadow, therefore, is conceived of as being related to the two instruments of poetic expression — the word and the sound — and to the two acts of poetic creation — writing and singing — which are responsible for the expression and the definition of Apollinaire's self.

The shadow, then, is an important image in Apollinaire's poetry.[31] In "La Chanson du Mal-Aimé" it is the central image of the *dédoublement* which makes for the series of pairs and of couples found in the poem. For example, the shadow of the poet's beloved and the shadow of a drunk woman are joined in one stanza to represent the degrading falseness of love:

> *J'ai pensé à ces rois heureux*
> *Lorsque le faux amour et celle*
> *Dont je suis encore amoureux*
> *Heurtant leurs ombres infidèles*
> *Me rendirent si malheureux* (8)

and in another passage of the poem Apollinaire addresses his shadow lying but a few feet away:

> *Et toi qui me suis en rampant*
> *Dieu de mes dieux morts en automne*
> *Tu mesures combien d'empans*
> *J'ai le droit que la terre me donne*
> *O mon ombre ô mon vieux serpent* (36)

> *Au soleil parce que tu l'aimes*
> *Je t'ai menée souviens-t'en bien*
> *Ténébreuse épouse que j'aime*
> *Tu es à moi en n'étant rien*
> *O mon ombre en deuil de moi-même* (37)

The shadow is a god, the last in which the poet can believe now that all his other beliefs, especially his faith in love ("dieux morts en automne"), have died. As his sole-surviving companion, it crawls along the ground measuring out his future grave (ll. 3-4). The empire claimed by the shadow is small indeed, for it is measured in "empans,"

---

[31] It occurs in a great number of poems; for example, in "Merlin et la vieille femme": "Qu'il monte de la fange ou soit une ombre d'homme" (*O. P.*, p. 89); in "Signe": "Une épouse me suit c'est mon ombre fatale" (*O. P.*, p. 125); in "Crépuscule": "Frôlée par les ombres des morts" (*O. P.*, p. 64); in "Le Larron": "L'ombre équivoque et tendre est le deuil de ta chair/Et sombre elle est humaine et puis la nôtre aussi" (*O. P.*, p. 94); in "Clotilde": "Il y vient aussi nos ombres/Que la nuit dissipera/Le soleil qui les rend sombres/Avec elles disparaîtra" (*O. P.*, p. 73); and in "Cortège": "Et je m'éloignerai m'illuminant au milieu d'ombres" (*O. P.*, p. 74), to name only a very few.

the distance between the thumb and little finger of a stretched hand. Yet, this faithful partner is also an alter ego ("Ténébreuse épouse"), an image of the dark, primitive, and destructive self represented earlier by the *voyou*.

Apollinaire's shadow is distinguished by its duality. It is lover both of the sun (l. 6) and of darkness ("Ténébreuse"). Although it belongs to the poet ("Tu es à moi") it is not a substance that he can hold, feel, touch, or love ("en n'étant rien"). It is a silent companion to his suffering, a mute witness unable to give either aid or comfort. In representing the shadow as both his wife ("épouse") and widow ("en deuil de moi-même") the poet underlines the paradoxical relationship between shadow and self. At any moment they are simultaneously united and separated, self and other, visible and invisible, within and without. Yet, a shadow, by definition, is created from the union of two contradictory things, light and matter. Thus, when the poet refers to it as both his "vieux serpent," crawling along the ground, and his "Ténébreuse épouse," joined inseparably to him — in other words as both male and female — he acknowledges not only the contradictory nature of the shadow, but its androgynous nature as well.

The hermaphroditic shadow represents the double sex of the self, in which male and female selves live in coexistence. Therefore, it is not surprising in "La Chanson du Mal-Aimé" to find Apollinaire's self playing both male and female parts. In one passage it becomes the wife of king Mausolus (st. 20), lamenting her husband's death; in another, it wears the costumes of both the Pharaoh and the queen of Egypt: "Je suis le souverain d'Egypte/Sa sœur-épouse son armée" (st. 3).

In the midst of this landscape of fog and shadow, as he watches a scarred, drunken woman, whose cruel and inhuman face resembles the beloved's, the poet becomes painfully aware of the falsity of love (st. 5). Suddenly, the London street disappears, and the poet thinks of happy kings who have enjoyed the devotion and fidelity of their wives:

> *Lorsqu'il fut de retour enfin*
> *Dans sa patrie le sage Ulysse*
> *Son vieux chien de lui se souvint*
> *Près d'un tapis de haute lisse*
> *Sa femme attendait qu'il revînt* (6)

> L'époux royal de Sacontale
> Las de vaincre se réjouit
> Quand il la retrouva plus pâle
> D'attente et d'amour yeux pâlis
> Caressant sa gazelle mâle (7)

A second dramatization here replaces the earlier dramatic episodes of the poet's encounter with the *voyou* and the drunk woman. Both dramatizations resemble two paintings hung side by side, one tableau depicting the falseness of love, the other illustrating the sincerity of love. Apollinaire dreams of a situation he had hoped would materialize between himself and the beloved. Ulysses and Doushmanta, the husband of Sacontale, are *personae*, who incarnate an aspect of the poet's self which longs to be the object of female devotion. But the poet also identifies with Penelope's loneliness, as she faithfully awaits the return of her spouse, and, above all, with Sacontale, who after being rejected by her husband, who had lost his memory, devotedly waited until he remembered her and took her back. As they had hoped to see their loved ones again, so the poet hopes to see his beloved; later in the poem he remarks: "Si jamais revient cette femme / Je lui dirai Je suis content" (st. 30). In his dramatization of what he calls the example of "ces rois heureux," Apollinaire's hermaphroditic self plays both male and female parts, both Ulysses and Penelope, Doushmanta and Sacontale: the proud, triumphant, inconstant loved one and the lonely, faithful, abandoned lover.

But this tableau is only a fleeting thought, a digression that only sharpens the cutting edge of the poet's suffering:

> J'ai pensé à ces rois heureux
> Lorsque le faux amour et celle
> Dont je suis encore amoureux
> Heurtant leurs ombres infidèles
> Me rendirent si malheureux (8)

The shadow of the beloved mingles with that of the drunken woman and is degraded. The final word of the strophe, "malheureux," is the first direct statement of feeling the poet has made; until now his unhappiness has been expressed indirectly through the *personae* of the poem. The stanza serves, then, as a bridge between the two dramatizations that have preceded and the confession that follows:

SONG: THE CATHARSIS OF SELF

> *Regrets sur quoi l'enfer se fonde*
> *Qu'un ciel d'oubli s'ouvre à mes vœux*
> *Pour son baiser les rois du monde*
> *Seraient morts les pauvres fameux*
> *Pour elle eussent vendu leur ombre*   (9)

> *J'ai hiverné dans mon passé*
> *Revienne le soleil de Pâques*
> *Pour chauffer un cœur plus glacé*
> *Que les quarante de Sébaste*
> *Moins que ma vie martyrisés*   (10)

Here, and throughout the poem, Apollinaire vacillates between remembrance of the past ("J'ai hiverné dans mon passé," "Je me souviens d'une autre année," "Je ne veux jamais l'oublier") and its rejection ("Qu'un ciel d'oubli s'ouvre," "Adieu faux amour"). Despite his efforts to forget, memory involuntarily returns, as when, after calling on Lethean skies to fall upon him, he remembers the beloved's kiss (st. 9). The poet then asks his memory if the time has not finally come to forget the past:

> *Mon beau navire ô ma mémoire*
> *Avons-nous assez navigué*
> *Dans une onde mauvaise à boire*
> *Avons-nous assez divagué*
> *De la belle aube au triste soir*   (11)

The poet's memory is a weary ship that has sailed and roamed the sea of the past ("De la belle aube au triste soir"), from the dawn of his love as described in "Aubade" to its sad twilight in London ("Un soir de demi-brume à Londres," st. 1) and in Paris ("Soirs de Paris ivres de gin," st. 57). But the sea of the past is filled with poisonous water ("une onde mauvaise à boire"). The word, "divagué," therefore, although it refers to the roaming of the ship, alludes also to the harmful effects that can come from a lengthy voyage into the past. "Divagué" suggests the rambling and roving of a drunk or of a madman, whose incoherent mind rambles from one thing to another. It implies that drinking the waters of the past may poison the poet, making him rave, talk nonsense, and perhaps even go mad.[32]

---

[32] The image of the past as a poisonous sea parallels the theme in Apollinaire's poetry of love as a slow-working poison:

The poet bids farewell to false love and to the beloved who has become confused with it:

> Adieu faux amour confondu
> Avec la femme qui s'éloigne
> Avec celle que j'ai perdue
> L'année dernière en Allemagne
> Et que je ne reverrai plus   (12)

Then, in a beautiful and melodious refrain that appears three times in the poem, he questions the stars about his future destiny:

> Voie lactée ô sœur lumineuse
> Des blancs ruisseaux de Chanaan
> Et des corps blancs des amoureuses
> Nageurs morts suivrons-nous d'ahan
> Ton cours vers d'autres nébuleuses   (13)

In the first three lines a feeling of satisfaction, plenitude, and refreshment dominates. The words convey this feeling in liquid *l*, luxurious *euses*, and long, rich, nasal sounds. The Milky Way, Chanaan, and the female bodies are described as sisters ("sœur"), and they appear to flow from the same milk-white source and to permeate the universe with their liquid purity. Cool, luminescent light emanates from the Milky Way, a galaxy of swirling stars. Milk and honey course through the streams ("ruisseaux") of the Promised Land. Sinuous, white bodies of goddess lovers ("amoureuses") invite their partners to the sexual embrace that is the flowing together of two bodies. The opening lines of this stanza, filled with the flow of stars, rivers, and bodies, represent three levels of experience, all of which are Edenic, for they calm, refresh, and renew the participants; they are mystical, or dream, experience ("Voie lactée"), religious experience ("Chanaan"), and sexual experience ("amoureuses").

Since the Milky Way, Chanaan, and the flesh of loving women are described as being fluid, the swimmer, by means of the coordinated

> Le pré est vénéneux mais joli en automne
> Les vaches y paissant
> Lentement s'empoisonnent
> Le colchique couleur de cerne et de lilas
> Y fleurit tes yeux sont comme cette fleur-là
> Violâtres comme leur cerne et comme cette automne
> Et ma vie pour tes yeux lentement s'empoisonne
>   ("Les Colchiques," *O. P.*, p. 60)

and harmonious movements of his body, can experience each one of them. His grace and fluidity make him a perfect symbol for the Edenic participant. But the swimmers in the poem, of which the poet is one, are dead ("Nageurs morts") or near death with exhaustion ("d'ahan"). Unable to propel themselves through the water, they float like dead bodies. Too exhausted to control their direction, they are pulled along by a strong current ("Ton cours"), while wondering to what future unknown experiences they may be destined ("suivrons-nous d'ahan/Ton cours vers d'autres nébuleuses"). In contrast to the beginning of the stanza, the last two lines are filled with an air of emptiness, sterility, and uncertainty. The swimmers appear to have been exiled from paradise, and now destiny pulls them where it will. Since the Milky Way is the only galaxy in the solar system, the poet asks whether it will drag him out of the universe toward other nebulae? The poet has no choice but to let himself be pulled by what he later, near the end of the poem, calls, "Destins destins impénétrables" (st. 51). The Milky Way represents the tide of destiny which flows irrevocably towards the future, and against which the strongest swimmer cannot swim.

The mysterious "Voie lactée" has yet another meaning. Many star images in *Alcools* refer to women. In "Le Brasier," for example, the poet describes a plain where,

> Les têtes coupées qui m'acclament
> Et les astres qui ont saigné
> Ne sont que des têtes de femmes
> (*O. P.*, p. 108)

and in "L'Ermite," the hermit looks at the sky and sees that a "squelette de femme innocente est pendu/A un long fil d'étoile..." (*O. P.*, p. 102). In "La Chanson du Mal-Aimé" the poet says of the beloved that,

> *Ses regards laissaient une traîne*
> *D'étoiles dans les soirs tremblants* (29)

and he describes the Milky Way as a "sœur lumineuse." The "Voie lactée" therefore, because it is a galaxy of many stars, is an image of concentrated femininity. Thus, when the poet asks his question, he desperately wants to know if, in those indistinct future nebulae toward which destiny is pulling him, he will find another woman, or if he has exhausted his share of love and will remain forever *le mal-aimé*.[33] Since, after their flight from Egypt and the long, painful journey across the desert, the Hebrews finally arrived at Chanaan, the poet wonders if he too, after his suffering, will be rewarded with milk, honey and the Promised Land of love. (Later in the poem he figuratively crosses this burning desert, when he experiences the "bûcher divin" of his own grief, and cries out, "Sur ma douleur quel holocauste," st. 33). Thus, the theme of the Exodus is a *leitmotiv* that expresses the poet's sad exile from love, and his fear that, like Moses, he may never again enter the Promised Land. In the "Voie lactée" strophe, therefore, it is the poet's question that stands out above all. In the two subsequent appearances of the refrain (sts. 27 and 49), however, other aspects will become important, for the meaning of the stanza changes with its position in the poem.[34]

The "Voie lactée" strophe is placed between a stanza bidding farewell to the past (st. 12) and one that recalls that past:

> *Je me souviens d'une autre année*
> *C'était l'aube d'un jour d'avril*
> *J'ai chanté ma joie bien-aimée*
> *Chanté l'amour à voix virile*
> *Au moment d'amour de l'année* (14)

This stanza introduces the "Aubade" interlude, and it constitutes the poet's reaction to what has just occurred in the preceding "Voie lactée" stanza. After facing the irrevocable fact that he will never see the beloved again (st. 12), the poet desperately interrogates the stars for a prophecy of the future (st. 13); and when the inscrutable skies do not answer, he returns to the past, taking the opium of memory to alleviate his pain and sorrow (st. 14).

The first interlude, entitled "Aubade chantée à Laetare un an passé" (sts. 15-17), evokes, therefore, "une autre année" (st. 14), a happy past when the poet sang of his love in a "voix virile" (st. 14). As a dramatization of a memory in the form of a pagan lyric, it

---

[33] This fear of not ever being loved again makes Apollinaire exclaim in "Zone": "L'angoisse de l'amour te serre le gosier/Comme si tu ne devais jamais plus être aimé" (*O. P.*, p. 41).

[34] See below, pp. 189, 204.

recalls the happiest moment of Apollinaire's love.[35] The beloved, referred to as "Pâquette," is invited by the poet to walk through a countryside overflowing with love and fertility:

> C'est le printemps viens-t'en Pâquette
> Te promener au bois joli
> Les poules dans la cour caquètent
> L'aube au ciel fait de roses plis
> L'amour chemine à ta conquête   (15)
>
> Mars et Vénus sont revenus
> Ils s'embrassent à bouches folles
> Devant des sites ingénus
> Où sous les roses qui feuillolent
> De beaux dieux roses dansent nus   (16)
>
> Viens ma tendresse est la régente
> De la floraison qui paraît
> La nature est belle et touchante
> Pan sifflote dans la forêt
> Les grenouilles humides chantent   (17)

As its title suggests, "Aubade" is a medieval lyric, sung on a Catholic holiday and expressing pagan joy. It combines three traditions: the medieval, since an *aubade* is a medieval song of greeting to the dawn; the pagan, for the poem is filled with the presence of the gods Mars, Venus, and Pan, and with allusions to erotic love, nudity, and the rebirth of spring; and the Christian, since "Laetare" is the name given to the mass of the fourth Sunday of Lent, which marks a brief moment of joy in the middle of the penitence of Lent. "Laetare," meaning "Rejoice ye," is the first word of the introit for the mass of this day ("Laetare Jerusalem"). During the service the celebrant and two deacons are dressed in rose vestments. And in keeping with the Laetare mass Apollinaire colors his poem rose; he describes the "roses plis" of a dawning sky and the naked "beaux dieux roses" who dance beneath the roses. However, the color "rose" in "Aubade" is without religious meaning. It refers to the pink flesh

---

[35] "Aubade" was probably composed around the time of Laetare Sunday of 1902, when Apollinaire and Annie were in Munich (Breunig, "Le Roman," p. 118). It forms, according to Apollinaire, "un intermède intercalé dans la *Chanson du Mal-Aimé*" (*Tendre comme le souvenir* [Paris: Gallimard, 1952], p. 70).

of the bodies of licentious gods and goddesses, and like the poet's joy, it is pagan. It is Eros, not Christ, that marches through the countryside ("L'amour chemine à ta conquête") to the whistling tune of the god Pan ("Pan sifflote dans la forêt"). "Aubade," according to one critic, celebrates "le triomphe du paganisme, sous le règne du dieu Pan." [36]

After the "Aubade" interlude and the joyful memory it resuscitates, Apollinaire returns to the unhappy present. Disconsolately, he mourns the death of all forms of love — erotic, courtly, and fraternal. The pagan, medieval, and Christian gods are all dead; Eros and Agape lie buried side by side along with Pan and Christ:

> *Beaucoup de ces dieux ont péri*
> *C'est sur eux que pleurent les saules*
> *Le grand Pan l'amour Jésus-Christ*
> *Sont bien morts et les chats miaulent*
> *Dans la cour je pleure à Paris* (18)

"La Chanson" again becomes a confession. The poet, abandoned by the gods of nature, love, and religion, weeps to the accompaniment of meowing cats, urban cries of lamentation that differ from the pastoral melancholy of the willows (l. 2). Dejection, moreover, has interfered with his ability to create poetry; rather than singing about his despair, turning it, that is, into poetry, he weeps about it. The proud self is disgraced by such behavior and exclaims in the strophe that follows:

> *Moi qui sais des lais pour les reines*
> *Les complaintes de mes années*
> *Des hymnes d'esclave aux murènes*
> *La romance du mal-aimé*
> *Et des chansons pour les sirènes* (19)

There is a striking contrast between the lachrymose ending of the previous stanza ("je pleure à Paris") and the loud affirmation of self that explodes in this one ("Moi qui sais"). The poet speaks of his considerable skill and knowledge in the art of creating poetry. He lists the repertoire of songs that his poetic self ("Moi qui sais") is able both to create and perform. The poetic talents of this self are formidable, and its orphic inventory is extensive, ranging from epic nar-

---

[36] Couffignal, *L'Inspiration biblique*, p. 83.

ratives ("romance") to shorter narratives ("lais"), from odes in praise of God, king, or country ("hymnes") to laments mourning one's ill-lived life ("complaintes de mes années"). The poetic self is a troubadour who performs before different audiences and who knows ("sais") the songs that each prefers. From queens to slaves, from seductive enchantresses ("sirènes") to a poorly loved man ("mal-aimé"), it knows how to create their favorite tunes. Its voices are many; few are the songs it cannot sing. An interesting work in its repertoire is the "hymnes d'esclave aux murènes." The allusion is to the Roman gastronomer, Vedius Pollion, who punished his servants by having them thrown into a tank of live carnivorous eels.[37] Their hymns, which the poet can imitate, are filled with the terror of a ghastly death.

While the stanza that preceded portrayed the self's anguish and desolation ("je pleure à Paris"), this strophe illustrates the poet's orphic power and skill. It overflows with the confidence of one who knows his craft well. But together both stanzas suggest a different meaning. The distinction between the weeping "je" (st. 18) and the creative "Moi" (st. 19) indicates the latter's disgrace at the former's behavior. The poet has lost the power of creation, and the poetic self, rather than boasting of its lyric feats, appears to be lamenting its sterile fate; it appears to be saying: "I, the poet, the creator, who know lays, plaints, hymns, and romances, I the song-maker, who once sang an *aubade* "à voix virile," and who know how to enchant the sirens, look at me now, weak, feeble, weeping, desperate, and useless." This stanza, like the "Voix lactée" refrain, is a *leitmotiv*. When it reappears as the final strophe of "La Chanson," it will be more affirmative and the poetic "Moi" will speak with more self-assurance, for by then the poet will have regained his poetic voice and his full poetic power.

Following the degradation of the poetic self, Apollinaire returns once again to the subject of his persistent faithfulness in love. Like

---

[37] Piron, p. 97. Hugo is another poet, M. Piron observes (*Ibid.*), who makes use of this classical allusion in "L'homme heureux" (*Odes*, IV, 8); it is probably from his poem that Apollinaire learned about it:

"Je m'ennuie au forum, je m'ennuie aux arènes;
    Je demande à tous: Que fait-on?
Je fais jeter par jour un esclave aux murènes,
    Et je m'amuse à peine à ce jeu de Caton."

the wife of Mausolus, who built a monument, one of the Seven Wonders of the world, to the memory of her husband, the poet has remained devoted to the memory of his beloved:

> L'amour est mort j'en suis tremblant
> J'adore de belles idoles
> Les souvenirs lui ressemblant
> Comme la femme de Mausole
> Je reste fidèle et dolent   (20)

Apollinaire then illustrates the intensity of his devotion and the extent of his attachment in stanzas that serve as an introduction to the poem's second interlude:

> Je suis fidèle comme un dogue
> Au maître le lierre au tronc
> Et les Cosaques Zaporogues
> Ivrognes pieux et larrons
> Aux steppes et au décalogue   (21)

> Portez comme un joug le Croissant
> Qu'interrogent les astrologues
> Je suis le Sultan tout-puissant
> O mes Cosaques Zaporogues
> Votre Seigneur éblouissant   (22)

> Devenez mes sujets fidèles
> Leur avait écrit le Sultan
> Ils rirent à cette nouvelle
> Et répondirent à l'instant
> A la lueur d'une chandelle   (23)

Apollinaire's allusion to the Zaporogian Cossacks merits a closer analysis. The Cossacks, a bellicose people of the Ukraine, were employed by Russian princes in the fifteenth century to colonize the Steppes and repulse Turkish and Tartar invasions.[38] Deeply attached to their land they refused all compromise with the invading Sultan of Constantinople, and it is this fierce devotion that Apollinaire dramatizes in the poem. The "Réponse" interlude was inspired in all probability by a series of paintings of the Cossacks composing a

---

[38] Georges Schmits, "Quelques strophes du 'Mal-Aimé,'" *Mercure de France*, CCCXXXVII (novembre, 1959), 538.

jeering reply to the Sultan, made famous at the end of the nineteenth century by the Russian painter, Repin (the most celebrated painting dates from 1891).[39] In these canvases the hilarious Cossacks are crowded around one of their number, who, by candlelight, composes the insolent answer. It seems quite probable that in the numerous readings of his youth Apollinaire may have come across a reproduction of Repin's painting and perhaps a copy of one of the counterfeit letters purported to be the Cossacks' reply.[40]

The Zaporogian Cossacks are a *persona* for the poet. Their rapport with Apollinaire goes as deep as his national identity, for these Cossacks are his slavic ancestors. On a personal level, their uncompromising fidelity to the land and to religion illustrates the poet's devotion to the woman he loves. But, as with most *personae* in the poem they are charged with ambivalence; in fact, they represent two contradictory aspects of the poet's self. As Apollinaire earlier in the poem played the roles both of Penelope and Ulysses and of Sacontale and Doushmanta, so here he plays both the Cossacks and the Sultan of

---

[39] Décaudin, *Le Dossier*, p. 103. Mr. Breunig observes that Apollinaire, like Gautier before him, is trying here "un simple exercice dans la transposition des arts" ("Le Roman," p. 118).

[40] Décaudin, *Le Dossier*, p. 103. The only existent letters of the correspondence between the Cossacks and the Sultan are counterfeits first circulated at the end of the seventeenth century and found in various Russian and Ukrainian versions. (For a discussion of these counterfeit versions see Élie Borschak, "La Lettre des Zaporogues au Sultan," *Revue des études slaves*, XXVI [Paris: Imprimerie Nationale, 1950], 99-105.) Apollinaire's "Réponse" has certain affinities in tone and vulgarity with these letters. (For a comparison, see Schmits, pp. 540-542.) More recently, the Russian critic N. I. Balachov has shown that from the point of view of words, sentences, sounds, and cadences "La Réponse des Cosaques Zaporogues au Sultan de Constantinople" in "La Chanson" is a precise translation of the seventeenth century letters, written in Ukrainian, which Apollinaire, who knew different slavic languages, had probably read:

> Le recours du poète à l'original,... peut seul expliquer la précision de son interprétation de la "correspondance" entre les zaporogues et le sultan, le fait qu'il en ait retrouvé l'esprit, la construction et même la structure rythmique. ("Apollinaire et les Zaporogues," *Europe*, nos. 451-452 [novembre-décembre, 1966], p. 281)

The "Correspondence" was published in Russian and Ukrainian many times during the nineteenth century, and Mr. Balachov suggests two sources where Apollinaire might have encountered it: a review dating from 1872-1873 and a book published in 1894. Based on his findings, Mr. Balachov concludes that it is highly improbable that Apollinaire was influenced, as many critics have believed, by "une source française" (*Ibid.*).

Constantinople, he who spurns and he who is spurned. Although the Cossacks exemplify Apollinaire's devotion to Annie, their scornful reply to the Sultan dramatizes the rejection he has suffered at her hands. As an appeal to the Cossacks to become the faithful, loving subjects of the Turkish Empire ("Devenez mes sujets fidèles"), the Sultan's letter resembles the many entreaties made by the poet to his beloved. The Cossacks' reply dramatizes in an exaggerated form Annie's repeated refusals.

The "Réponse des Cosaques Zaporogues au Sultan de Constantinople" (sts. 24-26), the poem's second interlude, is a violent discharge of anger and frustration:

>   Plus criminel que Barrabas
>   Cornu comme les mauvais anges
>   Quel Belzébuth es-tu là-bas
>   Nourri d'immondice et de fange
>   Nous n'irons pas à tes sabbats   (24)
>
>   Poisson pourri de Salonique
>   Long collier des sommeils affreux
>   D'yeux arrachés à coup de pique
>   Ta mère fit un pet foireux
>   Et tu naquis de sa colique   (25)
>
>   Bourreau de Podolie Amant
>   Des plaies des ulcères des croûtes
>   Groin de cochon cul de jument
>   Tes richesses garde-les toutes
>   Pour payer tes médicaments   (26)

After the delicate melodies of the preceding stanzas, the self explodes here in vehement anger, letting loose with a brutal, obscene attack directed at the beloved but well concealed by the *persona* of the Cossacks who utter the poet's words. The self exteriorizes its frustration by expressing it in the obscene language of the letter to the Sultan. The poet's anger is hidden because he has dramatized it beyond the point of immediate recognition. The use of the Cossacks as a *persona* enables Apollinaire to express himself cathartically, to purge his angry, pent-up emotions, while at the same time obliquely masking those same emotions. The Cossacks act out the drama going on within the poet's self.

In this short interlude, Apollinaire dramatizes many different faces of the self. He compares the fidelity of the Cossacks to his own; he relieves his frustration in vile denunciations spoken by others; he ridicules himself by dramatizing his own personal rejection in the Cossacks' hilariously irreverent repudiation of the Sultan; he exhibits his remarkable erudition; and finally, he shows an unusual talent for appropriating historical information for his own personal use. The "Réponse," therefore, contains a highly charged concentration of self in what appears to be at first glance only a dramatic reconstruction of an historical event.

The group of fifteen stanzas (sts. 27-41), which follows the "Réponse des Cosaques Zaporogues au Sultan de Constantinople" interlude and precedes the "Sept Epées" interlude, composes the heart of "La Chanson du Mal-Aimé." It constitutes the most frank expression in the poem of the poet's feeling, and it is the only confession uninterrupted by dramatized passages. Here the poet's self speaks faster and more intensely than anywhere else. A continuous stream of consciousness races through the stanzas; in them a torrent of ideas and images flows. The poet begins with a bitter attack on the beloved, then changes to a portrait of the self's liquidity; he addresses his burning grief and then his own shadow; his mind wanders from a countryside of disappearing snow back to the pain within his heart. Sorrow, grief, and suffering ("Douleur" and "Malheur") are the masters of the scene. The poet is so overwhelmed by them that the section as a whole is one long cry against their pain and against the destiny that has brought him under their power.

The confession begins with the "Voie lactée" refrain (st. 27), whose calm musicality puts an end to the vulgarity of the preceding interlude. When the refrain first appeared earlier in the poem (st. 13) emphasis was placed on the question which the poet addresses to the galaxy ("Nageurs morts suivrons-nous d'ahan/Ton cours vers d'autres nébuleuses").[41] Here, however, the emphasis has shifted to the lactescent bodies of imagined mistresses ("des corps blancs des amoureuses"), to the subject of erotic and carnal love. The stanzas that follow reveal the physical aspect of Apollinaire's love affair:

> *Regret des yeux de la putain*
> *Et belle comme une panthère*

---

[41] See above, pp. 180-82.

> *Amour vos baisers florentins*
> *Avaient une saveur amère*
> *Qui a rebuté nos destins* (28)
>
> *Ses regards laissaient une traîne*
> *D'étoiles dans les soirs tremblants*
> *Dans ses yeux nageaient les sirènes*
> *Et nos baisers mordus sanglants*
> *Faisaient pleurer nos fées marraines* (29)

Apollinaire, who later regretted the harshness of these lines,[42] explodes with bitterness. He calls Annie a whore. She has the vicious, terrible beauty of a panther, a beast of prey that has devoured his heart. Twice he refers to her seductive eyes, which are like those of a siren or of the Loreley.[43] Her looks are uncertain and fleeting ("une traîne/D'étoiles," "tremblants") as ephemeral and perhaps, in his mind, as insincere, as her love itself. Apollinaire becomes indiscrete, recalling the bitter taste of French kisses ("baisers florentins")[44] and

---

[42] In a letter to Madeleine (July 30, 1915) he wrote:

> Et bien des expressions de ce poème sont trop sévères et injurieuses pour une fille qui ne comprenait rien à moi et qui m'aima puis fut déconcertée d'aimer un poète être fantasque.
>
> (*Tendre comme le souvenir*, p. 70)

[43] The most striking aspect of Annie's beauty was in fact her eyes:

> Depuis son enfance on lui avait fait croire qu'il y avait quelque chose de honteux, de scandaleux dans sa beauté. Ses amies lui reprochaient ses "yeux pervers"; ses deux frères lui répétaient à chaque instant qu'elle devrait se couvrir la figure pour sortir....
> (Breunig, "Apollinaire et Annie," p. 641)

In many poems of the Rhine cycle Apollinaire refers to these "yeux pervers"; in "Mai," in "Les Colchiques," and above all in "La Loreley," which describes the legendary Rhine *ondine* whose eyes were fatal to anyone unfortunate enough to behold her:

> Je suis lasse de vivre et mes yeux sont maudits
> Ceux qui m'ont regardée évêque en ont péri
>
> Mes yeux ce sont des flammes et non des pierreries
> Jetez jetez aux flammes cette sorcellerie
> (*O. P.*, p. 115)

[44] An explanation of this expression, according to M. Décaudin, can be found in the *Dictionnaire comique, satyrique, critique, burlesque, libre et proverbial*... by Philibert Joseph le Roux, published in Amsterdam in 1718:

> "*Baiser à la Florentine*. Ce mot exprime l'action de deux personnes qui en se donnant l'un à l'autre des baisers sur la bouche se lancent tour à tour de petits coups de langue, pour servir comme

the violence of love-making ("baisers mordus sanglants"). Because of these intimacies the poet and his beloved have lost their innocence, for why else would their fairy godmothers who are responsible for their destinies, weep (l. 10).[45]

Yet, despite his anger and bitterness, the poet would gladly welcome back his beloved:

> *Mais en vérité je l'attends*
> *Avec mon cœur avec mon âme*
> *Et sur le pont des Reviens-t'en*

---

d'éguillonnement au plaisir. Cette sorte de baiser est appelée aussi en France baiser la langue en bouche etc."

(Michel Décaudin, "Compléments à Dossier, *R. L. M.*, nos. 69-70 [printemps, 1962], pp. 59-60)

[45] As Mme Morhange-Bégué has observed, what is interesting about these lines is not only the sensual relationship they suggest, but the fact that the "fées marraines" are weeping, for their tears reveal "le caractère *extraordinaire* d'une passion capable de susciter les larmes de celles qui, par leur nature même, connaissent ou font l'avenir, et qui, par conséquent, ne devraient pas être susceptibles d'émotion ni d'effroi au spectacle de destins auxquels elles ont présidé" (p. 115).

These lines also raise the much debated question regarding whether Apollinaire's love affair with Annie was physical or merely platonic. According to Annie it was platonic:

> "Il avait 20 ans quand je l'ai connu; il était follement amoureux et j'étais une petite stupide qui ne pouvais me laisser aller à l'aimer en raison surtout de mon éducation puritaine et aussi parce que la comtesse m'avait tant farci la tête d'histoires sur les hommes en général que je ne pouvais avoir ni confiance ni foi en Guillaume."
> (Durry, III, 24)

But, according to Apollinaire, who, in matters of amorous conquest, tended to embroider the truth, it was a physical relationship. In a letter from Germany to his friend James Onimus in July 1902 he describes Annie as his mistress:

> ...je vois toute l'Allemagne, et couche avec la gouvernante, anglaise 21 ans, épatante des nichons et un cul (!)
> (*Œuvres complètes*, IV, 715)

In July 1915 in a letter to Madeleine, he wrote of Annie: "...je l'aimai charnellement mais nos esprits étaient loin l'un de l'autre" (*Tendre comme le souvenir*, p. 70). Mme Durry, in her discussion of the poem "La Tzigane," which contains, in her view, a hidden allusion to the intimate physical relations of Apollinaire and Annie (III, 14-30), believes that Annie was a "demi-vierge" (p. 27), and that the two lovers "remplacent l'amour total par les ruses du corps. Sans se donner tout entière Annie ne refuse pas les substituts" (pp. 28-29).

> Si jamais revient cette femme
> Je lui dirai Je suis content   (30)

But the site chosen for this imagined reunion is a poor one. The bridge is a place where love does not return but passes away, as a decade later Apollinaire wrote in "Le Pont Mirabeau":

> Passent les jours et passent les semaines
>   Ni temps passé
> Ni les amours reviennent
> Sous le pont Mirabeau coule la Seine
>   (O. P., p. 45)

His wish to be reunited with the beloved is doomed from the start, since it contains its own contradiction.

But if love flows away, so does the self:

> Mon cœur et ma tête se vident
> Tout le ciel s'écoule par eux
> O mes tonneaux des Danaïdes
> Comment faire pour être heureux
> Comme un petit enfant candide   (31)

Sorrow transforms the poet's self — his feelings ("Mon cœur") and his spirit ("ma tête") — and the universe ("tout le ciel") into a liquid state; they both pour out of him in a torrent, leaving behind a void, an unfillable emptiness that resembles the leaky casks of the Danaides. Happiness alone can fill that void. But since nothing short of the beloved's return will make the poet happy, he is destined to feel empty for a long time to come. Sorrow has reduced the world to a state of continual flux, so that now nothing of substance, nothing permanent, remains. All that exists is the painful emptiness within and the flowing self without. With nothing concrete to hold onto, the poet is swept away by the torrent and risks being drowned in his own despair.

Happiness depends on stability, permanence, and continuity. For this reason, the child believes that happy moments will last forever; he is certain that characters in fairy tales will live happily ever after. But the adult, and especially the poet, know that such is not the case and that if there is any permanence in the world, it is the permanence of the flux. The poet wants to know how to recapture the candid joy of the child (ll. 4-5), but his question, since he already knows the answer, is less a question and more an anguished cry against fate, which makes the innocence and happiness of childhood forever irretrievable.

With the universe and the self flowing all around him the poet declares:

> *Je ne veux jamais l'oublier*
> *Ma colombe ma blanche rade*
> *O marguerite exfoliée*
> *Mon île au loin ma Désirade*
> *Ma rose mon giroflier*   (32)

The poet cries out for the permanence of memory, but he is hardly heard above the surging waters of the flux. Once again his wish is contradicted by what follows. He declares his intention of remembering the beloved but then describes her in a litany of ephemeral images: a bird that flies away ("colombe"), flowers that die (l. 5), an already dead and leafless plant (l. 3), and above all an island of dreams and pleasure ("Désirade") seen far away in the distance ("au loin").

The island and the harbor ("blanche rade") are images of the beloved, who now belongs to the past. The poet is at sea, either swimming along with the "nageurs morts" (sts. 13, 27), or sailing the "beau navire" of memory (st. 11), or floating in the waters of the self. He is tossed by the waves and exhausted from both the swimming (sts. 13, 27) and the sailing ("Avons-nous assez navigué," st. 11). In the distance he can perceive the restful shores of the island, its protective harbor and calm waters, just as he can see the past through the telescope of memory. Yet, as he cannot relive that past, so he can neither swim nor set sail for that island. The constant sight of the unattainable "Désirade," like the unending memory of the beloved, is perpetual anguish. It makes him aware of the distance and, therefore, of how much of the past he has already lost. Memory indicates not only what has been remembered but also what has been forgotten.

Sorrow, having subjected the poet to an experience of its emptiness, now makes him suffer its flames. From baptism by water the poet passes on to baptism by fire. The flames of grief and of unspent passion ("satyres," "égypans") burn within him:

> *Les satyres et les pyraustes*
> *Les égypans les feux follets*

> Et les destins damnés ou faustes
> La corde au cou comme à Calais
> Sur ma douleur quel holocauste   (33)

The second line restates the idea of the first in erudite synonyms. "Satyres" and "égypans," "pyraustes" — fabulous insects that live in fire — and "feux follets" are synonyms that double the expression of the poet's suffering. The fire splits the poet in two. As his body and spirit were earlier liquefied, so now they are being reduced by heat to an equally amorphous and uncertain state ("mon corps incertain"):

> Douleur qui doubles les destins
> La licorne et le capricorne
> Mon âme et mon corps incertain
> Te fuient ô bucher divin qu'ornent
> Des astres des fleurs du matin   (34)

But before the self can become totally melted down on that divine pyre that spells certain death, the poet flees. Although his suffering is great, he refuses to sacrifice the self, his last remaining possession, to any god. He will not capitulate to suffering by deifying his own despair. He refuses to serve the gods, "Douleur," or "Malheur" (st. 35), as either an insane priest or a weeping, imploring victim. To do so would be to destroy the self, replacing it with a consuming devotion to despair:

> Malheur dieu pâle aux yeux d'ivoire
> Tes prêtres fous t'ont-ils paré
> Tes victimes en robe noire
> Ont-elles vainement pleuré
> Malheur dieu qu'il ne faut pas croire   (35)

Over-involvement in one's grief requires the death of self; Apollinaire has saved himself from this fate by refusing to believe in the god "Malheur." The only god that he will recognize and that he will serve, however, is his shadow, image of the self:

> Et toi qui me suis en rampant
> Dieu de mes dieux morts en automne
> Tu mesures combien d'empans
> J'ai droit que la terre me donne
> O mon ombre ô mon vieux serpent   (36)

> *Au soleil parce que tu l'aimes*
> *Je t'ai menée souviens-t'en bien*
> *Ténébreuse épouse que j'aime*
> *Tu es à moi en n'étant rien*
> *O mon ombre en deuil de moi-même* (37)

After considering the self's fluidity, its passage through fire, and its double (the shadow), the poem switches to a landscape scene where winter is in the process of disappearing and spring in the process of being reborn. This lyric stanza, which probably describes the change of seasons along the Rhine, evokes a past moment of the poet's love:

> *L'hiver est mort tout enneigé*
> *On a brûlé les ruches blanches*
> *Dans les jardins et les vergers*
> *Les oiseaux chantent sur les branches*
> *Le printemps clair l'avril léger* (38)

And in the following stanza Apollinaire describes the same event but in a less lyric and more erudite language:

> *Mort d'immortels argyraspides*
> *La neige aux boucliers d'argent*
> *Fuit les dendrophores livides*
> *Du printemps cher aux pauvres gens*
> *Qui resourient les yeux humides* (39)

Apollinaire doubles the intensity of this memory by describing it twice; he also doubles some of the images. The expression, "argyraspides," which refers to an élite corps of silver-armored soldiers in Alexander the Great's army, is composed of the Greek words *arguros,* meaning "silver," and *aspis,* meaning "shields," which are restated in the expression "boucliers d'argent" of the following line. By repeating the image in a slightly different form Apollinaire reinforces the comparison between the melting snow and a retreating army.[46]

While the first stanza describes the death of winter in a traditional lyric vein, evoking gardens, orchards, and birds, the second stanza describes it in the form of a subtle and delicate allegory. According to M. Piron's reading of the stanza,[47] the snow, symbol of winter, flees the advent of spring and the advancing column of trees, the

---

[46] Piron, 95.
[47] *Ibid.*

"dendrophores livides." "Dendrophori" is the name given to the men — in Greece, slaves, in Rome, artisans — who carried sacred trees in pagan festivals honoring the gods Demeter and Dionysus. The trees, therefore, livid from their long, winter hibernation, advance on the snow, which retreats from the battlefield. But the snow's retreat is well guarded; it has shields and an élite corps of soldiers, the "immortels argyraspides." This rear guard is an image of those slow-melting patches of ice that remain under trees and rocks long after the main body of snow has disappeared.

But the renewal of spring and of hope is a memory that makes the *mal-aimé* even more dejected:

> Et moi j'ai le cœur aussi gros
> Qu'un cul de dame damascène
> Ô mon amour je t'aimais trop
> Et maintenant j'ai trop de peine
> Les sept epées hors du fourreau (40)
>
> Sept epées de mélancolie
> Sans morfil ô claires douleurs
> Sont dans mon cœur et la folie
> Veut raisonner pour mon malheur
> Comment voulez-vous que j'oublie (41)

These two stanzas, which introduce the third and final interlude of the poem, begin with one of those unexpected, scatological similes common to Apollinaire's poetry. The poet is desperate (l. 3); it is impossible for him to forget his love because its pain is a constant reminder (l. 4). After the emptiness, the fire, the memory, and all the internal suffering of the previous stanzas, his sorrow has become unbearable ("ô claires douleurs"); it is seven times greater. Seven blunt swords of melancholy pierce his heart like the Seven Sorrows of the Virgin Mary. Madness ("la folie") begins to make overtures in his direction. Thus, in a crescendo of despair this, the longest uninterrupted confession in the poem (sts. 27-41), comes to an end.

The "Sept Epées" interlude (sts. 42-48) is an obscure, allegorical dramatization of Apollinaire's love affair with Annie, and it has been subjected to more commentary, discussion, and exegesis than probably any other passage of "La Chanson":[48]

---

[48] James Lawler, "Les Sept Epées," *Le Flâneur des Deux Rives. Bulletin d'études apollinariennes*, no. 3 (septembre, 1954), pp. 10-13. Pol-P. Gossiaux,

La première est toute d'argent
Et son nom tremblant c'est Pâline
Sa lame un ciel d'hiver neigeant
Son destin sanglant gibeline
Vulcain mourut en la forgeant   (42)

La seconde nommée Noubosse
Est un bel arc-en-ciel joyeux
Les dieux s'en servent à leurs noces
Elle a tué trente Bé-Rieux
Et fut douée par Carabosse   (43)

La troisième bleu féminin
N'en est pas moins un chibriape
Appelé Lul de Faltenin
Et que porte sur une nappe
L'Hermès Ernest devenu nain   (44)

La quatrième Malourène
Est un fleuve vert et doré
C'est le soir quand les riveraines
Y baignent leurs corps adorés
Et des chants de rameurs s'y traînent (45)

La cinquième Sainte-Fabeau
C'est la plus belle des quenouilles
C'est un cyprès sur un tombeau
Où les quatre vents s'agenouillent
Et chaque nuit c'est un flambeau   (46)

La sixième métal de gloire
C'est l'ami aux si douces mains
Dont chaque matin nous sépare

"Recherches sur 'Les Sept Epées,'" *R. L. M.*, nos. 146-149 (1966), pp. 41-83; and his "Complément," *Du monde européen à l'univers des mythes. Actes du colloque de Stavelot (1968)*, ed. by Michel Décaudin (Paris: Minard, 1970), pp. 163-71; and his "Les 'Sept Epées' et l'astrologie," *R. L. M.*, nos. 249-253 (1970), pp. 165-69. Lionel Follet, "Images et thèmes de l'amour malhereux dans 'Les Sept Epées,'" *Europe*, nos. 451-452 (novembre-décembre, 1966), pp. 206-39; and his "Les Sept Epées," *Du monde européen à l'univers des mythes*, pp. 152-63. Claude Morhange-Bégué, "*La Chanson du Mal-Aimé d'Apollinaire*, pp. 160-90. Antoine Fongaro, "Encore les 'Sept Epées,'" *R. L. M.*, nos. 249-253 (1970), pp. 121-33. René Louis, "Lul de Faltenin," *Le Flâneur des Deux Rives*, no. 2 (juin, 1954), pp. 9-11; and his "Encore 'Lul de Faltenin,'" in *Ibid.*, no. 3 (septembre, 1954), pp. 7-9. (These last two articles deal only with the third sword.)

Adieu voilà votre chemin
Les coqs s'épuisaient en fanfares (47)

Et la septième s'exténue
Une femme une rose morte
Merci que le dernier venu
Sur mon amour ferme la porte
Je ne vous ai jamais connue (48)

According to Mr. Lawler's study,[49] the seven stanzas of the interlude contain the most personal and frank allusions to the love affair with Annie Playden ever revealed by Apollinaire; but these are presented behind oblique language, erudite riddles, and in general "sous une apparence pudique" (p. 10). It is Mr. Lawler's opinion that "toute l'histoire d'un amour, jusque dans ses détails les plus intimes, est contenue en ces sept enluminures très chastes" (p. 13).

Each stanza describes a different sword and thus dramatizes a different aspect of Apollinaire's love affair. Mr. Lawler sees the first sword, named "Pâline," a word composed of "pâle" and "câline," as a symbol of the beloved's virginal beauty about to be stained by love's bloody destiny (p. 11). The second sword, called "Noubosse," is a concealed allusion to the female sexual organ (p. 11); the rest of the stanza plays on the erotic meaning of the sword, as for example, the line, "Les dieux s'en servent à leurs noces." The third sword, "Lul de Faltenin," refers to the phallus and is described as "un chibriape," a neologism created by Apollinaire from the words "chibre" and "priape." This sword is carried on a cloth, like some holy relic, by "L'Hermès Ernest devenu nain," a god whose dwarfism is probably due to castration (p. 12).

The fourth sword, "Malourène," the poet calls a "fleuve vert et doré," and it evokes, according to Mr. Lawler, the fluid happiness of two lovers (p. 12). Different colors are enumerated, and Apollinaire describes memories of a love that once flourished along the banks of the Rhine, whose presence is suggested in the line, "Et des chants de rameurs s'y traînent." The next sword, "Sainte-Fabeau," is another phallic symbol, which the poet describes as "la plus belle des quenouilles," and as a cypress and a torch (p. 12). The sixth sword, which has no name, depicts a memory of the past, in which

---

[49] See above, p. 196, n. 48.

the poet quietly and tenderly takes leave of his beloved, while the morning sings around them (p. 13). The final sword, also nameless, dramatizes the end of the poet's love; it is the cruelest and sharpest of the seven. Another lover, whom the poet calls "le dernier venu," closes the door on love and memory, and the hurt Apollinaire denies the existence of Annie: "Je ne vous ai jamais connue" (p. 13).

In his long analysis of the "Sept Epées" interlude [50] Pol Gossiaux interprets the seven swords from a completely different point of view. His article contains a considerable amount of scholarly research into Apollinaire's symbols, and he offers some compelling ideas. The first stanza, according to M. Gossiaux, symbolizes the poet's sexual failure, his sterility as a lover (pp. 49-53). In the second stanza he experiences another failure, this one as a poet, for he questions "la valeur en soi de l'acte créateur et poétique, pour conclure à sa facticité" (p. 59). After doubting both his powers of physical and artistic creation, the poet finds himself in a state of suspension and incertitude, which he translates in the third strophe through images of hermaphroditism (pp. 60-65). The fourth stanza is a scene of transition. Haunted by the theme of hermaphroditism and the state of indecision and uncertainty it symbolizes, the poet feels forced to choose between male or female (p. 66). He makes his decision in the fifth stanza, declaring himself a poet, and his choice closes the door on love and its suffering (pp. 68-72). M. Gossiaux describes this stanza as "une description et une analyse imagée de la puissance créatrice, et une apologie de l'acte poétique" (p. 73). The sixth stanza is a continuation of the fifth, another defense of solitary poetic creation (p. 73). There is no explanation of the final stanza. In "Les Sept Epées," M. Gossiaux concludes,

> Apollinaire s'y libère de ses souffrances de mal-aimé, il y exorcise ses craintes de l'amour et son obsession de l'échec. Il s'y choisit poète.... (pp. 73-74)

Thus, in the creative act Apollinaire finds "une unité supérieure permettant de transcender l'incohérence de sa situation d'amoureux" (p. 74).

---

[50] "Recherches sur 'Les Sept Epées'"; see above, p. 196, n. 48.

Another interpretation of the "Sept Epées" interlude is given by Lionel Follet,[51] who seeks to explain the seven swords by comparing the many images and themes used in the interlude to similar uses of these themes and images in other poems by Apollinaire. For M. Follet, the interlude as a whole expresses "une vision globale de l'amour à travers les souffrances qu'il provoque" (p. 208). By insisting on the global quality of Apollinaire's description of love's pain, M. Follet transforms the personal mythology of the seven swords into a universal mythology.

The first sword, although appearing to announce the happiness of love, promises instead the inevitable betrayal resulting from all relationships between man and woman and due to "le destin de la femme [qui] interdit à jamais à l'homme de la saisir" (p. 215). "Noubosse," the second sword, represents the painful ephemerality of love, a theme that is further suggested by the rainbow (according to M. Follet, "signe d'un accord éphémère entre la terre et les dieux," p. 216), and by the wicked fairy "Carabosse" who gives the sword. According to legend, she was the fairy who as a means of revenge gave gifts that soon afterwards became maledictions. Love is a similar "cadeau funeste" (p. 216), remarks M. Follet, and what transforms its joy into misfortune is time. Moreover, he sees in the name "Noubosse" not only the suffix of "Carabosse," but also a rapport with the Latin words, "nubo," "nubere," meaning to "marry" and to "veil," themes that are germane to his interpretation of Apollinaire's notion of love (pp. 216-17). In the third stanza it is the poet in the form of the god Hermes who offers his own virility to the woman he loves as a form of sacrifice and thus becomes a dwarf, as the final line of the stanza reveals: "L'Hermès Ernest devenu nain." The stanza dramatizes a symbolic castration of the poet who is attracted to a physical love which robs him of his creative and procreative powers. "Noubosse" figures the "mensonge de l'étreinte" (p. 220). Another of love's deceptions is expressed by the fourth sword, "Malourène," which, since it is associated in the stanza with a flowing river (a common image in Apollinaire's poetry for the irrevocable passing of time), is an instrument of temporal destruction. It represents the temporality which lies at the heart of love and signals its eventual demise (p. 225).

---

[51] "Images et thèmes de l'amour malheureux dans 'Les Sept Epées' "; see above, p. 196, n. 48.

"Sainte-Fabeau," the next sword, makes this very clear by juxtaposing images of death with the theme of love. It evokes the death of love, but at the same time it reveals the death that is an integral and inseparable part of love and that is represented by "la traîtrise féminine" (p. 229). In the sixth stanza, love is already dead, but the pain it has caused, in itself a form of death, persists. The sixth sword is identified with the world of dreams, which the poet calls a friend ("l'ami") because it offers relief to all suffering and betrayed men; "le bonheur perdu revit dans les songes," remarks M. Follet (p. 232). The final sword represents forgetfulness, "la véritable mort de l'amour..., son abolition au cœur même de l'amant" (p. 233). The fact that not one detail of the stanza evokes the concrete image of a sword suggests that

> la septième douleur est donc différente des autres...: découvrir l'oubli, c'est encore souffrir, intellectuellement, de la finitude de l'amour, mais c'est aussi ne plus souffrir d'amour. (p. 233)

What makes itself felt in Apollinaire's description of love in the "Sept Epées" interlude is the basic incompatibility of man and woman whose "destins contraires les vouent, lui à souffrir, elle à trahir, et tous deux à l'incompréhension mutuelle" (p. 235). The interlude, M. Follet concludes, presents a universal condemnation of "toutes les amours humaines" (p. 236); it expresses "toute une philosophie pessimiste de l'amour" (p. 236).

While Mr. Lawler finds the key to understanding the "Sept Epées" interlude in Apollinaire's love affair with Annie, and M. Gossiaux locates it in the cathartic act by which Apollinaire symbolically resolves a psychological crisis of sterility and indecision and thus chooses to become a poet, and M. Follet discovers it in Apollinaire's pessimistic philosophy of love as revealed by a comparative analysis of themes, Mme Morhange-Bégué,[52] basing her interpretation on what she believes the structures of the poetic text alone can reveal to a careful and perspicacious reader, gives the most convincing and the most complete interpretation of the interlude, and the one that best describes the relationship of the interlude to the rest of "La Chan-

---

[52] *"La Chanson du Mal-Aimé" d'Apollinaire*; see above, p. 196, n. 48.

son."[53] She sees in the seven swords "une évocation des sept façons qu'a le souvenir d'infliger des blessures mortelles" (p. 159). The swords represent "l'impossibilité d'oublier" (p. 161), and they dramatize what has been a major preoccupation of le Mal-Aimé[54] throughout the poem, namely the desperate struggle to gain forgetfulness, "la seule solution à son tourment" (p. 159, n. 11).

Mme Morhange-Bégué describes the first sword, "Pâline," in terms of the three themes that are associated with it in the first stanza. While this sword is a rare and precious object (it is made of silver), it is also an instrument of death and betrayal (pp. 162-67). The second sword, "Noubosse," because of its strange sounding, unfamiliar name (a quality it shares with the other swords) creates an air of mystery, which is further compounded by the reader's surprise when, at the beginning of the stanza, he encounters images of beauty, color, light, and joy to describe what is, after all, "une épée meurtrière" (p. 168). The obscurity of the third sword, "Lul de Faltenin," goes deeper than the word itself, or even its meaning, and strikes at the very heart of the language used to represent it. Obscurity is "encodée

---

[53] Although criticizing the other commentators of the interlude for their reliance on biography, mythology, symbolism, and psychology, areas beyond the compass of any poetic text, Mme Morhange-Bégué does rely to a certain degree on some of their discoveries, but only when these discoveries do not do injustice to the autonomy and the self-sufficiency of the text.

[54] Mme Morhange-Bégué makes an important distinction between le Mal-Aimé, the 'voice' which speaks throughout the poem of its past, its suffering, and its grief, and le poète, the 'voice' of a transformed Mal-Aimé, which is heard only at the end of the poem, where it sublimates its grief, transforming it into song. It is worth noting that there is yet another more fundamental distinction which Mme Morhange-Bégué makes in her discussion of the voices that are heard in the poem:

> Derrière le je qui s'exprime au long du poème s'abrite en fait trois personnes: l'actant, le locuteur, l'auteur. Seul l'auteur est responsable du poème écrit que nous lisons, de même que l'actant seul en est le héros malheureux. Le locuteur, figure hybride qui emprunte à l'actant ses sentiments et sa métamorphose poétique, et à l'auteur l'œuvre ou part de l'œuvre que celui-ci a écrite, constitue en réalité le fondement de l'ambiguité de "La Chanson." Car celle-ci offre au lecteur, comme si c'était réalité, la double fiction d'une crise psychologique et morale en plein déroulement, et du poème résultant de sa résolution, l'un et l'autre étant superposés, parfois confondus. (pp. 268-69)

For the roles played in the poem by such diverse voices as the "Mal-Aimé," the "locuteur," the "protagoniste," the "actant," and the "narrateur," see pp. 30 (n. 1), 118, 150, 251-53, 268-70, 281-83.

dans le texte" (p. 170), by which Mme Morhange-Bégué means that it informs the vocabulary, the choice of images, and the syntactical structure of the stanza (pp. 170-71). This produces within the body of the stanza an opposition between appearance and reality, where reality, because it no longer supports or maintains appearance, constitutes "une forme de trahison" (p. 172). "Malourène," the fourth sword, is also associated with betrayal because it sets in motion a return to a past which in many ways — thematically, stylistically, and descriptively — is highly reminiscent of Apollinaire's early "poèmes rhénans." This stanza, remarks Mme Morhange-Bégué, presents "une mise en relief des puissances trompeuses du souvenir auprès d'une imagination prompte à se laisser leurrer" (p. 175). "Sainte-Fabeau," the next sword, is the most beautiful of all the swords because it is the most terrible in its power of destruction, a fact attested to by the plethora of death images which the stanza brings together: "quenouilles," "cyprès," "tombeau," and the winds that converge from the four cardinal points of the universe to do obeisance to death (pp. 176-77). The penultimate sword is associated with the themes of death and of betrayal, as the other swords had been, but it also announces a new theme not shared by the others, namely separation. The two lovers, who are seen taking their leave, are not departing with great tenderness, as Mr. Lawler believes.[55] Rather, there is present in the stanza "une sorte de rebuffade" (p. 180), which is evident in the poet's use of the word "adieu" and in the picture he gives of someone being brusquely shown his way out, as in the line: "Adieu voilà votre chemin." This rebuff transforms the roosters' "fanfares" from noisy, joyous cries of hope and promise, filling the morning air, to lies. The sword of the penultimate stanza thus condemns "la 'gloire' des matins d'amour heureux" (p. 181). The end of love comes in the last stanza, which bears witness to the rejection of the beloved and to an inevitable and final separation between her and *le Mal-Aimé*. This is represented syntactically by the change from the familiar pronoun "tu" (referring to the beloved) to the more formal and distant "vous." It is "ce rejet, ou le souvenir qu'il [*le Mal-Aimé*] garde de ce rejet, qui constitue la septième épée" (p. 183).

Thus, Mme Morhange-Bégué concludes, the "Sept Epées" interlude dramatizes the pain that *le Mal-Aimé* experiences because he

---

[55] See above, pp. 198-99.

cannot succeed in forgetting; his past is too much with him. Memory is shown throughout the interlude to be a power which

> embellit et transforme en chose rare et précieuse (thème de l'objet rare et précieux) une réalité trompeuse (thème de la trahison) qui n'aboutit qu'à la souffrance, voire à la mort (thème de la mort....) (p. 190)

Although the four interpretations of the "Sept Epées" interlude differ on many points, there is, nevertheless, one area on which they all would appear to be in agreement: namely, that the "Sept épées de mélancolie" (st. 41), whether they represent the intimate nature of Apollinaire's love affair (Mr. Lawler), or the triumph of the poet over sterility (M. Gossiaux), or the evolution of a universal, pessimistic attitude toward love (M. Follet), or the dogged persistence of memory (Mme Morhange-Bégué), constitute an image, a symbol, even a *persona*, by means of which Apollinaire dramatizes a deep and painful inner struggle in a poetic song so dolorous and intense that this obsessive struggle is ultimately exorcized. Not only are the swords instruments of a torture and a pain aggravated sevenfold, they are also instruments of expression and release, opening up wounds in the heart from which spill forth at once not only blood, but great outcries of pain, great lyric poems of suffering. It is this quality of dramatization and catharsis which joins the "Sept Epées" interlude to the rest of "La Chanson."

The final section of "La Chanson du Mal-Aimé" is introduced by the third and final appearance of the "Voie lactée" refrain (st. 49).[56] The stanzas that follow elaborate the theme of destiny contained in the refrain and symbolized by the Milky Way's eternal flow, its "cours vers d'autres nébuleuses." As the poet is pulled by the current toward other nebulae, so in a predetermined universe he is led by the demons of fate; his life and that of the human race is a *danse macabre* that he is powerless to stop:

> *Les démons du hasard selon*
> *Le chant du firmament nous mènent*
> *A sons perdus leurs violons*
> *Font danser notre race humaine*
> *Sur la descente à reculons* (50)

---

[56] See above, pp. 180-82, 189.

In the stanza that follows Apollinaire delineates the different kinds of fate which he is subject to:

>   Destins destins impénétrables
>   Rois secoués par la folie
>   Et ces grelottantes étoiles
>   De fausses femmes dans vos lits
>   Aux déserts que l'histoire accable   (51)

There is the destiny that strikes kings with madness (l. 2); the destiny of a trembling, perhaps, mad universe ("ces grelottantes étoiles"); the unfortunate destiny of men in love ("fausses femmes dans vos lits"); the fate of civilizations crumbling under the force of history (l. 5); and in the next stanzas the fate of two kings in particular, Luitpold and Louis II. Finally, in the last strophes of the poem the poet will face the reality of his own destiny.

The three stanzas concerning the insane King Louis II are a dramatic example of the force of destiny. Louis is the last *persona* to appear in the poem. As king of Bavaria from 1864 to 1886 he allowed his ministers to govern the country for him, while he shut himself away in his baroque and grandiose castles. (The most celebrated of these is Neuschwanstein.) When in 1886 he ordered all his ministers imprisoned, it was he instead who was interned in the castle of Berg. There, on the following day, he drowned himself in the lake of Starnberg. Since his brother and successor, Othon, was also mad, their uncle Luitpold took over the regency. Apollinaire refers to this in the opening lines of the dramatization:

>   Luitpold le vieux prince régent
>   Tuteur de deux royautés folles
>   Sanglote-t-il en y songeant
>   Quand vacillent les lucioles
>   Mouches dorées de la Saint-Jean   (52)

>   Près d'un château sans châtelaine
>   La barque aux barcarols chantants
>   Sur un lac blanc et sous l'haleine
>   Des vents qui tremblent au printemps
>   Voguait cygne mourant sirène   (53)

>   Un jour le roi dans l'eau d'argent
>   Se noya puis la bouche ouverte
>   Il s'en revint en surnageant

> *Sur la rive dormir inerte*
> *Face tournée au ciel changeant* (54)

Between the stanza about Luitpold and the one about Louis, Apollinaire inserts a quintain that belongs both to the death scene at hand and to his own personal life. It evokes the lyric melancholy and local color of the Rhineland ("aux barcarols chantants"). A calm sadness, suggested by the absence of women ("sans châtelaine"), by the delicate caress of the wind on the water, and by the dying swan, sets the scene for the king's suicide in the following stanza; but it also refers to the end of Apollinaire's love, which had begun in this same region of Germany. The swan that sings its last song ("Voguait cygne mourant sirène") refers to the symbolic death of Annie, in whose eyes "nageaient les sirènes" (st. 29).

At different times in "La Chanson du Mal-Aimé" the poet is seen as a swimmer exhaustedly floating in the changing sea of the self, besieged by tempests of suffering, and pulled by a strong current of destiny away from the past and the beloved (sts. 11, 13, 27, 49). Out at sea, the poet is far away from the peace and the bliss that he imagines on the island of "Désirade" and which he associates with the happy moment in the past when he was close to his beloved (st. 32). Yet, he can reach that island of rest and enjoy its tranquillity, if he is willing to follow the example of the insane King Louis. It is death that puts an end to the incessant flux and change found in the world. The drowned king sleeps peacefully at last ("dormir inerte," st. 54); death has carried him to that shore which is the final harbor, the ultimate "Désirade" ("Il s'en revint en surnageant / Sur la rive..."). His inert body faces the moving universe ("Face tournée au ciel changeant") as an example of permanence within the flux. But that sort of permanence is bought at a high price, one that the poet will not pay, no matter how intense his despair may be. For suicide, which ends suffering and brings peace, also murders the self. As long as the poet swims, as long as he moves, as long even as he suffers, the self remains alive.

Louis is a *persona* representing an aspect of the poet's self that is attracted by suicide and by the permanence and the immobility death promises, but that refrains, nevertheless, from acting destructively. Apollinaire is unable to commit suicide, a fact he admits in the next stanza of the poem where he is seen walking through Paris:

> *Juin ton soleil ardente lyre*
> *Brûle mes doigts endoloris*
> *Triste et mélodieux délire*
> *J'erre à travers mon beau Paris*
> *Sans avoir le cœur d'y mourir* (55)

With this stanza the poet returns to the confession form he has used extensively in the poem. It is June, and he is back in Paris; he alternates between describing the city and expressing his sorrow. Compared to the opening scene of the poem, where the poet walked the streets of London, this passage differs in every way but one. Instead of fog, there is sun. The time of the year is summer, not fall. The silence of the London street is replaced by the noise of Paris. Space is no longer presented as claustrophobic, but as airy and open (l. 4). And, finally, there is music. In fact, this stanza and each of the next four stanzas reverberate with either a sound or a song.[57] "La Chanson du Mal-Aimé" ends in a burst of music that stresses the power of song and artistic creation. And yet, there is one thing that has not changed since the beginning of the poem, and that is the poet's grief.

The poet refers to the June sun as an "ardente lyre" that burns his aching fingers (ll. 1-2), and his description conceals a statement about the creation of poetry. To play the burning lyre and create a song of heat and passion, the poet must endure pain; his fingers must be burned. Poetic creation involves pain and suffering. Poetry, he remarks in the next line, is a "Triste et mélodieux délire." The madness, the fury, and the emotion ("délire") of his sadness ("triste") is controlled and ordered by the musical form of his song ("mélodieux"). Both the "ardente lyre" and the "Triste et mélodieux délire" describe the act of poetic creation which occurs when the poet expresses his suffering.

The final stanzas of "La Chanson" describe the poet's wandering through Paris and evoke the city's sounds in a modernism that anticipates "Zone":

---

[57] In stanza 55 there is the "ardente lyre" of the sun and the "Triste et mélodieux délire" of the peripatetic poet. The following stanzas make mention of "les orgues de Barbarie" (56), the steely, mad music of "les tramways" (57), the cries of smoke-filled cafés with their busy crowds and nasal expresso machines (58), and finally, the songs, lays, laments, hymns, and romances of a poetic sensibility (59).

> Les dimanches s'y éternisent
> Et les orgues de Barbarie
> Y sanglotent dans les cours grises
> Les fleurs aux balcons de Paris
> Penchent comme la tour de Pise   (56)
>
> Soirs de Paris ivres de gin
> Flambant de l'électricité
> Les tramways feux verts sur l'échine
> Musiquent au long des portées
> De rails leur folie de machines   (57)
>
> Les cafés gonflés de fumée
> Crient tout l'amour de leurs tziganes
> De tous leurs siphons enrhumés
> De leurs garçons vêtus d'un pagne
> Vers toi toi que j'ai tant aimée   (58)
>
> Moi qui sais des lais pour les reines
> Les complaintes de mes années
> Des hymnes d'esclave aux murènes
> La romance du mal-aimé
> Et des chansons pour les sirènes   (59)

The final stanza of "La Chanson du Mal-Aimé" concerns the craft of the poet and begins with the affirmation of his creative self ("Moi qui sais..."). But before introducing this self, the poet in the preceding stanza has addressed the beloved in the following manner: "Vers toi toi que j'ai tant aimée." The repetition of the pronoun "toi" and the subsequent affirmation of the pronoun "Moi" in the next stanza create an important contrast between the poet's love, which is part of the past, and the poet's creative self, which has transformed that lost love into poetry. Moreover, there is another distinction to be made between the two stanzas, one that distinguishes between the poet's self which says, "j'ai tant aimée," and the self which declares, "Moi qui sais," between an active prosaic *je*, that has experienced love and suffering, and a creative, orphic *je* that is gifted with the knowledge of words and poetic forms. In creating poetry, the orphic self uses its knowledge and repertoire of lyric forms ("lais," "complaintes," "hymnes," "romance," and "chansons") to express the experience of love suffered and remembered by the affective self. From the collaboration between poetic self and affective self comes a lyric song of amorous sorrow, a *chanson du mal-aimé*.

In sum, "La Chanson du Mal-Aimé" is a poetic outpouring of feeling; it is indeed what Apollinaire calls a "Triste et mélodieux délire." The images of fluidity and of shadow, the confessions, the dramatizations, the *personae,* and the *dédoublement* all contribute to the externalization of suffering, pain, and sadness which lie deep within Apollinaire's self. From the opening foggy London street to the concluding smoky Paris café, the poem is an uninterrupted *catharsis of self.*

CHAPTER VII

CONCLUSION

> A poet's words
> Are signatures of self — the many selves
> Subsumed in one profounder sense that knows
> An all-according truth: a single eye
> Uncovering the countless constellations
> Of heart and mind. Wherefore the syllables
> Reach outward from the self in an embrace
> Of multitudes. [1]

For Apollinaire art articulates the self. Each of his poems can be envisaged as a space, a theater, in which a particular kind of presence, *a presence of being,* is created. This presence results from an encounter between poet and self so brief that it lasts but an instant, so changeable that it has already started to transform itself at the moment it appears, so immediate that it and the words expressing it are inseparably one, and so compelling that every poem strives to reproduce it. And Apollinaire's quest for the presence of being involves a voyage, not through any one poem, but through all his poems, each of which offers a fleeting glimpse of this presence. Every poem can be seen as a construction of words that moves towards, is *en route* to, the construction of a self, for only a poetry-in-movement

---

[1] Stanley Burnshaw, "Poetry: The Art," from *Early and Late Testament* (1952), in *In The Terrified Radiance* (New York: George Braziller, 1972), p. 147.

can hope to seize the self-in-movement. Apollinaire's poetic work constitutes a poetry of quest and passage whose very movement and mutability are sufficient to generate the presence of being he seeks.

In his "L'Esprit nouveau et les poètes" lecture of 1917 Apollinaire marvelled at the fact that he had seen the inside of his head:

> Quoi! on a radiographié ma tête. J'ai vu, moi vivant, mon crâne, et cela ne serait en rien de la nouveauté? [2]

And yet, his wonder at this scientific achievement is eclipsed by a poetic achievement of even greater magnitude. The knowledge of what lay inside his head is overshadowed by the knowledge of himself. The x-ray of his skull is nothing compared to the "x-ray" of the self, as it is presented in the fifty poems of *Alcools*.

The preceding chapters have attempted to define and analyze the different methods of self-exteriorization used by Apollinaire in a number of poems published in *Alcools*. Through such techniques as dramatization, montage, and catharsis the conflict lying deeply concealed within the poet and known as the drama of self is brought out into the open and placed in a poem for all to see. Such externalization of the self in a work of art has a twofold purpose. First, it arrests the

---

[2] p. 391. In "Les Collines" (*Calligrammes*) Apollinaire speaks of what the future will bring in the way of further explorations of man's inner world:

> Profondeurs de la conscience
> On vous explorera demain
> Et qui sait quels êtres vivants
> Seront tirés de ces abîmes
> Avec des univers entiers
>
> (*O. P.*, p. 172)

Apollinaire, it can be assumed, did not really know how far science would indeed go in exploring what he calls the "Profondeurs de la conscience." In an interesting study entitled "Comme un guetteur mélancolique: essai sur la personnalité d'Apollinaire" (*R. L. M.*, nos. 276-279 [1971], pp. 7-34) Guy Michaud uses the latest discoveries of morphopsychology and psychographology to study the forms of Apollinaire's face, as revealed in photographs, and the characteristics of his handwriting, as found in manuscripts, in an effort to define the nature of Apollinaire's personality. The features of Apollinaire's face and the traits of his handwriting constitute a system of signs: a language of *signifiants* (facial gestures, forms of handwritten letters) and *signifiés* (character traits) which add up to a semiology of Apollinaire's personality. M. Michaud then relates what he has discovered through the morphopsychological and psychographological approaches to that other important system of signs: Apollinaire's poetry.

fluctuating nature of the self by fixing it in an unchanging form, namely, the poem, and second, it preserves the self against the decay and change caused by time. While the self possessed by the poet will follow him to his grave, the self externalized in a work of art will be immortal. A final curtain will eventually fall on the drama of self; but the dramatization of self will give a continuous performance.

Throughout the poems examined in this study there has been a contrast between the future of the poet and the future of the poem. Merlin knows that a work of art will give him immortality; "Je m'éterniserai sous l'aubépine en fleurs," he says. Harlequin contemplates his future grandeur when he will grow to three times his present size. The poet in "Cortège" recognizes that his poetry will eventually grow in intensity and become a lasting monument to him, a "unique lumière." Yet, all three are well aware that the man, the creator of the creation, will die. And they know that this is as it should be, for in order to create an immortal work of art the poet must be mortal and participate in the changing rhythms of life.

Another contrast frequently found in Apollinaire's poetry is between the self and its double, the other, as, for example, in "Zone" when Apollinaire is simultaneously *je* and *tu*. Self and other are two names that describe the same thing seen from two different points of view: the self is the other subjectified; the other is the self objectified. A continual dialogue with the other is vital to the existence of the self. Without it the self would have no structure or content; instead, it would be vague, undifferentiated, and completely lacking in self-awareness. By objectifying and externalizing itself in the other, therefore, the self creates the distance necessary for self-contemplation and self-knowledge. The other is a device of self-objectification. It is a mask behind which the self conceals its identity, while, at the same time, revealing secrets about itself in voices, actions, and gestures that are not at first recognized. While there are many images of the self in *Alcools*, there are also many instances when the other appears; it is the poet's deriding laughter, the shadow he casts, the pronoun *tu* he uses, and the *personae* behind which he hides.[3] For Apollinaire, then, the other does not represent another person but another part or

---

[3] For a discussion of the relationship between the *I* and the *you*, the self and the other, in *Calligrammes*, see Renaud, pp. 335-39, 414-43, 457-65.

aspect of himself. The state of otherness in his poetry is very different from the concept of alterity developed by Hegel and Sartre.

The uniqueness of the relationship between the self and the other in *Alcools* becomes evident when compared with *I-you* relationships in the poetry of other poets. For example, in the poems of Paul Eluard an uninterrupted, unmediated relationship between two people in love, an *I* (the poet) and a *you* (the loved woman), which is represented through images of a reflected, reverberating light flowing from the eyes of one to the eyes of the other and back again, continuously and without interruption, gives a particular meaning and a definite structure to the meeting of the self and the other that occurs in these poems.[4] The relationship of the *I* and *you* is established according to an optics which Eluard's poems attempt to define and which Jean-Pierre Richard has described as that of the "regard regardé":

> Car si chacun s'y voit lumineusement dans le miroir qu'est devenu pour lui l'œil de l'autre, il y voit aussi l'autre le voir, se voir en lui, le voir en train de voir, et de se voir, si bien qu'il ne distingue plus en fin de compte quelle est, dans cette image récupérée de soi, la part de la seule réverbération et celle de l'interprétation, ou du message.[5]

There are no obstacles separating the *I* and the *you*. They possess one another through an act of union that can be described as an embrace of glances, an act of sensual intersubjectivity:

> Elle est debout sur mes paupières
> Et ses cheveux sont dans les miens,
> Elle a la forme de mes mains,
> Elle a la couleur de mes yeux,

---

[4] As Jean-Pierre Richard observes in his excellent essay on Eluard:

> Quelque chose se meut d'un partenaire à l'autre, cognant l'un, rebondissant sur celui d'en face, revenant sur le premier, repartant sur le second, en une circulation indéfinie. Comme deux joueurs de tennis se réexpédient la balle, nos yeux, dit Eluard, "se renvoient la lumière" (*l'Amour la Poésie*).

(*Onze études sur la poésie moderne* [Paris: Editions du Seuil, 1964], p. 106). My discussion of the *I-you* relationship in Eluard's poetry owes much to M. Richard's study.

[5] *Ibid.*

> Elle s'engloutit dans mon ombre
> Comme une pierre sur le ciel. [6]

The poet's self is defined and delimited by his encounter with the other, represented in the following line as a mirror:

> Je suis le seul qui soit cerné
> Par ce miroir si nul où l'ai circule à travers moi [7]

In fact, the self has no existence apart from the other, as M. Richard remarks:

> Avant les paroles, les images, les paysages même s'affirme, pour et devant le poète, la présence ardente d'un autrui, d'un *toi* miraculeusement jailli sur fond d'espace... *toi* par rapport auquel seul le moi pourra commencer à être... : dualité dans le cœur concave de laquelle ne vibre en réalité que l'intime, et pourtant aussi la spatiale, l'externe réciprocité d'un *nous*. [8]

The existence of the *I*, its survival, depends on its being penetrated by the glance of the *you*: "La courbe de tes yeux fait le tour de mon cœur." [9] The self both from within and from without is enveloped by the other; and so are the things of the world that surround this other:

> Le monde entier dépend de tes yeux purs
> Et tout mon sang coule dans leurs regards. [10]

> J'entends vibrer ta voix dans tous les bruits du monde. [11]

The presence of the other — her eyes and her voice — gives life, and so dependant is the poet's self on this other that the absence of the latter constitutes a form of death, inspiring in Eluard dark, despairing

---

[6] Paul Eluard, "L'Amoureuse," *Mourir de ne pas mourir*, in his *Œuvres complètes* ("Bibliothèque de la Pléiade"; 2 vols. Paris: Gallimard, 1968), I, 140.

[7] Eluard, "Celle de toujours, toute," *Capitale de la douleur*, in *Œuvres complètes*, I, 197.

[8] Richard, pp. 105-6.

[9] Eluard, *Capitale de la douleur*, in *Œuvres complètes*, I, 196.

[10] *Ibid.*

[11] Eluard, *Au défaut du silence*, in *Œuvres complètes*, I, 167.

poems, which are like negative prints of his joyous, celebratory songs of love. Where in the latter there are images of light, transparence, continuity, presence, movement, sight, and selfless love, in the former, antithetical images dominate: darkness, opacity, interruption, absence, paralysis, blindness, and narcissism. The *I* without the *you* is a person without life, without grounding, and without being. As M. Richard observes:

> Invisible à autrui, je ne pourrai me voir moi-même; coupé de tous, j'y serai surtout coupé de moi. [12]

What is significant is that in Eluard's poetry separation from the other, and the self-involvement it causes, rules out any possibility of self-knowledge. This is very different from Apollinaire's poetry where self-knowledge comes about almost exclusively in those moments when the poet is separated from a beloved and very much concerned with himself, having turned inward to feel the depths of his despair and sorrow. While for Eluard the self cannot exist without the loved woman, in Apollinaire the beloved always appears to be absent, to have disappeared into the past. Separation, from a woman, from the past, from himself, defines the world of Apollinaire's poetry and seems to be a condition for the search for self which lies at the heart of *Alcools*.

If the other in Apollinaire's poetry does not refer to a woman, for she is absent and even when remembered is still perceived *in absentia*, as a memory, to whom then does it allude, if not to Apollinaire himself. The other, therefore, unlike the other in Eluard's poetry, does not represent another person; rather, it is an exteriorized form, a double, of the Apollinarian self. While in Eluard's poetry the union of the *I* and the *you*, the self and the other, forms a *we*, in Apollinaire's poetry it creates an *I*. Apollinaire is always face to face with himself.

From the poems in *Alcools* it is clear that Apollinaire considers not only poetry to be invulnerable against time but memory as well. In "Cortège" he describes it as the "passé luisant" which will eventually create perfect poems in the future. As an event recedes into the past, the memory of that event grows in intensity. In "Mai" memory preserves the past in an unchanging, petrified state, so that

---

[12] Richard, p. 126.

it may endure in the present. It is, moreover, a powerfully creative force, for, like love, which produces a child, memory creates the poem.

Many of the poems in *Alcools* contain hidden statements about the creation of poetry; such poems are a disguised *art poétique*. Thus, Harlequin by his juggling act represents the magic, the music, and the acrobatics involved in poetic creation. Merlin's union with Morgane, moreover, symbolizes the creation of poetry that occurs when the poet is reintegrated with his memory or with a past self. In "Nuit rhénane," Apollinaire dramatizes the limits of poetry, those frontiers beyond which the poet cannot go, and in "La Chanson du Mal-Aimé" the orphic self translates the affective self's sorrow into a lasting song. Since the search for self is the focal point of these poems, and since poetic creation is the means to self-knowledge, it is not surprising to find that those poems which dramatize the drama of self also dramatize the creation of poetry.

In the course of studying the drama of self in Apollinaire's *Alcools* the self has been defined in many ways: as the fragmented, brightly colored costume of a harlequin; as an unfinished jigsaw puzzle from which pieces are always missing; as a kaleidoscope of interchanging fragments of glass; as a fixed lens through which the interior world of the self and the exterior world of the non-self are seen; as a moving camera that films simultaneous shots of different selves; as a shadow infiltrating the outer world; as a flowing song of despair; as a river whose only permanence is that it continually changes; as a cosmos populated with a diverse citizenry of past, present and future selves; and as a catharsis, a montage, and a dramatization. Since the creation of poetry for Apollinaire was inseparable from the search for self-identity, the poetic *œuvre* that he created and the self that he dramatized by that *œuvre* have both become his "unique lumière" ("Cortège"), that singular light radiating from all his poetry because fueled by an "inépuisable Moi." [13]

For Apollinaire, as for Paul Eluard, poetry is "l'art des lumières," [14] but of an extraordinary kind of light. [15] It is not only the light of

---

[13] Paul Valéry, "Fragments du Narcisse," *Œuvres* ("Bibliothèque de la Pléiade," 2 vols.; Paris: Gallimard, 1957), I, 126.

[14] *Avenir de la poésie*, in his *Œuvres complètes*, I, 527.

[15] M. Meschonnic points out that Apollinaire's fascination with light, which makes him perhaps "le plus grand poète méditerranéen," might have unconsciously inspired the choice of his pseudonym:

words growing in intensity as the words themselves move across the page on which a poem is in formation, like Mallarmé's famous constellation:

UNE CONSTELLATION
froide d'oubli et de désuétude
      pas tant
        qu'elle n'énumère
sur quelque surface vacante et supérieure
      le heurt successif
          sidéralement
d'un compte total en formation [16]

but the light of a self, also in formation, also growing in intensity, also radiating from a page, also shining forth from the center of a poem: a "feu oblong dont l'intensité ira s'augmentant / Au point qu'il deviendra un jour l'unique lumière" ("Cortège"). Constellations of words and constellations of selves, meeting on a page of paper and configuring simultaneously a poem and a self, this is the drama of Apollinaire's self because what these constellations do in fact create is the poet: "La lumière est ma mère" ("Merlin et la vieille femme").

Words are a source of light in Apollinaire's poetry:

> Tous les mots que j'avais à dire se sont changés en
>   étoiles
>   ("Les Fiançailles," O. P., p. 130)

And the selves expressed, voiced and, dramatized by those words are also a source of intense, creative light:

> Apollinaire s'est voulu dès le choix de son pseudonyme le poète de la lumière. "Apollon, mon patron" s'écrie-t-il dans *Que v'love*. On n'a peut-être pas jusqu'ici tiré toutes les conséquences de cette invocation au dieu du soleil, inventeur de la lyre.
>   ("Apollinaire illuminé au milieu d'ombres," p. 150)

Moreover, Apollinaire once wrote to the painter Robert Delaunay:

> ...je ne pense qu'une chose, cher ami, que je suis la tristesse même, mais non la vilaine et pauvre tristesse qui assombrit tout. La mienne brille comme une étoile, elle illumine le chemin de l'Art à travers l'effroyable nuit de la vie.
>   (*Œuvres complètes*, IV, 916)

[16] *Un Coup de dés jamais n'abolira le hasard*, in his *Œuvres complètes*, p. 477.

> Car c'est moi seul nuit qui t'étoile
> ("Lul de Faltenin," *O. P.*, p. 98)

It is light created by the self ("c'est *moi* seul"), engaged in an act of poetic expression, an act of lyric song powerful enough to transform the firmament and illuminate the cosmic night.

Constellations of words, galaxies of selves, these come into being in Apollinaire's poetry. His is a poetry of light, and this light, notwithstanding the many poems it shines out from, the innumerable words that bring it into existence, and the varied selves that generate it, is always the same light, the same "unique lumière," for as Apollinaire wrote of the flame in *Les Peintres cubistes*:

> La flamme a la pureté qui ne souffre rien d'étranger et transforme cruellement en elle-même ce qu'elle atteint. Elle a cette unité magique qui fait que si on la divise, chaque flammèche est semblable à la flamme unique. Elle a enfin la vérité sublime de sa lumière que nul ne peut nier.[17]

The "sublime truth of light": no finer description of Apollinaire's poetry has ever been written.

---

[17] p. 46.

BIBLIOGRAPHY OF WORKS CITED

A more complete bibliography of the works written by or about Apollinaire can be found by consulting the bibliographies in the following:

a. *Le Flâneur des Deux Rives. Bulletin d'études apollinariennes*, nos. 1-8 (mars, 1954 to septembre-décembre, 1955).

b. Guillaume Apollinaire, *Œuvres poètiques* ("Bibliothèque de la Pléiade"; Paris: Gallimard, 1959), pp. 1185-1235.

c. Michel Décaudin, *Le Dossier d'"Alcools"* ("Publications romanes et françaises," vol. LXVII; Geneva: Droz, 1965), pp. 235-40.

d. *La Revue des lettres modernes*: "Série Guillaume Apollinaire," 1- (1962 to date).

1. WORKS BY GUILLAUME APOLLINAIRE.

Chroniques d'Art (1902-1918). Ed. L.-C. Breunig. Paris: Gallimard, 1960.
"L'Esprit nouveau et les poètes," *Mercure de France*, CXXX (1er décembre, 1918), 385-396.
Œuvres complètes. Ed. Marcel Adéma and Michel Décaudin. 4 vols. and facsimiles. Paris: Balland et Lecat, 1966.
Œuvres poètiques. Ed. Marcel Adéma and Michel Décaudin. ("Bibliothèque de la Pléiade.") Paris: Gallimard, 1959.
Les Peintres cubistes. Méditations esthétiques. Ed. L. C. Breunig and J.-Cl. Chevalier. (Coll. "Miroirs de l'Art.") Paris: Hermann, 1965.
Tendre comme le souvenir. Paris: Gallimard, 1952.
Le Théâtre italien. Paris: Louis-Michaud, n. d.

2. WORKS ON APOLLINAIRE.

Adéma, Marcel. *Guillaume Apollinaire, le mal-aimé*. Paris: Plon, 1952.
Balachov, N. I. "Apollinaire et les Zaporogues." *Europe*, nos. 451-452 (novembre-décembre, 1966), pp. 281-82.
Bates, Scott. *Guillaume Apollinaire*. ("Twayne's World Authors Series," no. 14.) New York: Twayne Publishers, 1967.
Bergman, Pär. *"Modernolatria" et "Simultaneità": Recherches sur deux tendances dans l'avant-garde littéraire en Italie et en France à la veille de la

première guerre mondiale. ("Studia Litterarum Upsaliensia," vol. II.) Bonniers: Svenska Bokförlaget, 1962.
Bonnet, Marguerite. "A Propos de 'Cortège': Apollinaire et Picabia." *La Revue des lettres modernes,* nos. 85-89 (automne, 1963), pp. 62-75.
Breunig, L.-C. "Apollinaire et Annie Playden." *Mercure de France,* CCCXIV (1er avril, 1952), 638-652.
———. "The Chronology of Apollinaire's *Alcools.*" *PMLA,* LXVII (December, 1952), 907-923.
———. "The Laughter of Apollinaire." *Yale French Studies,* XXXI (May, 1964), 66-73.
———. "Le Roman du Mal-Aimé." *La Table Ronde,* LVII (septembre, 1952), 117-123.
Burgos, Jean. "Introduction" in Apollinaire, Guillaume. *L'Enchanteur pourrissant.* Ed. Jean Burgos. (Coll. "Paralogue," no. 5.) Paris: Minard, 1972, pp. v-clxii.
Carmody, Francis J. *The Evolution of Apollinaire's Poetics, 1901-1914.* ("University of California Publications in Modern Philology," vol. LXX.) Berkeley: University of California Press, 1963.
Chevalier, Jean-Claude. *"Alcools" d'Apollinaire: essai d'analyse des formes poétiques.* ("Bibliothèque des lettres modernes," vol. XVII.) Paris: Minard, 1970.
Couffignal, Robert. *L'Inspiration biblique dans l'œuvre de Guillaume Apollinaire.* ("Bibliothèque des lettres modernes," vol. VIII.) Paris: Minard, 1966.
———. *"Zone" d'Apollinaire. Structure et confrontations.* ("Archives des lettres modernes," no. 118.) Paris: Minard, 1970.
Davies, Margaret. *Apollinaire.* New York: St. Martin's Press, 1964.
Décaudin, Michel. "Apollinaire et le cinéma image par image" in *Apollinaire.* Ed. M. Bonfantini. Turin: Giappichelli and Paris: Nizet, 1970, pp. 19-28.
———. "Compléments à un Dossier." *La Revue des lettres modernes,* nos. 69-70 (printemps, 1962), pp. 57-61.
———. *Le Dossier d'"Alcools."* ("Publications romanes et françaises," vol. LXVII.) Geneva: Droz, 1965.
Durry, Marie-Jeanne. *Guillaume Apollinaire: Alcools.* 3 vols. Paris: Société d'Edition d'Enseignement Supérieur, 1964.
Follet, Lionel. "Du 'Palais' de Rosemonde à l'univers poétique" in Follet, Lionel and Poupon, Marc. *Lecture de "Palais" d'Apollinaire.* ("Archives des lettres modernes," no. 138.) Paris: Minard, 1972, pp. 15-102.
———. "Images et thèmes de l'amour malheureux dans 'Les Sept Epées.'" *Europe,* nos. 451-452 (novembre-décembre, 1966), pp. 206-239.
———. "Les Sept Epées." *Du monde européen à l'univers des mythes. Actes du colloque de Stavelot (1968).* Ed. Michel Décaudin. Paris: Minard, 1970, pp. 152-163.
Fongaro, Antoine. "Encore les 'Sept Epées.'" *La Revue des lettres modernes,* nos. 249-253 (1970), pp. 121-133.
Gossiaux, Pol-P. "Complément." *Du monde européen à l'univers des mythes. Actes du colloque de Stavelot (1968).* Ed. Michel Décaudin. Paris: Minard, 1970, pp. 163-171.
———. "Recherches sur 'Les Sept Epées.'" *La Revue des lettres modernes,* nos. 146-149 (1966), pp. 41-83.
———. "Les 'Sept Epées' et l'astrologie." *La Revue des lettres modernes,* nos. 249-253 (1970), pp. 165-169.

Hartwig, Julia. *Apollinaire*. Trans. Jean-Yves Erhel. Paris: Mercure de France, 1972.
Lawler, James R. "Les Sept Epées." *Le Flâneur des Deux Rives. Bulletin d'études apollinariennes*, no. 3 (septembre, 1954), pp. 10-13.
Lockerbie, S. I. "*Alcools* et le Symbolisme." *La Revue des lettres modernes*, nos. 85-89 (automne, 1963), pp. 5-40.
Louis, René. "Encore 'Lul de Faltenin.'" *Le Flâneur des Deux Rives. Bulletin d'études apollinariennes*, no. 3 (septembre, 1954), pp. 7-9.
———. "Lul de Faltenin." *Le Flâneur des Deux Rives. Bulletin d'études apollinariennes*, no. 2 (juin, 1954), pp. 9-11.
Meschonnic, Henri. "Apollinaire illuminé au milieu d'ombres." *Europe*, nos. 451-452 (novembre-décembre, 1966), pp. 141-169.
Michaud, Guy. "Comme un guetteur mélancolique: essai sur la personnalité d'Apollinaire." *La Revue des lettres modernes*, nos. 276-279 (1971), pp. 7-34.
Morhange-Bégué, Claude. "*La Chanson du Mal-Aimé*" *d'Apollinaire: essai d'analyse structurale et stylistique*. ("Bibliothèque des lettres modernes," vol. XVIII.) Paris: Minard, 1970.
Moulin, Jeanine. *Apollinaire: Textes inédits*. Geneva: Droz, 1952.
Navarri, Roger. "Apollinaire poète du déracinement." *Europe*, nos. 451-452 (novembre-décembre, 1966), pp. 133-141.
Orecchioni, Pierre. "Le Thème du Rhin dans l'inspiration de Guillaume Apollinaire." *La Revue des lettres modernes*, II (mars, avril, novembre, décembre, 1955), 161-190, 256-272, 529-544, 609-626; III (janvier, 1956), 1-48.
Piron, Maurice. "Sur quelques passages de *La Chanson du Mal-Aimé*." *La Revue des lettres modernes*, nos. 85-89 (automne, 1963), pp. 90-100.
Poupon, Marc. *Apollinaire et Cendrars*. ("Archives des lettres modernes," no. 103.) Paris: Minard, 1969.
Renaud, Philippe. *Lecture d'Apollinaire*. Lausanne: L'Age d'Homme, 1969.
Rouveyre, André. *Amour et poésie d'Apollinaire*. Paris: Editions du Seuil, 1955.
Salmon, André. *Souvenirs sans fin*. I. Paris: Gallimard, 1955.
Schmits, Georges. "Quelques strophes du 'Mal-Aimé.'" *Mercure de France*, CCCXXXVII (novembre, 1959), 536-543.
Virmaux, Alain. "*La Bréhatine* et le cinéma: Apollinaire en quête d'un langage neuf" in Apollinaire, Guillaume and Billy, André. *La Bréhatine*. Ed. Claude Tournadre. ("Archives des lettres modernes," no. 126.) Paris: Minard, 1971, pp. 97-117.
Warnier, R[aymond.] "Guillaume Apollinaire et l'Allemagne." *Revue de littérature comparée*, XXVIII (avril-juin, 1954), 168-190.

3. OTHER WORKS USED IN THIS STUDY.

Aragon, Louis. *Le Paysan de Paris*. Paris: Gallimard, 1926.
Arendt, Hannah. *The Human Condition*. Garden City: Doubleday Anchor Books, 1958.
Arnheim, Rudolf. *Film as Art*. Berkeley: University of California Press, 1957.
Baudelaire, Charles. *Œuvres complètes*. ("Bibliothèque de la Pléiade.") Paris: Gallimard, 1961.

Bergson, Henri. *Creative Evolution.* Trans. Arthur Mitchell. New York: The Modern Library, 1944.

———. *Le Rire, essai sur la signification du comique.* Paris: Presses Universitaires, 1962.

Bettelheim, Bruno. *The Empty Fortress. Infantile Autism and the Birth of the Self.* New York: The Free Press, 1967.

Bonnefoy, Yves. *Du Mouvement et de l'immobilité de Douve.* (Coll. "Poésie.") Paris: Gallimard, 1970.

Borschak, Elie. "La Lettre des Zaporogues au Sultan." *Revue des études slaves,* XXVI. Paris: Imprimerie Nationale, 1950, 99-105.

Burnshaw, Stanley. *In The Terrified Radiance.* New York: George Braziller, 1972.

Cendrars, Blaise. *Selected Writings.* New York: New Directions, 1966.

Chipp, Herschel (ed.). *Theories of Modern Art. A Source Book by Artists and Critics.* Berkeley: University of California Press, 1968.

Cirlot, J. E. *Dictionary of Symbols.* Trans. Jack Sage. London: Routledge and Kegan Paul, 1962.

Cocteau, Jean. *La Difficulté d'être.* Montana (Switzerland): Bottinelli, 1947.

Denis, Ferdinand. *Le Monde enchanté. Cosmographie et histoire naturelle fantastiques du moyen âge.* 1845; rpt. New York: Burt Franklin, n. d.

Eluard, Paul. *Œuvres complètes.* ("Bibliothèque de la Pléiade.") 2 vols. Paris: Gallimard, 1968.

Fowlie, Wallace. *Love in Literature. Studies in Symbolic Expression.* Bloomington: Indiana University Press, 1965.

Frazer, Sir James George. *The New Golden Bough. A New Abridgment of the Classic Work.* Ed. Dr. Theodor H. Gaster. New York: Criterion Books, 1959.

Gherardi, Evaristo. *Le Théâtre Italien de Gherardi, ou le recueil général de toutes les Comédies & Scènes Françoises jouées par les Comédiens Italiens du Roi, pendant tout le temps qu'ils ont été au service.* 6 vols. Paris: Briasson, 1741.

Heltzel, Virgil B. *Fair Rosamond. A Study of the Development of a Literary Theme.* ("Northwestern University Studies in the Humanities," no. 16.) Evanston: Northwestern University Studies, 1947.

Herdeg, Walter (ed.). *The Sun in Art.* Zurich: Amstutz and Herdeg, Graphis Press, 1962.

Hugo, Victor. *Œuvres poétiques.* I. ("Bibliothèque de la Pléiade.") Paris: Gallimard, 1964.

Kelly, Amy. *Eleanor of Aquitaine and the Four Kings.* Cambridge: Harvard University Press, 1950.

Langer, Susanne. "A Note on the Film" in her *Feeling and Form.* New York: Scribner, 1953, pp. 411-415.

Lemaitre, Georges. *From Cubism to Surrealism in French Literature.* Cambridge: Harvard University Press, 1945.

Mallarmé, Stéphane. *Œuvres complètes.* ("Bibliothèque de la Pléiade.") Paris: Gallimard, 1945.

Montaigne, Michel de. *Essais.* 2 vols. Paris: Garnier, 1962.

Nicoll, Allardyce. *The World of Harlequin. A Critical Study of the Commedia dell'Arte.* Cambridge: The University Press, 1963.

Niklaus, Thelma. *Harlequin Phoenix: or The Rise and Fall of a Bergamask Rogue.* London: The Bodley Head, 1956.

Ownbey, E. Sydnor. "Merlin and Arthur. A Study of Merlin's Character and Function in the Romances Dealing With the Early Life of Arthur. [Condensation of a thesis]." *Dissertation Collection Ph. D. Vanderbilt University*, IV, no. 5 (1932).

Paton, Lucy Allen. *Studies in the Fairy Mythology of Arthurian Romance.* 2nd ed., 1903; rpt. New York: Burt Franklin, 1960.

Read, Herbert. *Icon and Idea: The Function of Art in the Development of Human Consciousness.* Cambridge: Harvard University Press, 1955.

Richard, Jean-Pierre. *Onze études sur la poésie moderne.* Paris: Editions du Seuil, 1964.

Rimbaud, Arthur. *Œuvres complètes.* ("Bibliothèque de la Pléiade.") Paris: Gallimard, 1954.

Robbe-Grillet, Alain. *L'Année Dernière à Marienbad.* Paris: Editions de Minuit, 1961.

Rousset, Jean. *Forme et signification. Essais sur les structures littéraires de Corneille à Claudel.* Paris: Corti, 1962.

Seward, Barbara. *The Symbolic Rose.* New York: Columbia University Press, 1960.

Somville, Léon. *Devanciers du surréalisme. Les groupes d'avant-garde et le mouvement poétique 1912-1925.* ("Histoire des idées et critique littéraire," vol. 116.) Geneva: Droz, 1971.

Spicq, Ceslaus. *Agape in the New Testament.* Trans. Sister Marie Aquinas McNamara and Sister Mary Honoria Richter. 3 vols. St. Louis: B. Herder Book Co., 1965.

Stevens, Wallace. *Collected Poems.* New York: Alfred A. Knopf, 1964.

Symons, Arthur. "The World as Ballet" in his *Studies in Seven Arts.* London: Martin Secker, 1924, pp. 244-246.

Valéry, Paul. *Œuvres.* ("Bibliothèque de la Pléiade.") 2 vols. Paris: Gallimard, 1957.

Verlaine, [Paul.] *Œuvres poétiques complètes.* ("Bibliothèque de la Pléiade.") Paris: Gallimard, 1938.

Yeats, W. B. *The Collected Poems.* Definitive Edition. New York: Macmillan, 1956.

GENERAL INDEX

Adéma, Marcel, 62n, 165
African art, 160-1. *See also* cubism
angelism, 59n
Antonioni, Michelangelo, 120, 121
Aphrodite, 33
Apollinaire, Guillaume, 157; attitude toward women, 62n, 88ff., 149-51, 158-9, 181-2, 190; and despair, sadness, 86ff., 128-9, 131, 146-7, 149-50, 154-6, 157-8, 159-64, 169-70, 173-4, 182, 184, 189-95, 196-8, 203-4, 206, 207-9, 217n; and gourmandise, 35-7; his identity with immigrants, wanderers, gypsies, 70, 75, 116-7, 119, 157-8, 181-2; his imprisonment, 155-6; his laughter, 148n; literary influences on, 63-4, 114-5; and love, 62-3, 67-9, 75, 80, 149-51, 162-3, 166-7, 171-4, 176, 177-205, 206, 208; his loyalty to tradition and invention, 145; and obsession with repetition, 43n; his power of assimilation, 65-7, 79; his pseudonym, 216n; as reader of his own poetry, 165-6; and religion, 130, 135-41, 146, 160-2; his stay in Germany, 63ff.
Aragon, Louis, 119
Arendt, Hannah, 73
Les Argonautes, 106
Ariadne auf Naxos, 104n
Arlequinade, 104n
Arletty, 104n
Arnheim, Rudolf, 124
aubade, 183ff.
Avril, Jane, 92

Balachov, N. I., 187n
Barrault, Jean-Louis, 104n

Bates, Scott, 62n
Baudelaire, Charles, 87n, 112n, 116-7, 172
Bergman, Pär, 132n
Bergson, Henri, 52n, 60, 133
Bettelheim, Bruno, 15
Blériot, Louis, 132
Boileau, Nicolas, 39
Bonnefoy, Yves, 19
Bonnet, Marguerite, 41n
Boron, Robert de, 78
Borschak, Elie, 187n
Braque, Georges, 48n
Brentano, Clemens, 63
Breton, André, 145n, 148n
Breunig, L. C., 25n, 63n, 68, 80n, 148n, 166n, 167-8, 183n, 187n, 190n
Buffet, Gabrielle, 122-3
Buñuel, Louis, 163
Burgos, Jean, 79n, 83n
Burnshaw, Stanley, 210

Camus, Albert, 19n
Carmody, Francis J., 26n
Carnaval, 104n
La Carrozza d'Oro, 104n
Cendrars, Blaise, 129-30, 133-4, 137
Cézanne, Paul, 104n
Chaplin, Charlie, 104n
Chevalier, Jean-Claude, 17n, 18, 43n, 51, 88n, 121n
Un Chien andalou, 163
Christ, Jesus, 33, 37, 41, 100, 137, 139-40, 143, 161, 184; renunciation of, 162-3
Christianity, 86n, 98, 135-7, 150, 183, 196
cinema, 120-2, 140-1; techniques of,

as used by Apollinaire, 122, 124-8, 153, 159, 163
Cirlot, J. E., 143n
Clifford, Rosamond. *See* Rosamond
clowns. *See saltimbanques*
Cocteau, Jean, 146-7, 148n
Columbine, 107ff.
commedia dell'arte, 103ff.
Couffignal, Robert, 130n, 184
cubism, 25, 47, 48-9, 128n, 132, 135, 145, 160

Dalí, Salvador, 163
the dancer, as symbolist image, 89ff., 91-5, 96n
Davies, Margaret, 165n
death, 52, 53, 58, 72, 77-8, 82-9, 94ff., 98-9, 161-3, 181, 194, 201, 203, 204, 206, 212, 214-5. *See also* suicide
decapitation, images of, 162-4
Décaudin, Michel, 40, 106, 122n, 129, 130, 140, 143n, 167, 170, 190n
Degas, Edgar, 104n
Delaunay, Robert, 133, 134, 153n, 154n, 217. *See also* simultaneity
Les Demoiselles d'Avignon, 160
Dendrophori, 196
Denis, Ferdinand, 40, 41
Derain, André, 104n
Désirade, 193, 206
Doushmanta, 178, 187
dream, 35, 49, 201
Durry, Marie-Jeanne, 32, 86n, 98, 106, 107n, 191n

Eiffel Tower, 133-4
Eliot, T. S., 23
Eluard, Paul, 213-5, 216
Les Enfants du paradis, 104n
l'esprit nouveau, 28, 51, 79, 133, 145n. *See also* modernism

Le Festin d'Esope, 36n, 166
fire, flamme, 37-8, 43-4, 57-8, 193-4, 218
le flâneur, 119-22, 123-6
Fokine, Michel, 104n
Follet, Lionel, 38n, 200-1, 204
Fongaro, Antoine, 197n
Fort, Paul, 165
Fowlie, Wallace, 171n

Frazer, James George, 174n
Fuller, Loïe, 92
futurism, 26n, 136n, 145, 153

Gautier, Théophile, 187n
Gherardi, Evaristo, 112n, 113-4, 115
Ghil, René, 165
Gleizes, Albert, 48
Goffin, Robert, 63, 129
Gossiaux, Pol-P., 199-200, 201, 204
Greco-Roman tradition, 131-2; Apollinaire's rejection of, 132-5, 136n, 144-5, 161. *See also* modernism

Harlequin, 21, 103-18, 171n, 212, 216. *See also saltimbanques*
Harlequinade, 104ff., 118; *Arlequin, L'Empereur dans la lune*, 112; *Les Fées ou les contes de ma mère l'Oye*, 113-5; *La figlia disubbediente*, 104-5
Harlequin in April, 104n
Hartwig, Julia, 68n
Heine, Henri, 63, 71
Heltzel, Virgil B., 26n
Henry II, of England, 26, 27, 31
hermaphroditism, 170, 177-8, 199
Hermes, 198, 200
Hermes Trismegistos, 112, 115
Hiroshima Mon Amour, 121, 124
Hirsch, Charles Henry, 165
Hofmannsthal, Hugo von, 104n
Hugo, Victor, 67, 75n, 185n

Jacob, Max, 25, 36n
Jarry, Alfred, 133, 148n, 165
Jung, Carl, 15

Kelly, Amy, 34n

Laforgue, Jules, 116
La Goulue, 92
Langer, Susanne, 125
Laquedem Isaac, 98, 155
laughter, 59-61, 147-8
Laurencin, Marie, 106, 122, 131, 150, 159
Lawler, James, 170n, 198-9, 201, 203, 204
Lemaitre, Georges, 132-3
light, as metaphor, 42-5, 52, 90, 97, 175, 176, 216-9

Limelight, 104n
Lockerbie, S. I., 80n
London, 171-4, 177, 179, 207, 209
Louis, René, 197n
Louis II, of Bavaria, 205-6
love, 27-8, 30-2, 33-4, 62-3, 68, 72-3, 76-7, 81-91, 96-100, 149-51, 157-8, 162, 177-205, 208-9, 213-5
Luitpold, 205, 206

madness, 59, 155, 179, 196, 205-6
Mallarmé, Stéphane, 45, 87, 92-4, 116, 163, 173n, 217
Marceau, Marcel, 148n
Marconi, Guglielmo, 132
Marinetti, Filippo Tommaso, 26n, 136n
Mary, The Virgin, 149-50, 196
Mausolus, 177, 186
memory, 43-5, 52-3, 69, 72-8, 81, 87-9, 96-100, 121-2, 153, 179, 182, 192-3, 202-4, 215-6. See also temporality
Mercure de France, 136n
Mercury, 109
Merlin, 78-80, 81ff., 105, 110, 212, 216
Merrill, Stuart, 165
Meschonnic, Henri, 148n, 216n
Metzinger, Jean, 48
Michaud, Guy, 211n
Mocquet, Jean, 40
modernism, 119ff., 128-9, 132-6, 137ff., 140-1, 160-1, 163-4, 207-8; association of the mythic with the modern, 142-6. See also *l'esprit nouveau*; Greco-Roman tradition
Mollet, Jean, 166
Monet, Claude, 171
Montaigne, Michel de, 16, 17
Morgane, 81-2, 87-8, 89ff.
Morhange-Bégué, Claude, 169n, 191n, 201, 202, 203, 204
Moulin, Jeanine, 106n

Navarri, Roger, 157n
Nerval, Gérard de, 67
Nicoll, Allardyce, 103n
Niklaus, Thelma, 103n
Niniane. See Vivien
Nord-Sud, 36n
La Notte, 121

Onimus, James, 191n
Orecchioni, Pierre, 63n, 64n, 65, 66, 67
Orpheus, the myth of, 74n
Ownbey, E. Sydnor, 78n

paganism, 33, 142-4, 170, 183-4, 196
Pagès, Madeleine, 190n, 191n
Paris, 21, 119-64, 179, 206-7, 209
Paton, Lucy Allen, 80n
Pavlova, Anna, 104n
Penelope, 178, 187
Percy, Thomas, 34n
Picabia, Francis, 41, 122, 145n
Picasso, Pablo, 25, 47, 104n, 109, 116, 160
Piron, Maurice, 173, 185, 195
Playden, Annie, 63, 66, 67-9, 80, 166-7, 168, 171, 172, 188, 190, 191n, 196, 198-9, 201, 206
La Plume, 165
Poème et Drame, 39
poetry, 15, 19, 20, 79, 87, 92-4, 109-12, 163, 175, 210-1, and *passim*; and Apollinaire's orphic power, 184-5, 207-8; and creative imagination, 47-50; and criticism of symbolism, 89-95; as disguised *art poétique*, 81, 100, 207, 216; as gift of tongues, 38; and immortality, 52-3, 72, 81, 82, 88-9, 96-100, 115-7, 212; and incantation, 61; and light, 44-5, 52, 216-9; the limits of, 61; and magic, 109-12, 115; and memory, 44-5, 72, 74n, 76-7, 78, 81, 87-9, 96-9, 207-8, 215-6; and the modernization of language, 133-4, 136n; and poetic failure and sterility, 82-96, 199, 201; as the presence of being, 19, 210-1; repetition in, 42n, 88n, 163, 170, 195, 208; and self-knowledge, 38-9, 51-2, 199, 215, 216; as simultaneous creation of poem and self, 216-8; and suffering, 98-9, 184, 199, 204, 207. See also song
Pope Pius X, 136
Poupon, Marc, 130

Read, Herbert, 15n
recurrence, 74, 75-8, 85, 88, 91, 98-9,

212; permanence and flux, 192-3, 206. *See also* temporality
Régnier, Henri de, 95n
Renaud, Philippe, 21n, 53n, 74n, 95n, 212n
Renoir, Jean, 104n
Repin, Ilia Efimovitch, 187
Resnais, Alain, 120, 121
Reverdy, Pierre, 36n
Revue Littéraire de Paris et de Champagne, 25
the Rhine, 56, 58, 64-70, 71, 195, 198, 206
Richard, J.-P., 213, 214, 215
Rimbaud, Arthur, 20, 28, 30, 82
Robbe-Grillet, Alain, 126-7
Le Roman de Merlin, 78
Rosamond, 26-8, 30ff.; "The Ballad of Fair Rosamond," 34n
rose, as metaphor and symbol, 31-2, 83-6
Rouault, Georges, 116
Rousset, Jean, 19
Rouveyre, André, 27
Les Rubriques nouvelles, 80

Sacontale, 178, 187
Salmon, André, 160n, 166
saltimbanques, 106-7, 109-11, 116-7, 157n, 171n. *See also* Harlequin
Schmits, Georges, 186n, 187n
Schumann, Robert, 71
self, 22n, and *passim*; as called by different names, 15, 17n, 18n, 46, 50-1, 121, 128, 212-3; and confession, 168-70, 178-9, 184, 189-96, 207, 209; and the creation of a poetic work of art, 16, 18-20, 21n, 38-9, 51-3, 81, 88-9, 96-9, 115-8, 148, 175, 184-5, 199, 207-8, 210-2, 216-9; the *dédoublement* of, 126, 128, 168n, 170-1, 172, 176, 177, 194, 195, 212-3; the deprecation of, 25, 35-6, 59-61, 147-8, 185; the dispersion of, 21, 56-61, 78; the drama of, 17-21, 148, 217; the dramatization of, 17-21, 117-8, 148, 168-70, 178, 183-4, 188-9, 196, 204-5, 209, 211-2; and expressions of anger and violence, 159, 161-3, 172, 177, 188, 190; the fragmentation of, 14, 21, 22n, 25-53, 155; *I/you*, 213-5; and introspection, 40, 42-3, 46, 53, 121, 126-7, 129, 161, 215; the liquid expansiveness of, 169, 170-1, 172, 174, 180-1, 192-3; the montage of, 119-64; the objectification of, 19-20, 30, 40, 45-6, 50-2, 53, 60, 108ff., 118, 128, 147-8, 174-5, 211-2; and other, 20, 22n, 50-1, 83n, 118, 156-7, 174, 212-5; and *personae*, 50, 77, 79, 81, 87, 100, 103-6, 108, 117-8, 168, 169-70, 172, 178, 187-8, 204, 205, 206, 209, 212; its participation in the universe, 14-5, 58-9, 61, 65-6, 79, 87, 153n, 154n, 160n; the protean nature of, 15-6, 103-18; the reintegration of, 21, 62-100; the search for, 13-22, 81, 215, 216; and space, 175-7; and time, 44-5, 52-3, 83, 115-6, 117, 200, 212
"les Sept Epées," 196-204
Seward, Barbara, 31n
shadow, as image of self, 14, 97, 170, 174-7, 194-5
simultaneity, 121, 127-8, 134, 145, 152-4; "le contraste simultané" (Delaunay), 154n. *See also* temporality
Les Soirées de Paris, 36n, 122
Somville, Léon, 95n
song, 21, 56ff., 83n, 106, 167-8, 169-70, 171, 182-3, 184-5, 202n, 204, 207-9. *See also* poetry
Spicq, Ceslaus, 34n
Stevens, Wallace, 13, 163
Strauss, Richard, 104n
suicide, 22n, 112, 194, 205-7. *See also* death
Sultan of Constantinople, 186-9
sun, as image, 31-2, 33, 41-2, 44-5, 85-7, 88, 97, 138-9, 207; its ritual assassination, 161-3
surprise, the aesthetics of, 28, 140-1, 163
surrealism, 119, 121, 145, 163
Symbolism, 63, 80-1, 91-6, 99-100, 138ff.; criticism of, 93-5
Symons, Arthur, 93

temporality, 200; Apollinaire's attitude toward the future and to-

ward destiny, 44-5, 52, 88-9, 98-9, 115-7, 129, 157, 162, 180-2, 191, 204-5, 211, 212; his attitude toward the past, 41n, 44-5, 47-8, 52-3, 70-8, 87-9, 121-2, 125, 129, 138-46, 153, 157, 179, 182-4, 193, 195-6, 198-9, 200, 202-4, 206, 208, 215; his attitude toward the present, 125-8, 132ff., 138, 139-41, 143-4, 145-6. See also memory; recurrence; simultaneity
Toulouse-Lautrec, Henry de, 92, 116

Ulysses, 178, 187

Valéry, Paul, 101, 216
Vedius Pollion, 185
Verlaine, Paul, 28, 30, 106, 107n, 110n, 116

Vers et Prose, 39, 69n
Villon, François, 145, 156
Virmaux, Alain, 122n
vision, distant and proximate, 42ff., 45-6, 71, 73-4, 75, 154-5, 169n, 193; modes of, 213-5
Vivien, 80, 98, 99

Wagner, Richard, 64
Warnier, Raymond, 64n
wine, its pagan and Christian meanings, 57, 58, 59n, 139; *alcool*, 159

Yeats, William Butler, 93

Zaporogian Cossacks, 186-9

INDEX OF THE WORKS OF GUILLAUME APOLLINAIRE

Alcools, 13, 17, 18n, 20, 21, 22n, 27n, 36n, 43n, 64, 74n, 80, 81, 86, 100, 105, 122, 125, 148n, 153n, 159n, 162n, 181, 211, 212, 213, 215, 216: "A La Santé," 55-6; "Le Brasier," 14, 18n, 44, 79, 163n, 181; "La Chanson du Mal-Aimé," 14, 43n, 108n, 159n, 165-209, 216; "Clair de lune," 84n; "Les Cloches," 64; "Clotilde," 176n; "Les Colchiques," 68, 179n, 190n; "Cortège," 13, 18n, 39-55, 65, 79, 116, 176n, 212, 215, 216, 217, ("Brumaire," 40, 42); "Crépuscule," 22n, 105-18, 176n, 212, 216; "L'Emigrant de Landor Road," 14, 16; "L'Ermite," 17n, 80, 83n, 95n, 105, 148n, 163n, 165, 181; "Les Femmes," 64, 67; "Les Fiançailles," 14, 18n, 160n, 163n, 175, 217; "Le Larron," 17n, 80, 83n, 95n, 105, 148n, 160n, 176n; "La Loreley," 64, 65n, 80n, 105, 190n; "Lul de Faltenin," 218; "Mai," 43n, 62-78, 81, 88, 190n, 215; "Merlin et la vieille femme," 17n, 22n, 38n, 78-100, 105, 148n, 162n, 176n, 216, 217; "1909," 18n; "Nuit rhénane," 43n, 56-61, 64, 78, 79, 148n, 160n, 216; "Palais," 14, 25-39, 160n, 163n; "Poème lu au mariage d'André Salmon," 59, 160n; "Le Pont Mirabeau," 192; "Rhénane d'automne," 64, 65n, 67; "Rosemonde," 27n; "Saltimbanques," 105, 106; "Les Sapins," 64, 65n; "Schinderhannes," 64, 160n, 165; "Signe," 176n; "La Synagogue," 64, 65n, 67; "La Tzigane," 68, 75, 191n; "Zone," 13, 16, 36n, 43n, 45, 50-1, 60-1, 79, 86, 100, 121-64, 182n, 207, 212; "Vendémiaire," 14-5, 66, 79, 113n, 153n, 159n, 160n

L'Année Républicaine, 40, 149n, 150n, 151n

Le Bestiaire, 27n, 36n: "La Colombe," 150n

La Bréhatine, 122n

Calligrammes, 13, 22n, 36n, 45, 153n, 212n: "Chant de l'horizon en Champagne," 169n; "Les Collines," 14, 53, 211n; "Un Fantôme de Nuées," 117; "Les Fenêtres," 153n; "Fumées," 123; "La Jolie Rousse," 145n;

"Merveille de la guerre," 45, 154n, 169n; "Le Musicien de Saint-Merry," 15; "Ombre," 97n, 175; "Toujours," 53; "La Victoire," 135n, 175

Chroniques d'Art: "Realité, Peinture Pure," 154n; "Sculptures d'Afrique et d'Océanie," 160

L'Enchanteur pourrissant, 36n, 79, 83n, 98

"L'Esprit nouveau et les poètes," 28, 51, 79, 140, 143n, 145n, 148n, 211

Le Guetteur mélancolique, 64n: "Les Bacs," 64n, 70n; "Le Dôme de Cologne," 27n, 64n, 162n; "Mille Regrets," 64n; "Passion," 162n; "Plongeon," 70n; "Le Printemps," 71n; "La Vierge à la fleur de haricot à Cologne," 64n

L'Hérésiarque et Cie, 36n: "L'Amphion faux-messie ou histoires et aventures du baron d'Ormesan," 119-20; "Le Passant de Prague," 155; "Que v'love?", 217n

Il y a: "Dans le jardin d'Anna," 68

L'Œuvre du Divin Arétin, 36n

Les Peintres cubistes. Méditations esthétiques, 16, 25, 36n, 47, 48-9, 109, 135, 218

Poèmes de guerre, 22n

Poèmes retrouvés: "La Maison de cristal," 79

Poèmes rhénans, 56, 64-9, 70ff., 203

Le Poète assassiné: "L'Ami Méritarte," 36n; "Cas du Brigadier masqué c'est-à-dire le poète ressuscité," 36n

Le Théâtre italien, 114-5

Tendre comme le souvenir, 183n, 190n, 191n

NORTH CAROLINA STUDIES IN THE ROMANCE LANGUAGES AND LITERATURES

I.S.B.N. Prefix 0-88438

Recent Titles

CHARLES NODIER: HIS LIFE AND WORKS, by Sarah Fore Bell. 1971. (No. 95). -895-6.

RACINE AND SENECA, by Ronald W. Tobin. 1971. (No. 96). -896-4.

LOPE DE VEGA. "EL PEREGRINO EN SU PATRIA," edición de Myron A. Peyton. 1971. (No. 97), -897-2.

CRITICAL REACTIONS AND THE CHRISTIAN ELEMENT IN THE POETRY OF PIERRE DE RONSARD, by Mark S. Whitney. 1971. (No. 98). -898-0.

THE REV. JOHN BOWLE. THE GENESIS OF CERVANTEAN CRITICISM, by Ralph Merritt Cox. 1971. (No. 99). -899-9.

THE FOUR INTERPOLATED STORIES IN THE "ROMAN COMIQUE": THEIR SOURCES AND UNIFYING FUNCTION, by Frederick Alfed De Armas. 1971. (No. 100). -900-6.

LE CHASTOIEMENT D'UN PERE A SON FILS, A CRITICAL EDITION, edited by Edward D. Montgomery, Jr. 1971. (No. 101). -901-4.

LE ROMMANT DE "GUY DE WARWIK" ET DE "HEROLT D'ARDENNE," edited by D. J. Conlon. 1971. (No. 102). -902-2.

THE OLD PORTUGUESE "VIDA DE SAM BERNARDO," EDITED FROM ALCOBAÇA MANUSCRIPT ccxci/200, WITH INTRODUCTION, LINGUISTIC STUDY, NOTES, TABLE OF PROPER NAMES, AND GLOSSARY, by Lawrence A. Sharpe. 1971. (No. 103). -903-0.

A CRITICAL AND ANNOTATED EDITION OF LOPE DE VEGA'S "LAS ALMENAS DE TORO," by Thomas E. Case. 1971. (No. 104). -904-9.

LOPE DE VEGA'S "LO QUE PASA EN UNA TARDE," A CRITICAL, ANNOTATED EDITION OF THE AUTOGRAPH MANUSCRIPT, by Richard Angelo Picerno. 1971. (No. 105). -905-7.

OBJECTIVE METHODS FOR TESTING AUTHENTICITY AND THE STUDY OF TEN DOUBTFUL "COMEDIAS" ATTRIBUTED TO LOPE DE VEGA, by Fred M. Clark. 1971. (No. 106). -906-5.

THE ITALIAN VERB. A MORPHOLOGICAL STUDY, by Frede Jensen. 1971. (No. 107). -907-3.

A CRITICAL EDITION OF THE OLD PROVENÇAL EPIC "DAUREL ET BETON," WITH NOTES AND PROLEGOMENA, by Arthur S. Kimmel. 1971. (No. 108). -908-1.

FRANCISCO RODRIGUES LOBO: DIALOGUE AND COURTLY LORE IN RENAISSANCE PORTUGAL, by Richard A. Preto-Rodas. 1971. (No. 109). 909-X.

RAIMOND VIDAL: POETRY AND PROSE, edited by W. H. W. Field. 1971. (No. 110). -910-3.

RELIGIOUS ELEMENTS IN THE SECULAR LYRICS OF THE TROUBADOURS, by Raymond Gay-Crosier. 1971. (No. 111). -911-1.

THE SIGNIFICANCE OF DIDEROT'S "ESSAI SUR LE MERITE ET LA VERTU," by Gordon B. Walters. 1971. (No. 112). -912-X.

PROPER NAMES IN THE LYRICS OF THE TROUBADOURS, by Frank M. Chambers. 1971. (No. 113). -913-8.

STUDIES IN HONOR OF MARIO A. PEI, edited by John Fisher and Paul A. Gaeng. 1971. (No. 114). -914-6.

DON MANUEL CAÑETE, CRONISTA LITERARIO DEL ROMANTICISMO Y DEL POSROMANTICISMO EN ESPAÑA, por Donald Allen Randolph. 1972. (No. 115). -915-4.

When ordering please cite the *ISBN Prefix* plus the last four digits for each title.

Send orders to: University of North Carolina Press
Chapel Hill
North Carolina 27514
U. S. A.

NORTH CAROLINA STUDIES IN THE ROMANCE LANGUAGES AND LITERATURES

I.S.B.N. Prefix 0-88438

Recent Titles

THE TEACHINGS OF SAINT LOUIS. A CRITICAL TEXT, by David O'Connell. 1972. (No. 116). *-916-2.*

HIGHER, HIDDEN ORDER: DESIGN AND MEANING IN THE ODES OF MALHERBE, by David Lee Rubin. 1972. (No. 117). *-917-0.*

JEAN DE LE MOTE "LE PARFAIT DU PAON," édition critique par Richard J. Carey. 1972. (No. 118). *-918-9.*

CAMUS' HELLENIC SOURCES, by Paul Archambault. 1972. (No. 119). *-919-7.*

FROM VULGAR LATIN TO OLD PROVENÇAL, by Frede Jensen. 1972. (No. 120). *-920-0.*

GOLDEN AGE DRAMA IN SPAIN: GENERAL CONSIDERATION AND UNUSUAL FEATURES, by Sturgis E. Leavitt. 1972. (No. 121). *-921-9.*

THE LEGEND OF THE "SIETE INFANTES DE LARA" (*Refundición toledana de la crónica de 1344* versión), study and edition by Thomas A. Lathrop. 1972. (No. 122). *-922-7.*

STRUCTURE AND IDEOLOGY IN BOIARDO'S "ORLANDO INNAMORATO," by Andrea di Tommaso. 1972. (No. 123). *-923-5.*

STUDIES IN HONOR OF ALFRED G. ENGSTROM, edited by Robert T. Cargo and Emmanuel J. Mickel, Jr. 1972. (No. 124). *-924-3.*

A CRITICAL EDITION WITH INTRODUCTION AND NOTES OF GIL VICENTE'S "FLORESTA DE ENGANOS," by Constantine Christopher Stathatos. 1972. (No. 125). *-925-1.*

LI ROMANS DE WITASSE LE MOINE. *Roman du treizième siècle.* Édité d'après le manuscrit, fonds français 1553, de la Bibliothèque Nationale, Paris, par Denis Joseph Conlon. 1972. (No. 126). *-926-X.*

EL CRONISTA PEDRO DE ESCAVIAS. *Una vida del Siglo XV*, por Juan Bautista Avalle-Arce. 1972. (No. 127). *-927-8.*

AN EDITION OF THE FIRST ITALIAN TRANSLATION OF THE "CELESTINA," by Kathleen V. Kish. 1973. (No. 128). *-928-6.*

MOLIÈRE MOCKED. THREE CONTEMPORARY HOSTILE COMEDIES: *Zélinde, Le portrait du peintre, Élomire Hypocondre,* by Frederick Wright Vogler. 1973. (No. 129). *-929-4.*

C.-A. SAINTE-BEUVE. *Chateaubriand et son groupe littéraire sous l'empire.* Index alphabétique et analytique établi par Lorin A. Uffenbeck. 1973. (No. 130). *-930-8.*

THE ORIGINS OF THE BAROQUE CONCEPT OF "PEREGRINATIO," by Juergen Hahn. 1973. (No. 131). *-931-6.*

THE "AUTO SACRAMENTAL" AND THE PARABLE IN SPANISH GOLDEN AGE LITERATURE, by Donald Thaddeus Dietz. 1973. (No. 132). *-932-4.*

FRANCISCO DE OSUNA AND THE SPIRIT OF THE LETTER, by Laura Calvert. 1973. (No. 133). *-933-2.*

ITINERARIO DI AMORE: DIALETTICA DI AMORE E MORTE NELLA VITA NUOVA, by Margherita de Bonfils Templer. 1973. (No. 134). *-934-0.*

L'IMAGINATION POETIQUE CHEZ DU BARTAS: ELEMENTS DE SENSIBILITE BAROQUE DANS LA "CREATION DU MONDE," by Bruno Braunrot. 1973. (No. 135). *-934-0.*

ARTUS DESIRE: PRIEST AND PAMPHLETEER OF THE SIXTEENTH CENTURY, by Frank S. Giese. 1973. (No. 136). *-936-7.*

JARDIN DE NOBLES DONZELLAS, FRAY MARTIN DE CORDOBA, by Harriet Goldberg. 1974. (No. 137). *-937-5.*

When ordering please cite the *ISBN Prefix* plus the last four digits for each title.

Send orders to: University of North Carolina Press
Chapel Hill
North Carolina 27514
U. S. A.

NORTH CAROLINA STUDIES IN THE ROMANCE LANGUAGES AND LITERATURES

I.S.B.N. Prefix 0-88438

Recent Titles

MYTHE ET PSYCHOLOGIE CHEZ MARIE DE FRANCE DANS "GUIGEMAR", par Antoinette Knapton. 1975. (No. 142). *-942-1.*

THE LYRIC POEMS OF JEHAN FROISSART: A CRITICAL EDITION, by Rob Roy McGregor, Jr. 1975. (No. 143). *-943-X.*

HISTORIA Y BIBLIOGRAFÍA DE LA CRÍTICA SOBRE EL "POEMA DE MÍO CID" (1750-1971), por Miguel Magnotta. 1976. (No. 145). *-945-6.*

THE DRAMATIC WORKS OF ÁLVARO CUBILLO DE ARAGÓN, by Shirley B. Whitaker. 1975. (No. 149). *-949-9.*

POETRY AND ANTIPOETRY: A STUDY OF SELECTED ASPECTS OF MAX JACOB'S POETIC STYLE, by Annette Thau. 1976. (No. 158). *-005-X.*

STYLE AND STRUCTURE IN GRACIÁN'S "EL CRITICÓN", by Marcia L. Welles. 1976. (No. 160). *-007-6.*

MOLIERE: TRADITIONS IN CRITICISM, by Laurence Romero. 1974 (Essays, No. 1). *-001-7.*

CHRÉTIEN'S JEWISH GRAIL. A NEW INVESTIGATION OF THE IMAGERY AND SIGNIFICANCE OF CHRÉTIEN DE TROYES'S GRAIL EPISODE BASED UPON MEDIEVAL HEBRAIC SOURCES, by Eugene J. Weinraub. 1976. (Essays, No. 2). *-002-5.*

STUDIES IN TIRSO, I, by Ruth Lee Kennedy. 1974. (Essays, No. 3). *-003-3.*

VOLTAIRE AND THE FRENCH ACADEMY, by Karlis Racevskis. 1975. (Essays, No. 4). *-004-1.*

THE NOVELS OF MME RICCOBONI, by Joan Hinde Stewart. 1976. (Essays, No. 8). *-008-4.*

FIRE AND ICE: THE POETRY OF XAVIER VILLAURRUTIA, by Merlin H. Forster. 1976. (Essays, No. 11). *-011-4.*

THE THEATER OF ARTHUR ADAMOV, by John J. McCann. 1975. (Essays, No. 13). *-013-0.*

AN ANATOMY OF POESIS: THE PROSE POEMS OF STÉPHANE MALLARMÉ, by Ursula Franklin. 1976. (Essays, No. 16). *-016-5.*

LAS MEMORIAS DE GONZALO FERNÁNDEZ DE OVIEDO, Vols. I and II, by Juan Bautista Avalle-Arce. 1974. (Texts, Textual Studies, and Translations, Nos. 1 and 2). *-401-2; 402-0.*

GIACOMO LEOPARDI: THE WAR OF THE MICE AND THE CRABS, translated, introduced and annotated by Ernesto G. Caserta. 1976. (Texts, Textual Studies, and Translations, No. 4). *-404-7.*

LUIS VÉLEZ DE GUEVARA: A CRITICAL BIBLIOGRAPHY, by Mary G. Hauer. 1975. (Texts, Textual Studies, and Translations, No. 5). *-405-5.*

UN TRÍPTICO DEL PERÚ VIRREINAL: "EL VIRREY AMAT, EL MARQUÉS DE SOTO FLORIDO Y LA PERRICHOLI". EL "DRAMA DE DOS PALANGANAS" Y SU CIRCUNSTANCIA, estudio preliminar, reedición y notas por Guillermo Lohmann Villena. 1976. (Texts, Textual Studies, and Translation, No. 15). *-415-2.*

LOS NARRADORES HISPANOAMERICANOS DE HOY, edited by Juan Bautista Avalle-Arce. 1973. (Symposia, No. 1). *-951-0.*

ESTUDIOS DE LITERATURA HISPANOAMERICANA EN HONOR A JOSÉ J. ARROM, edited by Andrew P. Debicki and Enrique Pupo-Walker. 1975. (Symposia, No. 2). *952-9.*

MEDIEVAL MANUSCRIPTS AND TEXTUAL CRITICISM, edited by Christopher Kleinhenz. 1976. (Symposia, No. 4). *-954-5.*

SAMUEL BECKETT. THE ART OF RHETORIC, edited by Edouard Morot-Sir, Howard Harper, and Dougald McMillan III. 1976. (Symposia, No. 5). *-955-3.*

When ordering please cite the *ISBN Prefix* plus the last four digits for each title.

Send orders to: University of North Carolina Press
Chapel Hill
North Carolina 27514
U. S. A.

The Department of Romance Studies Digital Arts and Collaboration Lab at the University of North Carolina at Chapel Hill is proud to support the digitization of the North Carolina Studies in the Romance Languages and Literatures series.

www.ingramcontent.com/pod-product-compliance
Lightning Source LLC
Chambersburg PA
CBHW022014220426
43663CB00007B/1075